NORTHERN SPHINX

NORTHERN SPHINX

*Iceland and the Icelanders
from the Settlement to the Present*

by

SIGURDUR A. MAGNÚSSON

MCGILL-QUEEN'S UNIVERSITY PRESS
Montreal 1977

First published in the United Kingdom by
C. Hurst & Co. (Publishers) Ltd., London
Published in North America by
McGill-Queen's University Press, Montreal

© 1977 by Sigurdur A. Magnússon

ISBN 0 7735 0277 7

Legal Deposit 1st Quarter 1977
Bibliothèque Nationale du Québec

Printed in Great Britain by
Billing & Sons Limited,
Guildford, London and Worcester

Foreword

This book is intended as a general introduction to Iceland, past and present, with special reference to cultural trends in its historical development. Although it expresses a personal view, it makes no claim to being a particularly original work; I gratefully acknowledge the immense help I have received from authorities in the various fields, some of whom are directly quoted, while others are fondly remembered as sources of information and inspiration. Since the book is primarily conceived as an introduction, I have kept the bibliographical notes to a minimum, but have appended a selected list of books in English on some of the main subjects dealt with.

There are always certain technical difficulties connected with reproducing Icelandic names in English. In this I have, in the first two sections, followed the general rule, adopted by many previous authors, of using the accusative case, which is the stem of every word, dropping the final -r or -ur of the nominative case, writing for instance *Olaf* for *Ólafr* or *Ólafur*, *Sigurd* for *Sigurdur*, etc. The same rule has been applied to names with double consonants in the nominative case, such as *Egill* and *Ódinn*, which are here rendered in the accusative *Egil* and *Odin*. There is only one exception to the accusative rule, that of names ending in -ir in the nominative case, like *Sverrir* or *Grettir* (they drop the final -r in the accusative), and in names ending in -i in the nominative case, like *Helgi* or *Snorri*. In the third main section of the book the nominative case is used throughout, e.g. *Gudmundur, Thórarinn, Egill*, since it might seem inappropriate to modify the names of living or newly deceased persons. Many Icelandic names are of course the same in both nominative and accusative, names like *Jón, Jóhann, Jóhannes, Hannes, Hans* (five different forms of the English name *John*); those ending in -ar, like *Gunnar, Gardar*; in -ús and -úst, like *Magnús* and *Ágúst*; and a host of others, like *Björn, Örn, Jakob, Rafn* (or *Hrafn*), *Matthías, Konrád, Tómas*, etc. The accent over some of the vowels does not denote a stress, since every Icelandic word has the stress on the first syllable, but a different sound of the vowel. Thus *a* is pronounced like *a* in 'Alabama', while *á* has the sound of *ou* in 'house'; *e* sounds like *e* in 'end', but *é* like *ye* in 'yes'; *i* sounds like *i* in 'inferno', but *í* like *ee* in 'deed'; *o* sounds like *o* in 'order', but *ó* like *o in 'hope'*; *u* sounds like *u* in 'tureen', but *ú* like *oo* in 'pool'; *ö* sounds like *u* 'turn' and *ae* or *æ* like *i* in 'wild'. Throughout I have avoided the peculiar Icelandic letters 'þ' and 'ð' (*th* hard and soft), replacing 'þ' with *th* and 'ð' with *d*. This should make Icelandic names and words less forbidding to the uninitiated reader.

I owe special thanks to Dr Jónas Krisjánsson, Director of The Arnamagnæan Institute in Reykjavík, and to Professor Sigurdur Líndal of the University of Iceland for their helpful criticisms and suggestions after reading my manuscript. I am also indebted to Mr Peter Kidson, formerly First Secretary of the British Embassy in Reykjavík, now a naturalized citizen of Iceland under the name Pétur Karlsson (Icelandic law compels immigrants to adopt native names and drop family names in favour of patronymics), for going over the manuscript and correcting my English syntax. Finally, my very special thanks go to Mr Christopher Hurst, my publisher, for his patient and perceptive work in revising, compressing and restructuring the third section of the book, so as to make it more symmetrical and coherent. But, needless to say, all faults of fact, sense and style are mine.

Reykjavík
November 1976   SIGURDUR A. MAGNÚSSON

Contents

'To me Iceland is sacred soil. Its memory is a constant background to what I am doing. No matter that I don't make frequent references to the country; it is an equally important part of my life for all that. I may be writing about something totally unrelated, but it is still somewhere close by. It is different from anything else. It is a permanent part of my existence, even though I am not continually harping on it. I said it was a kind of background, that's right. I could also say that Iceland is the sun colouring the mountains without being anywhere in sight, even sunk beyond the horizon.'

—W. H. Auden, in a newspaper interview,
Reykjavík, April 1964

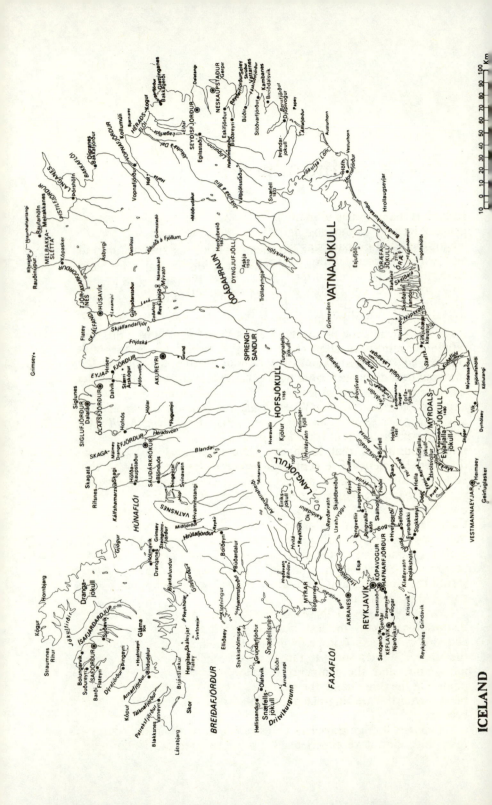

ICELAND

Introduction

Iceland is many things to many foreign races. To Scandinavians in general Iceland is the nostalgically romantic 'Isle of the Sagas' where their Viking past was preserved in splendid literary works, and where Nordic culture saw its finest flowering some seven centuries ago. To well-informed Germans Iceland is likely to be the only source of knowledge of the pre-Christian culture of the Teutonic peoples, from which, for instance, Richard Wagner derived the material for his *Ring der Niebelungen*. To the French it is the magical scene of novels by Jules Verne and Pierre Loti, the refuge of numerous shipwrecked French fishermen in the last century, and the destination of various scientific expeditions. To the Irish Iceland is the former base of ferocious red-bearded pirates who harried the coasts of Ireland centuries ago, looted their homes and abducted their women. To the British, Iceland is the stubborn adversary of the notorious 'cod-wars' of 1958, 1972 and 1975-6, and a favourite haunt of travellers. To the Americans Iceland is the native country of that foolhardy adventurer Leif Erikson who discovered America five centuries before Columbus and had the bad taste to lose it again, as well as being the site of one of those secluded bases to which American soldiers are relegated to their own discontent and with the grumbling consent of Congress. To Canadians Iceland is the original home of a sizeable segment of their population, including the great Arctic explorer Vilhjalmur Stefansson and one of the greatest poets to have lived in Canada, Stephan G. Stephansson, who wrote in his native tongue. To the rest of the world Iceland is an island on the Arctic Circle where ice and cold predominate.

Obviously, many of these conceptions are partial, blurred and distorted, especially the last, since Iceland has one of the mildest climates in Western Europe owing to the Gulf Stream surrounding the island. Winter snow is rare in South Iceland, except on the mountains, and the temperature seldom drops below freezing point. On the other hand, the southern part of the country seems to be a favourite meeting-place of all kinds of gales, winds, and breezes.

Of course, foreign travellers know much more about the country than this: they have experienced hazardous journeys in the wild interior, camping on glaciers, fishing in the rich salmon rivers, hunting the reindeer in the eastern part of the country and witnessing volcanic eruptions at close quarters, both offshore and inland. To geologists, botanists and ornithologists, Iceland is a paradise. Engineers are intrigued by the tremendous quantities of natural hot water, used for the central heating of the capital and other towns, and for hot-house cultivation of exotic fruits and flowers. They are also amazed at the enormous amount of water power in the rivers which, if harnessed on a large scale, would produce electricity far beyond the country's domestic needs. Philologists and literary students in the Germanic field are drawn to Iceland's ancient literary treasures which are in some ways unique and constitute a significant branch of world literature.

There are few tangible historical monuments in Iceland more than about two centuries old, though there are some ruins surviving from the early settlement of the country. But few nations are more historically conscious or have closer links with their past than the Icelanders, which can be a curse as well as a boon. This is due to the extensive written records going back to the twelfth century and covering the entire history of the nation from its very inception. These records have, literally, been in the possession of the whole people throughout the centuries and have shaped the way of thinking and feeling of every individual. Even though historical remains are scarce, the identification with the past has been kept alive not only through the written records but also through the preservation of all the old names of farms and other historic sites. Almost every inhabited spot in Iceland is closely linked with some well-known event in the Sagas or the turbulent history of later centuries. In few other countries, not excepting Greece or Italy, is the historically initiated traveller so over-whelmed by a sense of unbroken historical continuity.

A Norwegian literary historian was travelling in Iceland and came on foot to a farm where he overheard two Icelanders having a lengthy discussion over some deceased person. One of them deplored that the individual in question should have died so young, and the other mused romantically what such a gifted man could have done for his country. When the Norwegian politely inquired who this deceased person was he was told in a matter-of-fact way that they were discussing Skarphédin Njálsson, one of the heroes of the thirteenth-century *Njál's Saga*.

This lively sense of historical continuity is the mainspring of all the national endeavours of the Icelanders today. Their past glories as well as their age-long misfortunes are a source of inspiration and determination to overcome obstacles on the road to self-realization.

This book is meant as an introduction to Iceland and its people, its history and its present affairs. Obviously, such a brief account can only skim the surface, but it might whet the reader's appetite and induce him to delve deeper into some of the subjects touched upon in these pages. This is a personal account, dwelling mainly on aspects that the author finds most rewarding or important. Needless to say, many significant things have been left out.

The procedure will be to present some of the historical data at the outset, concentrating on the celebrated epoch at the dawn of Icelandic history when Iceland was an independent Commonwealth of tiny chieftaincies and when the most distinguished literary works were produced. That period came to a close towards the end of the thirteenth century, followed by a long, dark period of foreign domination and internal distress extending until the beginning of this century. Those six hundred years were an interlude when little of political or cultural consequence happened, so that during the first half of the twentieth century greater social and cultural changes took place than during the preceding six or seven centuries. Indeed, the survival of the nation during those dark ages was frequently in doubt. The last five chapters will deal with modern Iceland, picking out some of the characteristic traits of the country and the people and describing the various cultural, political, economic and social activities of the present age.

The settlement of Iceland is directly related to two significant historical facts. It came at the height of that extraordinary period called the Viking[1] Age, and it was effected by the unification of Norway under a single king. To gain some perspective, we shall have to review briefly the events that led up to this.

Our first written records of the North are stray references in various Mediterranean writers, more or less reliable. Thus Pytheas of Massilia (Marseilles), a Greek geographer of the fourth century B.C., had made a journey to Northern Europe, and various references to a lost book of his indicate a fair knowledge of that region. A land which he visited, and named *Thule,* has been taken to refer to Iceland, but it seems probable from his descriptions that it was the Scandinavian peninsula he had in mind.

Another Greek geographer at about the time of Christ, Strabo, quoted Pytheas, but did not believe him. He mentions the Cimbri, then a dominant tribe in Jutland (Himmerland). Pliny the Elder (*ca.* A.D. 23-79) had been in Germany as a Roman military officer and mentions 'Scatinavia' in his *Natural History,* but he was evidently a very credulous listener and his accounts from the North are filled with fantastic tales. Tacitus, the Roman historian, wrote his *Germania* about A.D. 98 and makes interesting observations on Northern customs and religion. Among others he mentions the *Suiones* (Swedes?), a powerful tribe in the North. Among other early writers who made references to the North was Ptolemy, who wrote his *Geography* about A.D. 150 and mentioned various Scandinavian tribes.

Then after centuries of oblivion came two writers who possessed a fairly accurate knowledge of the North, Procopius and Jordanes in the sixth century. Procopius wrote mostly about the wars of the Byzantine Emperor, Justinian the Great (527–65), against the Ostrogoths and other tribes. Jordanes, probably a Gothic priest or monk, wrote a *History of the Goths*, filled with legends and fairy-tales.

In the meantime great changes had taken place in the North and all over Europe. The great Migrations had flooded Europe, and by no means the smallest stream had come from Scandinavia. Many of the most warlike and powerful tribes before, during and after the Migrations in Europe may have stemmed from there: the Lombards, the Burgundians, the Cimbri, the Teutons (from the Danish district Ty), and the Goths, to name only the best known, had scattered all over Europe and become powerful kingdoms, some even threatening Rome and others succumbing to the Huns. The kingdom of the Ostrogoths (Eastern Goths) extended in the fourth century from the Baltic to the Black Sea, under the great king Ermanaric, only to be swallowed up by the Huns. The great Burgundian kingdom in Germany was similarly defeated by the Huns sixty years later (437). The remnants of this tribe settled in France, in the province of Burgundy. These two greatest defeats of the Germanic tribes were linked with the story of Sigurd (Siegfried) the Dragon-slayer in the heroic Niebelung cycle, to which we shall revert.

These waves of expansion and conquest, the causes of which have never been clearly explained, continued intermittently well into historical times (which begin in Scandinavia around 800) and did not die away finally until the end of the Viking Age in the eleventh century. In the later period, however, they assumed a different form. Instead of the migration of a whole tribe or nation *en masse* to new more or less permanent settlements, the later waves were in the forms of marauding bands, often quite large, seeking wealth or new lands for temporary settlements. Of course, some of these bands settled permanently in their new homes and were then assimilated by the previous inhabitants.

The Viking Age proper is usually considered to extend from about 800 to the beginning of the eleventh century. If the earlier migrations have about them an air of aimless vagrancy, the Viking conquests are on the whole well-organized expeditions to coasts where there was something to gain. We have an account of London being attacked by 350 ships around 850, and by 490 ships in 994. Such expeditions presuppose a high degree of organization and resolute leadership.

It has been said that internal dissension abroad drew the Vikings like a magnet, and we see on many occasions how they would strike where the resistance was weakest due to strifes and quarrels among the leaders, notably in France and England.

The miscellaneous tribes of Sweden and Denmark were welded into national states by the dominant tribes in these areas, the Swedes and the Danes—states that were not necessarily always intact or unified, but at least the *idea* of a common cause and a common state was there. Norway, on the other hand, remained until the Viking Age a land of petty tribal kings who because of the topography of the country with its many fiords and formidable mountain ranges, often had little contact with each other.

What brought about the Viking movement has been endlessly debated. Some ascribe it to a tremendous increase in population; others have pointed to climatic changes. The true reasons are probably to be found in the fact that after the consolidation of fairly peaceful national states the scope for activities at home was limited, harrying was almost impossible, and wealth could only be amassed slowly. What was more natural than to seek fame, wealth and adventure on foreign shores?

These untiring conquerors seem to have feared nothing and balked at no obstacle. With an almost religious zeal they went from land to land, ravaging city after city until they were the terror of half the world, and were bought off by the most powerful of kings and emperors. They raided the entire Atlantic coast of Europe, from North Germany to Gibraltar, they went to North Africa and Italy, and would have attacked Rome had they not mistaken its position. The British Isles were for centuries the main quarry of Scandinavian wealth, and for long periods Northern kings ruled in parts of England, Scotland, Ireland and the surrounding islands. These 'western' Vikings were mostly Norwegians and Danes.

The eastern part of Europe was equally in the grip of the Viking. Since early times Swedish merchants had travelled round the coasts of the Baltic and to Russia. In their wake came 'merchant-Vikings' who made expeditions farther inland, now trading, now plundering. They sailed up Russia's rivers, along the Dniepr, the Dniester, and the Volga. At an early stage they made a permanent settlement in Novgorod (Hólmgard) and in 862 founded a Scandinavian empire in Kiev (Kaenugard). Fifty years later (907) they were at the gates of Constantinople and tried to take the imperial city. These Swedish rovers were referred to variously as *Rhos, Rus* and *Rûs* by Greek, Slavonic and Arab chroniclers. The name derives from a province in Sweden, and the word *rus* originally means 'rower'. In Finnish this old name, *Ruotsi,* is still used of Sweden. Thus the Swedish Vikings founded the Russian empire, and gave it its first rulers and the name that is still in use—Russia, or in the Scandinavian languages, Rusland.

In the Byzantine Empire the Northmen were well known and in time came to constitute the Emperor's bodyguard. They were usually referred to as *Varangians,* in Slavonic *variag,* in Greek *barangoi.* Their proper Nordic name, *vaeringjar,* still current in Iceland, originally meant 'those bound together by a pledge', but it came to be used exclusively of the Emperor's bodyguard. We have in the Icelandic Sagas numerous accounts of young men making their way to Constantinople (in Icelandic *Mikligardur*—'Great City') to win fame and fortune.

Thus at the height of their activity the Northmen traversed half the globe, from Russia to America, from Africa to Greenland. Yes, we even have an account of a single man—later known as Harald Hardruler, king of Norway—who served the Byzantine Empress Zoë and went on expeditions to Italy, Sicily and Africa, staying there several years, conquering some eighty cities and amassing great wealth. Having been refused the hand of a princess in Constantinople, he left the city and on his way back to Norway married the daughter of King Yaroslav of Novgorod. Later Harald was engaged in various wars in Northern and Western Europe, for instance in the historic battle at Stamford Bridge in England in September 1066, where he fell.

The Norse language, which is spoken in Iceland today with very slight modifications, was thus for a time a 'world language'. It was spoken all over Scandinavia, and at the courts of the Scandinavian rulers in England, Scotland, Ireland, France and Russia. It was the recognized language of the Emperor's bodyguard in Byzantium. And it was the first European language spoken on the shores of America.

The Northmen brought home with them not only rich treasures but also a vastly enriched knowledge of the world and the ways of other men, a wider horizon, and a cosmopolitan outlook that was bound to leave its stamp on their creative activities. Like the Greeks of antiquity, they learned to organize states in their new settlements, and indeed in Normandy they laid the 'foundation of the most highly organized state in Europe and prepared the way for the Norman conquest of England'.[2]

In all his savage conquests the force of the Viking is usually coupled with a high degree of wisdom of a practical kind. These two trends in Norse life we shall have occasion to observe in various manifestations in the following pages. Whether they were innate in equal measure is quite another question. It seems plausible that this was a fusion of foreign and native, for that is usually the case with great achievements, as is perhaps best seen in ancient Greece and Elizabethan England. The Vikings provided a stimulus to European culture in general, but they also derived great stimuli from the peoples with whom they came into contact. They conquered and were conquered at the same time.

We have noted earlier that the realms of Denmark and Sweden were unified by single strong tribes, from whom they derive their names. In Norway the course took a different direction. Here a single strong man brought about the unification of the petty kingdoms in the late ninth century. Hence the name of Norway does not derive from a tribe, but from that country's position with regard to Denmark and Southern Sweden: *Norvegr*—'Northern Way'.

This event was of paramount significance for Iceland, since it was one of the principal causes of its settlement. When the ambitious Harald Finehair,[3] himself a petty king from Southern Norway, succeeded in subjugating the rest of Norway during ten years of continuous wars, there were according to the Sagas only three possibilities open to the country's aristocracy. They could enter the king's service and thus receive some concessions. They could resist him, perhaps at the cost of their lives, and certainly of their property. Or they could escape abroad, thus saving their honour, their lives and some of their property. All three ways were taken. Many resisted and fell, or were driven out of the country. Some prudently entered the king's service, and were allowed to keep their property and even some of their titles. But a great number left without further ado to settle in other lands, first of all the British Isles, already a favourite hunting ground. A little earlier some unfortunate voyagers had been carried off course and taken to a distant island in the northern seas, a peaceful virgin island whose natural beauty and wealth were praised in many reports. The result was that increasing numbers of Norwegian noblemen directed their ships to this island, which was already known by the name 'Iceland'.

Many of the settlers had already lived in Ireland or Scotland for a generation or two, and moved to Iceland when their power and prosperity was waning in the British Isles owing to greater native resistance. Others came directly from Norway, but often harried the coasts of the British Isles on their way to make up their retinues which had been diminished on leaving the homeland. There are numerous accounts of settlers coming from Norway with a number of Irish slaves, who in due time were given freedom and provided with homes in Iceland.[4]

This was the time of Iceland's emergence into history. It was a time of worldwide conquest, by force or by daring enterprise, a time of cultural interchange, enrichment and flowering. A time when the foundations were laid for many an edifice that was destined to defy the law of time and decay. It was the springtime of a race, when all its budding forces broke out in one marvellous and bewildering play of the brightest colours.

Notes

1. The word Viking is probably derived from *vík,* and Old Norse word for 'bay', still used in Icelandic: e.g. Reykjavík, 'Smoky Bay'. This appellation stems from the fact that the Vikings usually operated from landlocked and placid inlets or bays. A less plausible explanation is that the word derives from *wic,* Anglo-Saxon for 'camp'.

2. Allen Mawer, *The Vikings,* Cambridge 1913, p. 79.

3. The epithet of King Harald has been rendered into English as 'Fairhair', but the Old Norse *fagr* simply means 'fine', 'beautiful', not 'light' as the English use of 'fair' implies. G. Turville-Petre uses 'Finehair'.

4. The first human beings known to have lived in Iceland were not Norsemen, but Irish monks and hermits (*papar*). As early as A.D. 795 we have an account of some Irish hermits staying in Iceland from February to August. When the Norsemen came to Iceland in the ninth century they met some of these Christian hermits who, loath to mingle with pagans, fled, probably to Greenland.

It has been calculated on the basis of the *Book of Settlements,* that 84 per cent of the settlers came from Norway, but that 12·6 per cent were from the British Isles. It is interesting to note that of the latter some 33 per cent were of noble birth, but only 6 per cent were slaves—an improbable proportion. Jón Steffensen maintains that the Celtic element in the early Icelanders was almost certainly stronger than our sources would lead us to believe. Steffensen has not only analysed the texts, but made use of anthropological material. He has found a marked difference between ancient Icelandic and Norse iron-age skulls, but he found ancient Irish skulls to be closer to the ancient Icelanders than those from the Scandinavian peninsula. Hence a 'larger number of settlers than indicated in the *Book of Settlements* calculations are from countries outside of the Scandinavian countries'.

There is also some evidence of Celtic influence in Icelandic literature. Some of the most distinguished heroes of the Sagas have Celtic names such as Kormák, Njál and Kjartan (the last-named was the grandson of an Irish princess who had been enslaved by Norse Vikings and sold to a prominent Icelander). Many of the prominent families in Iceland were undoubtedly of mixed descent, and a great number of place-names indicate Irish origins.

The mingling of Celtic and Nordic blood in Iceland cannot unreasonably be assumed to have given a new dimension to its culture, created new potentialities, without however essentially changing the Norse cultural heritage. Iceland presents us with the last expression of Germanic culture before that culture was permeated by Christianity. That expression was all the more vigorous and memorable for the new potentialities created by the Celtic admixture. (The references to Steffensen are to *Samtíd og saga,* Vol. III, Reykjavík 1964, p. 275.)

PART ONE

THE ICELANDIC COMMONWEALTH

1. A Unique Polity

The settlement of Iceland was in every respect remarkable and in some respects unique.

No other nation in Europe possesses a record of its history from its very inception such as the Icelanders have in their *Book of Settlements* (*Landnámabók*), a record containing the names, genealogies and short biographies of all the principal settlers. These numbered a little over four hundred, and we have other sources for additional settlers.[1]

This book gives us an account of the discovery of Iceland as well as an explanation of how it came by its 'chilly misnomer'. The first Norsemen known to have come to Iceland were a Norwegian and a Swede, the former drifting there by accident, the latter seeking the island at the direction of his second-sighted mother. Both of them returned home, having given the island names that would not stick.

Having heard about the new land a Norwegian Viking, Flóki, set out to settle it. We are told that instead of a compass Flóki took with him three ravens. Once out on the ocean he sent his ravens reconnoitring. The first flew back to Norway, the second cam back to the ship, but the third flew ahead in the direction of Iceland. This account calls to mind Noah's raven and three doves, and Utnapishtim's dove, swallow, and raven, employed in similar fashion (*The Gilgamesh Epic*), but in other respects the account of Flóki has few legendary traces.

Having reached his destination Flóki became so absorbed in fishing that he neglected to provide hay for his stock, with the result that most of his animals died during the following winter. Disgusted, he decided to go back home, but before leaving he happened to see a fiord filled with drift-ice, which gave him the idea of naming that ill-fated island Iceland. Back in Norway he had no favourable reports of the newly discovered land, but one of his shipmates was of a different opinion and reported that in Iceland 'every blade of grass was bedewed with butter', for which he was thenceforth called Thórólf Butter. Flóki was later to revise his views, for he did settle in Iceland during the Age of Settlement.

The first permanent settler of Iceland is considered to have arrived in the year 874, and a thousand years later the place he settled was to become the capital of Iceland, Reykjavík. This settler was named Ingólf, and his descendants enjoyed a special distinction in the Icelandic Commonwealth. The place he settled was, however, not entirely his own choice. The gods had a hand in it. When he sighted land he threw overboard the wooden high-seat pillars, which he had carried away from his home in Norway. These had elaborate mythological carving, somewhat like totem-poles. The high-seat pillars were the most sacred part of every home, and their removal to the new home was symbolic in much the same way as were fire and earth to ancient Greek colonists. Wherever the high-seat pillars touched land the settlers would build their new homes. This seems to have been a common heathen custom.

The Age of Settlement lasted for some sixty years (874-930). At the end of it most of the coastal areas were settled, the interior being uninhabitable. There have been different guesses as to the total population by 930, varying from 20,000 to 45,000. By the year 1100 the inhabitants are supposed to have been around 70,000. This conclusion is reached by counting the leading men of the country and estimating approximately how great a household and following each of them had. It must be remembered that the settlers were followed not only by their families but by friends, relatives, freedmen, servants and slaves, forming a considerable colony when every head was counted. It is said of one man that he had fourteen slaves, and when he rode from one of his estates to another he was accompanied by eighty men. A famous female settler had with her twenty freedmen, most of them with their own families.

Each settler would take extensive tracts of land and then parcel it out to his followers and freedmen, and to later immigrants who might join him. When land became scarce the rule was made that no settler might take more land than he and his shipmates could carry fire around in one day. The fires were built from sunrise to sunset in one day, and had to be visible one from the other, in much the same way as the ancient Greeks built fires on mountain tops when they wanted to convey a speedy message. There was a different rule for women. They could take as much land as a two-year-old heifer could run around in one day.

For an idea of the daily life of the settlers we may quote a passage from one of the Sagas. It tells about one of the more prosperous settlers, but it is no doubt representative of the living conditions of many leading men in Iceland:

Skallagrím was a great man for work. He always kept a lot of men on hand, and sought busily after such supplies as might be found thereabouts which could prove useful to them; for the first they had little livestock compared with what was needed for the number of men they had there. However, what livestock there was found its own food in the forest through winter. Skallagrím was a great shipbuilder, nor was there any shortage of driftwood west of the Mýrar. He had a farm built at Álftanes, and had a second home there, from which he had men go out rowing for fish and seal-hunting and egg-collecting, for there was abundance of all these provisions, and also driftwood to be fetched back home. At that time too there were numerous whale-strandings, and harpooning them was free for all. And all creatures were at their ease in the hunting grounds, for men were unknown to them.

The third home he had was by the sea in the western Mýrar. This was even better situated for waylaying driftwood, and he had ground sown there and called it Akrar. Offshore lay islands where whales were to be found, and these they called Hvalseyjar. Skallagrím also had men of his own up on the salmon river for the fishing. He put Odd Live-alone on Gljúfrá to look after the salmon fishing there; he lived under Einbúabrekkur, and it is from him that Einbúanes gets its name. Then there was a man called Sigmund whom Skallagrím put on Nordrá. He lived at the place which used to be called Sigmundarstadir but is nowadays known as Haugar. From him Sigmundarnes gets its name. Later he shifted his dwelling over to Munodarnes, where he found it handier for the salmon fishing.

Once Skallagrím's livestock showed a substantial increase, all the sheep went up on the high ground for the summer. He could see a big difference, how the stock which went on the heath grew better and fatter, and also how sheep did well over the winter in the high valleys, even if they were not fetched down. As a result, Skallagrím had a farm built up on the fell, and owned a house there, and had his sheep tended there. It was Gríss who looked after his house, from whom Grísartunga gets its name. Skallagrím's estate was now standing on more legs than one.[2]

Most of the leading settlers of Iceland had been powerful chieftains in Norway and the British Isles, and not a few had been religious leaders by virtue of owning a temple, if we are to believe the Sagas and other ancient sources. We are told that one of the first acts of many of these leaders was to build a temple in the new home, thus acquiring religious and political authority in their neighbourhood. But all our written sources are from the Christian period and may well be coloured by Christian ideas concerning religious practices. Some scholars have maintained with convincing evidence that temple worship was not practised in the Nordic countries in heathen times, and that the authority of the chieftain rested on his noble birth and following, as in other Germanic nations.[3] On the other hand, the Icelandic terms for chieftain and chieftaincy, *godi* and *godord,* denote a religious function. According to the Icelandic sources, whether true or false, worship at the temple was not free, but a privilege bought by a certain degree of submission to the chieftain. His followers paid him a small tax, and he was obliged to keep up the temple at his own expense. The office was never remunerative, and one of the sources is explicit that the chieftaincy was 'power but not wealth'. Thus we may presume that only a wealthy man had the possibility of becoming a chieftain. It must also be kept in mind that in the ninth century the pagan religion was on the wane, so that chieftain's power did not rest primarily on his religious authority, but rather on his personal authority and his ability to handle public issues. This became obvious after the adoption of Christianity in the year 1000.

During the Age of Settlement the authority of the chieftain was in no way clearly defined. It was his duty to take care of the interests of his followers, and this was not merely an imposed or unwelcome duty, but the very condition for his power and success: if he were negligent he might lose his followers to other chieftains. The chieftaincies were never limited by geographical boundaries, although the tendency was obviously to support the chieftain closest at hand. We have numerous accounts of chieftains losing their followers to other more successful chieftains, sometimes living in remote districts.

Roughly, the situation in Iceland in the beginning was not far removed from what it had been in Norway before it was united or, for a further analogy, what it had been in the Greek city-states at one stage of their development. Here were a number of independent mini-states, ruled by individuals whose power rested on their ability to give their subjects a just and effective rule.

It was soon apparent, however, that this state of affairs could not continue for long. A land without common law or some attempt at harmonizing the disparate elements might be torn apart by civil strife. It is a lasting testimony to the political genius of the Icelanders that they managed to solve this thorny problem without much friction and in a way which remains unique to this day.

There had been a few successful attempts at setting up local *Things* or Assemblies in individual districts, and in one case several districts set up a common *Thing*, where disputes were settled by the chieftains with the aid of specially appointed courts. But this might prove inadequate. In the case of disputes between men from widely separate districts it was hard to effect settlements, and impossible if either chieftain refused to co-operate.

It was for this reason that a wise and experienced man, Úlfljót—the Solon of Iceland—was sent abroad about the year 920 to study the laws of South-western Norway and recommend a new code of law for Iceland. His foster-brother, Grím Goatee,[4] was sent around the island in search of a suitable site for the national assembly. To anyone who has travelled in Iceland it must seem that Grím was guided by divine spirits, for the place he selected is one of the most impressive in the whole island.

The year 930 marked the foundation of the *Althing* (literally: General Assembly) and the beginning of the Icelandic Commonwealth which was to stand for the next 330 years. The site was properly named *Thingvöllur* (Assembly Plain), nowadays commonly used in its plural form, *Thingvellir*.

The Althing was a great national experiment; it came to be the focal point of the Commonwealth, and remained so to the very end. It has been called the first parliament in history with some justification, but actually it was not a parliament of the modern type. It was at once something more and something less. It was attended every summer by a large part of the population, but the government rested entirely with the chieftains, who were thirty-six at first and thirty-nine after 965.

The Althing was divided into a law-making and a judicial body, both composed of the chieftains, and each with its distinct functions. This distinction was far in advance of other nations in the Middle Ages. In 965 the system was modified in that the judicial body was replaced by four quarter-courts, each quarter being composed of three judicial districts, which in turn were made up of three chieftaincies. The Northern quarter was composed of four such districts, as the people there would agree to nothing less. The inhabitants of each quarter had to seek justice at their own court.

Thus the whole Commonwealth was composed of thirteen districts with their own local *Things*, each district comprising three of the thirty-nine chieftaincies. The local *Things* were held in the spring and lasted between four days and a week. They were presided over in turn by the three chieftains, each of whom appointed twelve of the thirty-six judges. Another session of two days was held two weeks after the Althing in order to make its decisions known to those who had not been able to attend the session at Thingvöllur.

The district *Things* in the spring came to play a very important role in the Commonwealth, as we see clearly in the Sagas, and only such suits as could not be settled in the district were brought to the Althing.

The Althing itself was to be in session two weeks every summer, starting on the Thursday between 18 and 24 June. Each chieftain had to be there before sunset on the opening day, or he might forfeit his chieftaincy, unless he had a legitimate excuse.

There was much formalism, even primitive ritual and insistence on exact formulae, in the procedures of the Althing. The law-making body convened within sacred boundaries, sitting in a circle round a central space on three successive rows of benches. On the central bench sat the thirty-nine chieftains, together with nine additional members, three from each of the quarters having only nine chieftains, chosen in order to give all the quarters equal representation. These forty-eight members had the voting powers, but each of them also had two counsellors, occupying the front and the rear benches. Thus the entire body consisted of 144 men. The law-making body alone had the right to interpret, 'correct' or enact laws, grant pardons, reduce prescribed punishments, issue permits, elect the Law-speaker, and represent the country as a whole *vis-à-vis* foreign powers. A simple majority was sufficient to pass or interpret laws, but in a tie of equal votes the vote of the Law-speaker was decisive.

In the judicial branch of the Althing the four quarter courts were composed of thirty-six judges, the nine chieftains of the quarter each choosing four judges, except in the Northern quarter where each of the twelve chieftains chose three judges. The conditions for being elected a judge were that the candidate be a male of twelve years or older, that he be mature enough to be fully responsible for his words and oaths, and that he be a free man with permanent domicile. Those who had not spoken the Norse language from childhood could only be chosen to the court after three years' residence in the country. According to the law, people were of age at sixteen, but for some reason the age limit for judicial functions was four years younger. A decision of the quarter court was preceded by a presentation of the prosecution and the defence by two of the judges. Since every breach of the law had a fixed fine, the judges merely had to decide whether the culprit was guilty or innocent. Even if differences of opinion existed among the judges, a decision was regarded as unanimous if the number of dissenting votes did not exceed six. If the number of dissenting votes exceeded six, a *vefang* arose, the two groups each trying to persuade members of the other. If the number still remained too large, each group would render its decision, both decisions being void and both groups taking the *vefang* oath that they had decided in accordance with what they considered to be just and lawful.

Around the year 1004 a superior of Fifth Court was created owing to the incompetence of the quarter courts in dealing with certain disputes between the quarters. There were forty-eight judges elected to this court by the chieftains and the *ad hoc* 'chieftains' in much the same way as to the law-making body of the Althing. But both plaintiff and defendant were supposed to reject six judges each, and if the plaintiff did not use this privilege the defendant rejected twelve judges; so that for any given case only thirty-six judges remained. The Fifth Court handled all suits which failed of final decision at the quarter courts, both as a court of appeals and as the supreme court. Similarly it had jurisdiction in a certain class of cases including perjury, false verdicts, bribery, and rescuing or helping outlaws and runaway debtors, slaves or vicars. Owing to the importance of the court two men had to pledge their honour in support of each person who made an oath upon any matter. In this tribunal a simple majority sufficed to reach a decision, but in case of a tie (18:18) a fine was imposed, except when the tie occurred in cases upon which another court had been unable to agree or reach a verdict. In such cases the rules were quite complicated, but the main rule was to make the decision by lot. The establishment of the Fifth Court led to the elimination of the duel as a primitive way of settling disputes. After the establishment of this tribunal there were no constitutional changes in the Icelandic Commonwealth except that the bishops were admitted to the central bench of the law-making body of the Althing after the bishoprics were founded in 1056 in the South and in 1104 in the North.

This has been a rather extensive account of the organization of the Althing, and yet may have failed to give a clear and comprehensive picture of the eminently legalistic and painfully correct procedures with which the young Commonwealth was held together. The Althing constituted a definite victory over the seething, anarchical forces that obviously were at work in the young society, as in any frontier community. It was in many ways ineffective, but if we compare early Iceland with the American West in its early days, we shall see both the tremendous obstacles facing the Icelanders, and their great achievements, in a clear light.

We can hardly look for any analogy in history that enables us to understand better the political organization of the Commonwealth. It was not tyranny, not oligarchy, not theocracy, not republic—and it was democracy only in a limited sense. Far-fetched though it may seem, the closest analogy is probably the modern United Nations Organization.

In actuality, each of the thirty-nine chieftaincies was autonomous and took care of its internal affairs, even though there were only very loose boundaries to mark it off from other chieftaincies. They were political, not geographical, states. These 'dwarf-states' set up a General Assembly to preserve the peace among themselves and to settle disputes between members of two or more chieftaincies. These states did indeed have the same language and the same culture, but that does not necessarily imply a single statehood (in this the analogy of the independent states of Latin America suggests itself). The Althing was entirely in the hands of the chieftains in much the same way as member-governments run the General Assembly of the United Nations.

What is so striking in the Icelandic Commonwealth is that there was no executive authority of any kind, no military, naval or police forces to enforce the law or protect the citizens—in short, no ruler, no central power. The sole official of the Commonwealth was the *Law-speaker* who was to be unanimously elected for his first three-year term, during which he had to recite the entire body of the law. What he omitted was no longer valid, if no one called attention to the omission (an admirable way of doing away with obsolete laws). The Law-speaker might be re-elected indefinitely, requiring only a simple majority for re-election. The functions of the Law-speaker were purely procedural. He conducted the meetings of the Althing, made announcements and called meetings when necessary during the session, but he could neither pass judgments, prosecute, nor carry out punishments. The chieftains had taken good care not to invest him with any trace of executive authority. He was, in effect, an 'international' civil servant not much different from the Secretary General of the United Nations.

It may be an over-simplification to talk of democracy in the Icelandic Commonwealth, but there was nevertheless a certain amount of political freedom in that all free men of Iceland had the privilege to choose whatever chieftain they wanted to serve and support.[5] The chieftains were, as we have seen, not heedless of popular sentiment. They were in no sense absolute rulers. Moreover, they were bound by certain legal obligations which it might prove perilous to disregard. These obligations were mostly imposed by the Althing and related to it— and here the Commonwealth had some essential differences from the United Nations. Every chieftain was obliged to attend the Althing—and be punctual—or he might lose his office. The chieftains had to take part in all the deliberations of the Althing and be present whenever there was voting. Moreover—and this is superior to all modern parliamentary practices—every single chieftain had to explain his vote on every single issue. This required a thorough grounding in all the laws of the land, and an intimate acquaintance with every detail of any given issue. If ever there was a real-life approximation to the Platonic ideal of the enlightened ruler, we find it among the Icelandic chieftains. They might on occasion resort to force, but they were well versed in the laws, excellent orators, and deeply devoted to the rule of reason over passion.

The chieftaincy had a dual aspect, as it were. It was both a public institution and a personal property, subject to sale or transfer by succession. It could be distributed to many individuals, but in such cases one was commissioned to discharge the duties of the chieftain on behalf of the others, or they might do so in rotation. On rare occasions it happened that a chieftaincy was wrested from its owner. In every chieftaincy there were a number of geographical units (parishes) with elaborate social-security and insurance systems, of which any modern welfare state could be proud.

The Commonwealth presents us with an extraordinary unity in diversity. The Althing became the rallying point of all the independent chieftaincies, and it did, at least indirectly, reflect the popular will. It was a unifying force in somewhat the same way as were the Olympic Games in ancient Greece. It harmonized the divergent elements.

The Icelandic Commonwealth was the last bastion in Europe of democratic government, where the common man had his influence, if not the actual power. This was a far cry from the rest of Europe where kingdoms and empires swelled to enormous proportions, and the people as a political entity were completely stamped out, stripped of their dignity and self-respect. The same had happened earlier in Greece and Rome, where tyrants and emperors replaced 'popular' governments. It was to happen in Iceland at the end of the thirteenth century when the king of Norway arrogated the power over the strife-torn Commonwealth.

Perhaps the clearest and most interesting example of the acute political instinct and common sense of the Icelanders was the introduction of Christianity in the year 1000 (or 999). This event stands out in bold contrast to the headlong and savage behaviour we have been accustomed to associate with the Norse Vikings.

We have records of a number of Christians among the settlers of Iceland. Most of these came from Ireland and the Hebrides where they had either inherited the new religion or adopted it because of personal conviction or, more often, for reasons of expediency. Some of these settlers are presented to us somewhat 'mixed' in their religion, worshipping Christ and Thór as two helpful comrades-in-arms with different spheres of influence. Many of the early Christian families returned to paganism after they settled in Iceland, and there is very little evidence of Christianity in Iceland for the first one hundred years. At the same time it must be remembered that the ancient religion had lost much of its force. It appears to have been more a matter of tradition and conservatism than of religious conviction for the Icelanders to keep faith with the old gods. At the same time we find even among the pagan chieftains a new kind of consciousness. We are told that when a noble and learned Law-speaker, the grandson of Ingólf Arnarson the first settler, felt death to be imminent, he ordered his servant to carry him outside his house, and there he commended himself to the care and mercy of the Power which had created the sun. This is related in a Saga from the Christian period and may well be coloured by the new ideas of Christianity.

At the same time Christianity was making headway in Europe,

and its influence in Scandinavia was fast increasing. Occasionally a young Icelander, travelling abroad, would be so impressed that he submitted to baptism, but these converts rarely found themselves compelled to start missionary work among their fellow-countrymen. It was not until 981 that a serious attempt in this direction was made. The missionary was a young Icelander of noble birth who had been converted in Germany. He was a curious blend of the ideal Viking and the Christian saint, with the former element tipping the scales to the detriment of his missionary activities. He made considerable progress, but his violent temper proved his undoing, and he left Iceland after five turbulent years, having been outlawed by the Althing. This first real missionary of Iceland ended his days as a recluse in a Russian monastery, but he has always been dear to the Icelanders. His name was Thorvald the 'Widely Travelled'.

There were other missionaries after Thorvald, most of them his inferiors, some of them outright bandits. But the group of converts increased steadily, partly through conversions abroad, especially at the court of King Ólaf Tryggvason of Norway who had become a zealous, not to say fanatical, champion of Christianity. He was intent on Christianizing all the Norse settlements, and he was behind the events that took place in Iceland in the year 1000.

By that time many of the leading families of Iceland had adopted Christianity; and no doubt a large section of the common people followed their example. It had come to such a pass that the chieftains were losing many of their followers, who now ranged themselves under the support of the new Christian chiefs, who however had no place in the organization of the Commonwealth.

At the Althing in the year 1000 there was a clear division of pagan and Christian forces, and headstrong men in both camps urged a conclusion by force. The more sober-minded elements averted disaster, but a division of the Commonwealth seemed imminent. The Christians wanted to set up their own Commonwealth and their own Althing and sever all ties with the old system.

On 23 June the tension had reached breaking-point, and very little was needed to start a conflagration that would have been fateful to the whole people. Each group seceded from the law and from the existing order, intending to establish a new Commonwealth. The situation was grave indeed, for the chieftains were loath to renounce their ancient gods who, indirectly at least, were the source of their power. The Christians were equally loath to worship idols and live in a wholly pagan order. They therefore chose their own Law-speaker, and the breach seemed irreparable. But the Christian Law-speaker, Hall of Sída, was one of the wisest and most temperate men of his time. Foreseeing the consequences of the actions of his own party, he entered into an agreement with the Law-speaker of the old regime whereby the latter should proclaim the law. We are told that Thorgeir, the pagan Law-speaker, accepted the responsibility and went to his booth where he retired under a cloak which he pulled over his head, so that no man might speak to him. Thus he remained in solemn meditation all day and the following night.

On the morning of 24 June Thorgeir summoned the Althing and made perhaps the most important oration ever delivered in Iceland. He pointed out that affairs would have come to a dangerous pass if the elements of disunity and immoderation carried the day. Security rested on one common law, he said, and a division of the Commonwealth would only lead to bitter and prolonged struggles. He went on: 'It seems to be advisable that at this juncture those who counsel extreme measures upon either side be not permitted to rule, but that we so compromise the matter in controversy that each side shall not wholly surrender its position, and that all of us recognize the authority of one system of law and custom throughout Iceland. It will prove true that when we sunder the law we end the peace.'6

It speaks well for the respect and authority enjoyed by this noble Law-speaker that nobody raised a voice against him, and he took binding oaths from both parties that they would abide by laws which he proclaimed. He then went on to say: 'This is the foundation of our laws that all men in this land are to be Christians and believe in one God—the Father, the Son and the Holy Ghost—and that they are no longer to worship idols, nor expose children, nor eat horsemeat. If any man is found guilty of these practices, he shall be condemned to outlawry, but if he carries them on in secret, there shall be no punishment involved.'7 Allowing for certain scribal modifications and Christian colouring, we may trust that this was the substance of what Thorgeir said on that historic occasion. It was indeed a speech worthy of a Solon.

When we keep in mind that the people involved in this wise compromise were the very same men, or their descendants, whose fierce and warlike spirit had inspired the people of the British Isles and of the European mainland to pray, 'From the wrath of the Norsemen, O Lord, deliver us', we realize that in this instance reason and good sense were winning one of their most remarkable victories over passion and anarchy.

It stands to reason that a compromise of this sort did not lead to any radical changes or revaluations. Nominally, the Common-wealth was Christian and Christ took the place of the ancient gods, indeed often retaining their functions. But the entire political and social life of the Commonwealth remained much the same as it had been. The pagan spirit was so far from dying out that toward the end of the Commonwealth a new 'Viking Age' set in, a period of

civil strife and savage killings which in no respect lagged behind
the Viking activities in their heyday. The pagan deities might be
dead, but the ancient spirit of pride and feud flourished to the end.
The only difference was that in the later age many devices from the
Christian South were introduced, such as tortures and mutilations.

It is of paramount importance to literature that the progress of
Christianizing the Icelanders was so slow. The church in Iceland
was for a long time a national rather than an international
institution, and it was instrumental in preserving the national
culture. The ancient treasures of myth, legend and heroic tales
remained sacred to the people, and there is evidence that many of
the Sagas were written down in monasteries by clerically educated
men.

This is another indication of the essentially rational bent of the
Icelandic mind. These people had a sane, practical outlook, devoid
of superstition and fanaticism. There is a delightful illustration of
this characteristic in a little episode which took place at the
Althing when Christianity was being adopted.

During the deliberations, we are told, a man came running to
the Assembly saying that 'earth-fire' or volcanic eruptions had
started not far from the meeting place, and that it would overrun
the homestead of one of the chieftains. Then the pagans began to
say, 'It is no wonder that the gods are angry at such speeches.'
Then Snorri Godi, one of the most influential chieftains, retorted,
'What were the gods angry at, when the lava on which we now
stand was burning here?'

But reason did not always govern the actions of the Icelanders,
and the first 400 years of their history are packed with dramatic
events in the perennial struggle between the sage and the warrior,
the law and the passions of headstrong individuals or families.
When we consider that the period from the settlement of Iceland
to the collapse of the Commonwealth is longer than the period of
the European settlement in North America and almost twice the
duration of the American Republic, it will be easy to understand
that there were ups and downs in Iceland as later in America.

The four hundred years from the beginning of the settlement to
the collapse of the Commonwealth may be divided roughly into
the following periods:

874-930: Age of Settlement.
930-1030: Saga Age, the period during which most of the events
occurred which are recorded in the Sagas of Icelanders. It was in
many ways a very turbulent period, as we shall see later.
1030-1120: Peace Age, when life in Iceland became relatively
stabilized and Christianity began to take root. During this period
Iceland had its first bishops, some of them of outstanding learning

and intellect, and great political ability. It is even reported that for a while the custom of carrying arms passed out of use. This period saw the first vernacular translations of foreign religious works, mostly homilies, which had a profound influence on Icelandic prose.

1120-1230: Writing Age, when the national literature of Iceland was developed and perfected. This was a period of prosperity and great intellectual activity, both artistic and scholarly.

1230-64: Sturlung Age, named after the most powerful family of the time. This was a period of violent civil strife and clashing interests between kinsmen as well as families which resulted in the fall of the Commonwealth (1262-4). During and after this last period some of the finest Sagas were written. With some justification it has been called the Icelandic Renaissance.[8]

Everything considered, it is a marvel that an organization like the Commonwealth lasted so long, as it had some undoubted flaws which made it vulnerable, and which indeed caused its destruction in the end. It is worth considering these briefly, for they present us with a paradox which has been tenacious in human society. It is the perennial problem of reconciling common law with unrestricted personal liberty.

Iceland was settled by men who put their love of liberty and independence above any other consideration. Icelandic society was in fact the last expression of the Germanic Heroic Age in that here everything revolved around the family, and loyalty to kin was the highest duty, for it was in his kinsman that the individual found his strength and protections. Contrary to the paradox of Ibsen, a solitary man was conceived of as a weak man. But the family is always part of a larger context, the community. And in a community of strong and independent families there are bound to be clashes that may result in violence. Wherever family feeling is particularly strong the expediency of the blood-feud as a social institution seems to be accepted. This is evident around the Mediterranean, for instance in Corsica, Italy and Greece where the *vendetta* continued to be practised until this century. The same holds true for certain countries of Latin America and Asia.

But a community with any sense of responsibility and a will for survival recognizes the danger of extinction if the blood-feud is given free rein. Hence the necessity for a common law whereby the community may preserve some degree of order and prevent unbridled slaughter. In a community with a strong central authority the implementation of the law is fairly easy. Thus, in the individual districts the chieftains of Iceland usually managed to keep the peace and prevent bloods-feuds among their followers.

But in a society without any central power, such as the

Commonwealth, the maintenance of law and order becomes a difficult, if not an impossible task. The Commonwealth made its laws and passed its judgments, but when it came to carrying them out there was but one way open. It had to be left to the individual families. In other words, the man who sought the law had himself to execute the judgment once it had been passed. Obviously, there was the temptation to by-pass the courts and take the law into one's own hands, as happened on numerous occasions. This was one of the principal weaknesses of the otherwise admirable system of the Commonwealth; and in passing it may also be noted that this is one of the limitations of the United Nations.

As in Greece or Afghanistan, the feuds in ancient Iceland had numerous causes, the most common of which was a personal insult. Living in a heroic age, the Icelanders had an amazingly touchy sense of honour. Almost anything might become a valid reason for killing. They called this *skapraun*—the trial of condition, the test of temper and manhood. The nature or significance of the insult was irrelevant. Whether a hearty joke or an argument over who should be first to cross a stream, it had to be faced squarely and might result in the loss of many lives. A sense of humour and a sense of honour have often proved hard to reconcile.

The family feuds are obviously antagonistic to the communal law, but they are very close to the conditions whereby an individual has himself to carry out the judgment of a communal court. In other words, it might become a matter of mere formality whether a case was taken to court or just settled privately. Even at the court physical strength not infrequently played a part in the settlement of a suit, if we may trust the Sagas, but for obvious reasons they tend to emphasize and embellish such events.

Taking these things into account, it is all the more remarkable how decisive a role the law played in Iceland. For it was clearly by law that the Commonwealth was kept together for so long. It was a matter of great honour to win a lawsuit, and many of the heroes of the Sagas are described as just and law-abiding men. But the relative frequency of blood-feuds in the Sagas clearly stems from the fact that feuds are usually better narrative material than peaceful settlements.

Gwyn Jones, in his lucid introduction to *Four Icelandic Sagas* (New York 1935), discusses the legal aspects of the Icelandic Commonwealth, and the crucial part the family played in it. He points out that an 'injury was conceived of as on a personal and not a legal basis', and hence it was the family, not the community as a whole, that was interested in bringing about justice. In other words, legal suits were in fact a more civilized form of the family feud.

There were three courses open to the Icelander when a dispute had arisen. The injured party might settle the matter on his own account, taking the law into his own hands. Secondly, a reconciliation might be brought about, either directly between the parties concerned, or through arbitration. Thirdly, the case might be brought before a court, either without the litigant's having asked for compensation or after it had been denied him. Gwyn Jones, quoting Andreas Heusler, shows that of more than 500 cases of feud in the Sagas, less than one-tenth came to a legal settlement. Considerably more than half were cases of private action by the parties concerned, ending in vengeance. One-fifth were examples of pure agreement, while roughly another tenth consisted of cases of legal procedure which declined into arbitration and agreement. The exact figures are: total cases 520; private vengeance 297; pure agreement 104; legal cases becoming agreement 60; legal cases 50; legal cases wrecked 9.

Gwyn Jones then goes on to discuss each of the three courses and points out that the family or kin supplied the double means of self-preservation and mutual aid, at a time when the two ideas were intimately connected, forming a defensive and warlike alliance for the support of its members. The family always stuck together and struck together; guilt and loss were shared equally by all its members. Therefore 'the offending blood could be spilled from any vein that bore it, provided that the object of revenge was *vápnfærr*, or old enough and of the right sex to bear weapons and fight for himself'.

But the loss of a member of the family, Gwyn Jones points out, was material as well as emotional; that is to say, the members of the family were its material possessions, and their loss was not only a matter of sentiment and emotion, but also a matter of diminished property and security. Therefore a loss could be assessed in terms of current values; it could be restituted by the payment of a money fine or atonement. Blood vengeance might provide an emotional satisfaction, but the acceptance of financial compensation was a material restoration which in some cases at least was equally desirable. The family or kin in general contributed to the *wergeld* paid for a slain person, and they benefited from a *wergeld* paid for one of their own members, so that they had some say in the matter when the method of conducting a feud was decided. The comparative frequency of composition in feud is in large measure due to these circumstances

There were two ways of settling a dispute peacefully out of court. It could be done by an agreement in which both parties took part directly. But the more usual method was arbitration by a third party. Each side would select its own umpire or umpires, promising to accept the findings of this third party. But both sides might also agree on *one* arbitrator who had the power to impose his will on both sides. Usually the arbitrator was a man of great repute, and it was considered an honour to be called upon to settle disputes. Another mode of settlement was the so-called 'selfdoom', an arrangement whereby one party gave to the other the absolute right to decide the terms of a settlement. The right of selfdoom might at times be arrogated by a powerful and resolute adversary, but it was often also generously conferred on an opponent in recognition of the justice of his position.

The settlement by direct agreement or arbitration was much more elastic and adatable than the legal settlements of the courts, where everything had to follow exact, well-defined rules of procedure.

Legal settlement was, as we have seen, the rarest mode of resolving a dispute, at least according to the Sagas. One reason may be that at least three, and sometimes four, steps had to be taken after a killing (the most common cause of feud in the Sagas) before a lawsuit could be brought before a court.

The first was notification (*víglýsing*) when the killer announced his deed, so as not to be found guilty of murder. An open slaying was a homicide, and less serious than a secret killing which was murder and carried the heaviest penalty, outlawry.

The two next steps were taken by the pursuant. Right after the killing he had to go to the field of action and give notice against the killer (*lýsa vígum*), thereby starting his lawsuit. Then in the spring he rode on the appointed days before the Thing and summoned (*stefna*) the killer to the Thing where the lawsuit would be pleaded. The summons had to occur at the killer's home or within his hearing, and this frequently led to acts of violence and bloodshed. The fourth step was only taken under certain circumstances, and it was left to the defendant. He could 'unhallow' (*óhelga*) the killed man, thereby justifying his deed. It might be self-defence, but the reason might also be that the killed man had broken an agreement and thus put himself outside the law.

If a man was found guilty of killing at the courts of the local Things or the Althing, the judges could only sentence him to full outlawry which carried with it a death sentence. The outlaw was outside the law in that he could not be a party to any lawsuit nor expect his family to pay for his depredations if he supported himself by preying on the neighbours. He was outside the peace in that he could be attacked and killed by any man without fear of legal or compensatory consequences. All his social ties were dissolved—marriage, kinship, right of inheritance and succession— and all his property was forfeit at the Court of Execution.

Lesser outlawries were imposed by the arbitrators. They might mean banishment overseas for a period of time, usually three winters, but sometimes for life or until the death of a certain individual. There was also the district banishment. Some of these banishments were accompanied by money fines. On the whole the lesser outlawries had the same aims as the *ostracisms* in ancient Greece, namely to remove dangerous or disruptive elements for a period of time, until tempers had cooled or until more favourable circumstances had arrived.

Gwyn Jones concludes his admirable introduction by saying: 'This overwhelming importance of the personal element was the great difficulty with which Icelandic law had to contend, a difficulty aggravated by the extent of personal participation in the legal procedure of the time. In those cases which touched a man to the quick, the death of a kinsman or sworn brother, or a bitter personal insult, every instinct urged him to settle the matter himself, without the all but unendurable respite which an appeal to the law must entail. The compulsion of both kin obligation and manhood drove him to individual action and not legal procedure as the true means of satisfaction.'

But it still holds true that the law did curb the anarchy of unbridled blood-feuds. It was the preserving force of the Commonwealth. The best example of what the law meant to the ancient Icelanders is found in the events which took place at the Althing in the year 1000. There can be no doubt that the Icelanders were genuinely devoted to the sword. They were the true sons of Thór with his all-smashing hammer. But they were in equal measure devoted to reason and order. They were also the sons of Ódin, who had sacrificed one of his eyes in order to master wisdom. In fact, everything we know of ancient Icelandic culture points to the twin rule of Ódin and Thór—mind and might of arm.

The settlement of Iceland took place during the middle of the Viking Age which extended well into the eleventh century. To make the brief outline of that age in the Introduction a little more complete it remains to say a few words about two 'conquests' in the far west which are often left out of Viking histories, mainly because they were not Viking conquests in the usual sense, but rather, like Iceland, accidental discoveries.

In the case of Greenland the task is comparatively easy in that we have two extensive records of the settlement there, and these are supported by archaeological finds. The first Northman to *see* Greenland was an Icelander by the name of Gunnbjörn Úlfsson, but the discovery is usually credited to Eirík the Red, an outlaw from Norway settled in Iceland, who having been outlawed from Iceland for three years made a planned discovery of Greenland in 982 or 983. He had in mind to set up a colony in the new land, and having completed his three years of exile, he sailed back to Iceland, gathered a great number of prospective settlers (some 800) and sailed for the new land to which he had wisely given the name Greenland. Twenty-five ships set out, of which eleven had to return owing to bad weather. But it seems probable that they made another attempt and reached their destination. At any rate Greenland became the home of two fairly large and quite prosperous settlements, one on the south coast near Cape Farewell, the other on the west cost near the modern Godthaab. As has been pointed out, this migration was unique in history, in that it was first undertaken, and the settlement of a large and prosperous colony was brought about, on the sole basis of a people's reliance on the wisdom and integrity of one single man.

Later research has proved that climatic conditions in Greenland in the eleventh, twelfth and thirteenth centuries were much milder than they are at present—which clearly explains the prosperity of the colony and the willingness of so many well-to-do Icelanders to move there. By the fourteenth century conditions had greatly deteriorated, and the colony probably came to an end some time in the fifteenth century. It has been suggested that the Northmen in Greenland perished at the hands of the natives after all contact with Iceland had been severed. Others believe there may have been an assimilation between natives and Icelanders, and point to the presence of blond and blue-eyed Eskimos when Greenland was 'rediscovered' by Christian missionaries, who had hoped to find some remnants of the Northmen but searched in vain.

We have some literary records concerning Greenland which were preserved in Iceland. Chief among them are the accounts of the Greenland settlement and the discovery of America. One of the better preserved legendary poems in the *Poetic Edda* carries the name 'Greenlandic Lay of Atli', indicating that it was composed there. That may well be the case, as the lay is markedly different from other Eddic poems.

The discovery of America was a direct result of that of Greenland, but due to lack of archaeological findings it has often been discredited. However, it has been shown with almost conclusive evidence that America was visited by several expeditions, both Greenlandic and Icelandic.

The discovery of America was similar to the previous one of Greenland in that the continent was first sighted by a mariner, Bjarni Herjólfsson, who brought the news to Greenland. His voyage was one of the greatest navigational feats of all time. Having heard the news, the energetic son of Eirík (Erik) the Red, Leif, made a well-planned voyage to the unknown land. First he came to a barren country with glaciers in the highlands and slabs (the snouts of the glaciers) by the coast, and named it *Helluland* (Slabland). Then he reached a flat, wooded country which he called *Markland* (Woodland). These places are generally thought to be Baffin Island and Labrador respectively. Finally Leif came to a wooded and fertile place which he named *Vínland* (Vineland). Here he built his dwelling *Leifsbúdir* (Leif's Booths) and stayed through the winter, returning home the following spring. Leif went ashore in all three places and was thus the first European to set foot on the American continent.

Following Leif's voyage, another was made by his brother, Thorvald, who managed to find the place where Leif had built his house. Thorvald stayed two years, made some explorations and came into contact with the natives with the result that he was killed, the first European to die on American soil. Thorvald had obviously intended to settle permanently in the new world. A third brother, Thorstein, made an unsuccessful attempt to reach America.

Then followed the historic voyage made under Thorfinn Karlsefni, a man from North Iceland who set out to colonize America with at least a hundred people. His expedition lasted three years, but he too had to return, having come into contact with the warlike natives and lost some of his men. Evidently these prospective settlers neither had the manpower nor the means to set up a colony in the new world.

There have been long and conflicting discussions about the places reached by these voyagers. They will probably never be conclusively established, but there are a number of remarkable leads worthy of consideration.

Edward Reman has advanced views which seem tantalizingly convincing. He has followed the procedure of consulting the so-called Greenlandic records for the voyages made by the Greenlanders, and the Icelandic records for the voyage of Karlsefni. This, he thinks, clears up some muddled points. According to Reman, Leif reached the Bay of Fundy in Maine and there built his house, later found by his brother, while Karlsefni went into Hudson Bay, stopping in Ungava Bay, Chesterfield Inlet and Nelson River. These conclusions he reaches after a thorough study of the texts and extensive explorations on the North American coast.

Moreover, in the absence of any archaeological finds to prove the visits of Northmen to America, Reman points out certain significant details in the text which come close to proving the accuracy of the accounts. We are told in the story of the second voyage that Thorvald found on one of the islands a wooden *kornhjálm*, a container for storing grain. There is evidence that Indians of later times used this kind of receptacle. When thoroughly dry the corn 'was usually stored in caches, although it was sometimes placed in wooden receptacles about three feet high, made by cutting hollow logs into sections'.[9] Later we are told that a great number of natives appeared in 'hide boats', a reference which was long believed to indicate confusion with the Eskimo boats in Greenland. However, it has now been proved that 'boats of moose-hide were actually made and used by the ancient Indians of northern and central Maine and Nova Scotia, however rare their use may have been among American Indians elsewhere'.[10]

In the account of Karlsefni's voyage we are told that the natives attacked them and used 'war slings'. We have evidence that the Algonquin Indians inhabiting the region between Hudson Bay and the Atlantic seaboard used slings, often of considerable size and power. Then we are told later on that Karlsefni's men killed five natives on the shores (of Hudson Bay, according to Reman), and these had with them a container filled with a mixture of animal marrow and blood, which 'corresponds well with the sausages the Red Indians used to prepare'. The Neskaupee, a Northern Algonquin people, used to preserve marrow and blood 'in the form of a thickened pudding'.[11]

These minute details reinforce the veracity of the accounts, and Reman's thorough and scientific examination of the texts as well as climatic conditions, flora, fauna, landscape, currents, and anthropological evidence comes close to dispersing any doubts about the discovery of America by these early voyagers.

Other evidence, however, points in other directions. When Helge Ingstad was exploring the northern tip of Newfoundland in the early 1960s he met an old man, George Decker, who lived in the fishing village L'Anse-aux-Meadows. He pointed out some old ruins near his village, which were called 'Indian Camp', which he believed to be remains of the dwellings of Norse Vikings. Excavations there have brought to light a charcoal pit, an old 'smithy' and some slag that indicate the former presence of ironworkers, but neither the Indians nor the Eskimos, the original inhabitants of the country, were able to work in iron. The charcoal found there has been determined by the C-14 method as being from about the year 900, the date in question being when the wood ceased to grow and not when the coal was made.[12]

We are told that Leif's brother, Thorvald, was killed by an arrow, most likely shot by an Indian. In the ruins of the Sandnes farm in Greenland (where Thorstein, Thorvald's brother, lived) a stone arrow was found a few years ago. The Danish ethnologist Jørgen Meldgaard considers that arrowhead to be exactly of the type used by the Indians in Labrador. Thorvald's comrades might well have brought it back with them to Greenland. At any rate, Meldgaard considers this arrowhead alone as sufficient proof that the people in Greenland had contact with the American mainland.

Notes

1. Professor Thórhallur Vilmundarson of the University of Iceland has adduced cogent arguments to the effect that the *Book of Settlements* should not be taken as a reliable historical source. He has shown with numerous examples that many of the persons mentioned in that book are imaginary creations used to explain certain place-names. His theory is that the place-names derive from natural characteristics in the landscape. His conclusions have been supported by Halldór Laxness, who has long been interested in medieval history, and by Professor Sigurdur Líndal of the University of Iceland, who has put forth strong arguments for supposing that the first settler of Iceland, Ingólf Arnarson, is very doubtful as a historical personage. These exciting theories are bound to be intensely debated in the coming decades.

2. *Egil's Saga*, translated by Gwyn Jones, New York 1960, pp. 81-2.

3. Olaf Olsen, *Hørg, hov og kirke. Historiske og arkæologiske studier.* Copenhagen 1966.

4. The epithet of Grím is usually rendered *geitskór*, meaning 'goatshoe', but some scholars maintain that this is a misreading for *geitskör*, meaning 'goatee', which seems probable.

5. See Einar Ól. Sveinsson, *The Age of the Sturlungs*. Translated by Jóhann S. Hannesson. New York 1953, p. 9.

6. Quoted from *Pioneers of Freedom* by Sveinbjorn Johnson, Boston 1930, p. 200.

7. *Njal's Saga*, translated by Bayerschmidt and Hollander, New York 1955, pp. 219-20.

8. Hans E. Kinck, quoted in *The Age of the Sturlungs*, p. 62.

9. Edward Reman, *The Norse Discoveries and Explorations in America*, California 1949, p. 104, quoting C.C. Willoughby in *American Anthropologist*, Vol. VIII, p. 131.

10. Ibid., p. 110, quoting Frank G. Speck, *Penobset Man*, 1940, p. 66.

11. Ibid., p. 175, quoting William Hovgaard, *The Voyages of the Norsemen in America*, 1914, p. 190, and Frank Speck, *Neskapi*, 1935, p. 92.

12. Thórhallur Vilmundarson, 'The Vinland Voyages', *Iceland Review*, Vol. 3, No. 1, 1963, p. 11.

2. Individuals

We have already mentioned that Christianity was adopted in the year 1000, and that Icelandic literature had its beginnings around the middle of the twelfth century. There is clearly a connection between these two events in so far as the church introduced an alphabet which was soon adapted to the vernacular. Moreover, the chieftains endeavoured to function as religious leaders, along with their secular activities, by building churches and taking holy orders or appointing priests who were their dependants. This made for a high degree of learning among the ruling class, as many of them went abroad to study and came home to organize schools, which in time produced some of the most distinguished scholars of the Commonwealth. It became the fashion to be 'learned', or well versed, not only in religious matters but equally in history and poetics. Some of these learned men would enter the service of the church and translate foreign religious literature which in many ways influenced secular Icelandic literature. Others did not make direct use of their religious learning, but devoted their time and talents rather to preserving from oblivion the past of their proud race. The first written records in the vernacular were the laws of the land which were codified in 1117-18. And as time passed, stories and poems which had been passed down orally, sometimes for centuries, were committed to writing.

The names of a number of historians of early Iceland are known, while those of the authors or compilers of the Eddic poems and the numerous Sagas have never been discovered. These historians are worth considering briefly, for there is an intimate connection between the Sagas and history proper, and it has never been possible to determine conclusively how much in the Sagas is history. All we know is that some of the historians learned much from the technique of the Sagas, and that the Saga-writers often used historical records, such as genealogies or accounts of specific historical events.

The first historian of any note in Iceland was Saemund Sigfússon (1056-1133), the grandson of Hall of Sída, the Christian Law-speaker who was instrumental in preserving the peace in the year 1000. Saemund studied in Paris at an early age and became a master of Latin, surpassing all contemporary Icelanders. He and his prodigious learning became the subject of many legends, and he was erroneously credited with having written the *Poetic Edda*. Saemund became a priest at Oddi, a famous estate in South Iceland and a great centre of learning under his direction and that of his descendants.

Saemund had a great influence and was an important historian, specializing in chronology, mainly the genealogies of the Norwegian kings of earlier ages, for whom he established a Christian chronology up till 1047. His works, which were written in Latin, have all been lost except for references in other books.

A contemporary of Saemund, Ari Thorgilsson (1067-1148), was the first historian to write in the vernacular. He wrote *Islendingabók* (Book of the Icelanders) of which his abbreviated version is still extant. Here he gives an objective survey of Icelandic history from the beginning of the settlement down to around 1000, which became a model for later Icelandic histories. Ari starts his work with a declaration: 'Whatever is misstated in this account, it is imperative to prefer whatever proves to be more correct.' It indicates Ari's painstaking endeavour to record only what may be verified, and he goes to great pains to enumerate his souces. In these Ari was exceptionally fortunate, for he had informants of great learning and good memories. One of them was Hall Thórarinsson, his foster-father from the age of seven, who could remember his own baptism by one of the Christian missionaries in 998, when he was three years old. He died in 1089 at the age of ninety-four. He had travelled extensively abroad and been in the service of King Ólaf of Norway (*d.* 1030), who after his death became St Ólaf.

Ari had a profound influence on later historians and on the writers of the Sagas. Snorri Sturluson, probably referring to his lost book, speaks of his history as remarkable; and he is named in many of the Sagas as the most reliable source of information. It has been shown that Ari was probably the author of the original version of the *Book of Settlements,* now lost, and that all later versions are ultimately traceable to him.[1] Besides being of inestimable value as a historical source, Ari's existing work 'is no less precious as a literary monument, for it is the oldest example of narrative prose in a Scandinavian language'.[2] Like Saemund, Ari bore the epithet '*fródi*' ('the wise' or 'the learned') and was a priest. He was the great-grandson of Hall of Sída on one side, and on the other the great-grandson of Gudrún, the renowned heroine of *Laxdaela Saga*.

Many of the monks of the small Icelandic monasteries distinguished themselves as historians, especially of Norwegian history. Eirík Oddsson wrote a work of Norwegian history, now lost, around 1160, and Abbot Karl Jónsson wrote the history of King Sverrir of Norway, partly at the dictation of the king himself.

Two monks in North Iceland, Odd Snorrasọn and Gunnlaug Leifsson, wrote histories of the Norwegian king Ólaf Tryggvason in Latin. Gunnlaug also wrote biographies of two famous bishops in Iceland. There exist a great quantity of bishops' biographies in Icelandic, written from around 1200 to 1350, but most of them are anonymous.

Whatever the reasons, the ancient Icelanders seem to have felt a special mission to preserve the past from oblivion, not only the past of their own country, but also that of their cousins in Scandinavia. The absence of writing in the other Nordic countries is conspicuous, and it is interesting to note that the only historian of any consequence outside Iceland, the Danish Saxo Grammaticus, who wrote a history of his own nation in Latin around the year 1200, has this to say of 'the industrious Icelanders':

They are happy to spend their whole life promoting knowledge about the deeds of other peoples. It is their pleasure to study the affairs of all nations and tell about them to others, and they take just as much pride in presenting the acts of virtue and manhood of others as in performing such acts themselves. I have diligently consulted their treasures of true stories, which I have made the basis of a great part of my work, and I would not reject such authorities well versed in all ancient matters.

It was from Saxo that Shakespeare derived the material for *Hamlet,* and Saxo undoubtedly had his story from Iceland, where many independent traditions of the famous prince were in existence (his name, *Amlódi* in Icelandic, has become a synonym for an irresolute or inactive person).

A Norwegian author who wrote a history of the Norwegian kings in Latin about the same time as Saxo wrote his history, referred to the Icelanders for a point of chronology, and added: 'Undoubtedly, above all nations of the North, they have always been the most inquiring and the best informed in all such questions.'

But Iceland was still to see the giant in the field of historical writing, the man who would combine the vast knowledge of a great historian with a creative mind, artistic instincts and independent judgment. This man was Snorri Sturluson (1178-1241) who wrote two of the most significant works of Norse literature, the so-called *Prose Edda* and *Heimskringla,* the history of the kings of Norway from the pre-historic times up to the high Middle Ages. Snorri is probably also the author of *Egil's Saga,* one of the best and most renowned of the *Sagas of Icelanders.*

Snorri Sturluson lived during one of the most chaotic periods in Icelandic history, a period exceeding in savagery anything previously known in Iceland. This period down to the collapse of the Commonwealth derives its name from Snorri's family, the

Sturlungs (descendants of Sturla). His father Sturla was an ambitious, ferocious and influential upstart chieftain who had married into a very prominent family and had three legitimate sons, all outstanding men who played a tragic part in the history of their age.

In a sense Snorri's greatest fortune was caused by a feud between his father and a protégé of one of the most powerful chieftains of the country, Jón Loftsson, grandson of Saemund Sigfússon the Wise of Oddi and of King Magnus Bareleg of Norway. Sturla had been stabbed in the cheek by the wife of his opponent at a meeting of the contending parties and demanded a compensation far in excess of the legal penalty for such an injury. The arrogant demand was rejected, and Sturla's opponent found many strong supporters, among them Jón Loftsson. Sturla agreed to let Jón judge the matter and was awarded a mere eighth of the sum claimed. But in order to placate Sturla, Jón offered to act as foster-father to his son Snorri, then aged three. The offer was a great honour which Sturla willingly accepted, and thus it came about that Snorri was reared at the great cultural centre of Oddi, steeped un an atmosphere of history, poetics and Latin, where he remained till early manhood. There was a large collection of manuscripts to be delved into by a curious and intelligent young man, and Snorri evidently made ample use of the opportunity. Moreover, his foster-father was one of the most learned and brilliant men of his age, a man of goodwill and peace, even though he stood firmly on his own right. He probably instilled in the young Snorri love for law and literature, and modified the warlike disposition he had inherited from his turbulent father.

Sturla died in 1183, when Snorri was five, and his second son Sighvat inherited the chieftainship. Snorri's share of the inheritance was mostly wasted by his mother, so that he had few resources when Jón Loftsson died in 1197. Two years later, when Snorri was twenty-one, his eldest brother Thórd arranged for him to marry Herdís, only daughter of Bersi the Wealthy, who owned the estate of Borg, which had been the home of his maternal ancestor, the great poet and warrior Egil Skallagrímsson. When Bersi died in 1202, Snorri moved to Borg and acquired a chieftainship, probably by inheritance from Bersi. He also shared another chieftainship with his maternal uncle Thórd Bödvarsson. Now Snorri plunged into the politics of his time with all the impetuousness of youth, quickly amassing a fortune, most likely by the same unscrupulous and ruthless methods which he used in his later dealings. Snorri's marriage to Herdís was probably no more than a cold-blooded means of acquiring wealth.

In about 1206 Snorri left his wife and their son and daughter at Borg, himself moving to Reykholt, some twenty-five miles away, a large estate of which the owner was old and incapable of running it efficiently. Snorri took over the property and undertook to support the old man and his family in exchange. In this way he both increased his wealth and his power. One of the very few archaeological remains in Iceland is the work of Snorri, a walled circular basin in Reykholt, some three feet deep and about twelve feet across, filled with water from one of the many hot springs in the valley. It was probably roofed over in Snorri's time, so that it could be used at any time of the year.

By this time Snorri had already begotten one bastard child, and from now on for many years he kept a series of concubines by whom he had several more children. This did not prevent him from being twice elected to the distinguished office of the Law-speaker, first from 1215 to 1218 (when he went abroad), and again from 1222 to 1231. He proved himself an outstanding jurist and an accomplished diplomat.

At the age of forty, in 1218, Snorri sailed for Norway where he was welcomed by the regent, Earl Skúli Bárdarson, uncle of King Hákon Hákonarson, who was only fourteen years old at the time. Skúli and Snorri, both of them ambitious, unscrupulous and indecisive, became close friends and allies. The following spring Snorri went to the Swedish island of Gotland, and then returned to Earl Skúli with whom he stayed for the next year and a half. In the spring of 1220, when Skúli's court journeyed from Túnsberg to Bergen, Snorri made himself exceedingly useful intervening in a dispute between Icelanders and the townsmen of Bergen which had assumed ominous proportions, almost threatening a military expedition to Iceland. It had been the ambition of several Norwegian kings to subject Iceland to their rule, as they had done to the Orkneys and the Faroes, and the clash in Bergen had suggested this again to both Earl Skúli and King Hákon. But Snorri was able to dissuade them by convincing them that it would be better to win the friendship of the chief men in Iceland and induce them to give their allegiance to the Norwegian king. However, on his returning to Iceland he did nothing to promote this idea, probably because he never intended to do so, but merely wanted to save his country from warfare and destruction. Snorri was met with distrust when he returned, since rumours of the secret agreement with the Norwegian crown had gone before him. But he was able to dispel all suspicions with his diplomatic skill and regain the confidence of this compatriots with the consequence that he was re-elected Law-speaker in 1222, holding that most influential post for ten years. He was soon again the most powerful man in Iceland, having married his three daughters to outstanding leaders of three powerful families, and himself having set up house with the richest woman in Iceland, the widow

Hallveig Ormsdóttir, arranging that they should hold all property in common and that he should also be in charge of the property of her two sons by her previous marriage. That made him by far the richest man in Iceland. It was probably in this period that Snorri composed the literary works which place him in the forefront of medieval European writers.

For all his wealth and prestige, Snorri's position in Iceland was not as secure as might have been expected. One of his sons-in-law was killed in 1228, and his two other sons-in-law, both powerful chieftains, divorced their wives. Snorri also fell out with his eldest brother, Sighvat, who had a just complaint against him because of the depredations of Snorri's ungovernable favourite son (a bastard), Óraekja. To avenge himself, Sighvat attacked Snorri in 1236 and drove him out of house and home in Reykholt. On the occasion Snorri showed little physical courage or determination. Snorri was also on bad terms with his sons: he refused to part with lands on which his legitimate son Jón Murt had intended to settle, and later refused a similar request from Óraekja.

In 1237 Snorri sailed for Norway accompanied by his son Óraekja who had been castrated by his uncle and cousin, Sighvat and Sturla, and exiled. Sturla Sighvatsson had spent two years in Norway and Rome, and was on friendly terms with King Hákon who had probably made him his special emissary in Iceland with the promise of appointing him supreme chieftain there once Iceland was brought into subjection. King Hákon therefore had little use for Snorri, who attached himself to Skúli, who had now risen to the rank of a duke and was not on good terms with his nephew. In the autumn of 1238 news was brought to Norway that both Sighvat and Sturla had been killed by Snorri's former son-in-law, Kolbein the Young, who now ruled the whole of North Iceland. Snorri was deeply moved by his brother's death and expressed his grief in a verse which he sent to one of Sighvat's two surviving sons, but he also saw a new chance of regaining his properties and influence. The following spring he therefore set out for Iceland, in direct disobedience of the king's express order, but with the connivance of Duke Skúli. On seeing the king's letter, he merely remarked 'I am homeward-bound', and it was said that Duke Skúli had conferred on him the title of earl.

Snorri succeeded in regaining all his former chieftainships and even increasing his wealth. He also helped Sighvat's surviving son, Tumi, to obtain compensation for his father from Kolbein the Young and from Gizur Thorvaldsson who had also been a leading antagonist in the battle in which Sighvat and Sturla were slain. Kolbein and Gizur, both of them estranged sons-in-law of Snorri Sturluson and both belonging to families of long-established power, seem to have been determined to prevent him from rebuilding his position at their expense. At about the same time Snorri lost Hallveig, whom he appears to have held in great esteem, and was faced with the heavy task of sharing out her estates with his two stepsons. When he evaded a final settlement they turned for help to their uncle Gizur Thorvaldsson, who was only too eager to pick a quarrel with his former father-in-law. He had a letter from King Hákon ordering him to bring Snorri to Norway, with or without his consent, or else kill him for committing an act of treason in leaving Norway against the king's command. With sixty men, among them one of the stepsons and a former son-in-law of Snorri, Gizur surprised him in Reykholt in the nigh of 23 September 1241, and had him killed. The king claimed Snorri's properties. In a sense his death was the prelude to the collapse of the Commonwealth twenty years later, when Gizur Thorvaldsson became the Norwegian king's earl over Iceland.

Whatever may be said about Snorri Sturluson's intrigues, avarice, political ambitions and ruthless legal manipulations, he is the author of two of the most significant works of Norse literature, the so-called *Prose Edda* and the *Heimskringla (Orb of the World)*, and probably of *Egil's Saga*, one of the major *Sagas of Icelanders*.

The first and most important part of the *Prose Edda* takes up the myths of the *Poetic Edda* and tells them in prose in the framework of a continuous tale of great literary merit and engaging wit. This is a very valuable source of information about ancient Germanic mythology, since Snorri has filled in many of the gaps that exist in the *Poetic Edda* as we have it today. The first part is called *The Deluding of Gylfi* and tells of the travels of a Swedish king, named Gylfi, to Asgard, the home of the tribe of Aesir (singular: *As*) or gods, to learn their wisdom and find out about their origins. Interestingly enough, Snorri places Ásgard in Asia, and has the great gods live in Troy as chieftains with Odin as the king or overlord. Odin then sets out and travels to the North through Germany, Denmark, Sweden and Norway, over each of which he places one of his sons as a ruler.

Gylfi, disguised as an old man, reaches his destination after long travels and meets three kings who in reality are three different incarnations of Odin. They call themselves High, Just-as-High, and Third. Gylfi asks them many questions and they tell him all about the origin of the world and the events of antiquity. At the beginning Snorri's account is coloured by his Christian outlook, and he tries to explain the pagan religion by two rationalizations. The first is that the gods were great men of former ages who came to be worshipped as gods: this is a Greek interpretation (euhemerism) which Snorri probably found in foreign books. The other rationalization is closer to that in vogue among nineteenth-century scholars who tried to explain the origins of religion.[3]

Snorri says:

They observed that in many respects the earth and birds and beasts have the same nature and yet exhibit different behaviour, and they wondered what this signified. For instance, one could dig down into the earth on a mountain peak no deeper than one would in a low-lying valley and yet strike water; in the same way, in both birds and beasts, the blood lies as near to the surface of the skin of the head as of the feet. Another characteristic of the earth is that every year grass and flowers grow on it and that in the same year they wither and die; similarly fur and feathers grow and die every year on beasts and birds. There is a third thing about the earth: when its surface is broken into and dug up, grass grows on the topsoil. Mountains and boulders they associated with the teeth and bones of living creatures, and so they looked on the earth as in some way a living being with a life of its own. They knew it was inconceivably ancient as years go and, by nature, powerful; it gave birth to all things and owned all that died, and for that reason they gave it a name and reckoned their descent from it. They also learned from their ancestors that the same earth and stars and sun had been in existence for many centuries, but that the procession of stars was unequal; some had a long journey, others a short one. From things like this they guessed that there must be someone who ruled the stars, who, if he desired, could put an end to their procession, and that he must be very powerful and strong. They reckoned too that, if he controlled the primal elements, he must have existed before the heavenly bodies; and they realized that, if he guided these, he must rule over the shining of the sun and the dew-fall and the growth of plants resultant on these, and the winds of the air and storms of the sea as well. They did not know where his kingdom was, but they believed that he ruled everything on earth and in the sky, heaven and the stars, the ocean and all weathers. In order that this might be related and kept in mind, they gave their own name to everything, but with the migrations of peoples and multiplication of languages this belief has changed in many ways. They understood everything in a material sense, however, since they had not been given spiritual understanding, and so they thought that everything had been made from one substance.[4]

For a thirteenth-century writer these are interesting specu-lations, but as soon as Snorri starts relating the various stories of the gods he forgets all such 'scientific' endeavour for sheer delight in story-telling. With great skill he makes the gods come to life again. Most of these stories are found in the *Poetic Edda* to which we shall return in the next chapter.

In the second section of Snorri's *Edda*, called *Language of Poetry*, it is Bragi, the god of poetry, who has the floor and explains the origin of his divine art in Suttung's Mead, another reference to the Eddic lays. This section is actually a textbook for the *skald* or court poet, containing instructions on the preparation and use of poetic images from the world of myth. Here Snorri was making a last unsuccessful attempt to revive the skaldic poetry, which was declining rapidly during his lifetime.

The last section of the book is a *tour de force* on Snorri's part, giving concrete examples illustrating the preceding section. It consists of 102 stanzas, each in a different metre, with complicated variations. This performance is of little significance artistically, but Snorri reveals himself a supreme master of form—of which he was rightly proud. This section has been called a display of fireworks in versification rather than a poetic achievement.

But Snorri was yet to write his major work and reveal still another of his many and prodigious talents. This he did in the *Heimskringla*, a history of the kings of Norway from the earliest times down to 1177 when King Sverrir, whose history we possess, took the reins in Norway. This work is widely regarded as the outstanding historical work of the Middle Ages. Snorri was a careful and scientific historian who showed great acumen in his choice of sources and would have nothing to do with myths and legends. Whenever possible he omitted them or rationalized them, as comparison with his sources readily demonstrates. Snorri placed great store by skaldic poetry, which in his opinion was least likely to misrepresent events, due to reasons which he put forth in his prologue:

There were skalds with Harald [Finehair], and men still know their poems, and the poems about all the kings who have since ruled in Norway. And we take our statements most of all from what is said in those poems which were recited before the rulers themselves and their sons. We accept as true all that is found in these about their exploits and battles. It is certainly the custom of poets to praise most highly the person they are addressing, but no one would have dared to recite to the man himself exploits which he and all the hearers knew to be false and feigned; that would have been mockery and not praise.

Snorri also made use of the historical research of Ari, whom, he showed, there was every reason to trust, as he had only made use of first-class sources.

Snorri concentrated on the essential points of the separate stories of the kings and brought them into a connected whole, making an artistic unity out of a conglomeration of disconnected facts. He had the artist's broad vision and unsurpassed skill in the handling of language. But his outstanding ability was his power of characterization, of psychological penetration and portraiture. There can be little doubt that in this respect Snorri benefited from his knowledge of the *Sagas of Icelanders,* some of which had already been written by his time. But it is equally probable that Snorri's writing had a profound impact on all later Saga-writing, for that genre only reached its peak after his time. What is striking is the dramatic quality of Snorri's work, a quality which probably owed something to the *Sagas of Icelanders,* and perhaps even more to the Eddic poetry, with which he was so eminently familiar.

In his *Heimskringla* Snorri makes the kings the sole carriers of the history of Norway, thus magnifying their role and finding a centre of gravity for his whole work. The vital problem in that history is the struggle between king and nobility, the one representing large national ideals, the other small, selfish interests. This makes for unity in the work, while Snorri is careful not to use sweeping generalizations. The character of each king is at the forefront and defines the particular action and policy in each case. The central character of the whole work is the missionary king St Ólaf (*d.* 1030), whose story comprises about one-third of the entire *History,* and is in reality an independent work. The *locus classicus* of Snorri's characterization is the one where he compares the two brothers and kings, St Ólaf and Harald Hardruler, and shows that no two men were actually more alike in character, although Ólaf was regarded as a saint and Harald as a tyrant.

There have been conflicting views as to whether Snorri wrote other works, and many scholars doubt it, but the leading Icelandic authority Sigurdur Nordal has proved beyond reasonable doubt that he is the true author of *Egil's Saga,* which we shall discuss in a later chapter. This is one of the very greatest of the *Sagas of Icelanders,* and the only one whose author is reasonably established.

If any man was an embodiment of the whole of medieval Icelandic culture, that man was Snorri Sturluson. He was the warrior and the sage: on the one hand historian, poet, mythologist, lawyer and Saga-writer; and on the other chieftain, Viking, and lover of wealth and women. He was in a fuller sense than pehaps any other man the perfect example of the 'Renaissance Man', for he excelled in most of the things he undertook, and drained the cup of life to its very last drop. If we look for a Greek analogy, we shall have to combine salient traits from such different individuals as Herodotus, Alcibiades, Themistocles and possibly Pericles. Of the ancient Romans Cicero would seem most akin to Snorri: both were greedy for wealth and power, and occupied high offices; both were great writers and masters of language; both were wicked and ruthless, but preferred others to do their dirty work; both were fickle-minded artists with opposing tendencies fighting in their souls, but lacking the fortune to check their ambitions and assess their achievements, with the result that both were killed by more ruthless villains, neither of them trying to defend himself.

The last great historian of the Icelandic Commonwealth was a nephew of Snorri's and his collaborator for some time, Sturla Thórdarson, to whom we owe our detailed knowledge of the last turbulent phase of the Commonwealth. Sturla also wrote biographies of Norwegian kings and some skaldic poetry with which he won the favour of the son and successor of the Norwegian king who had caused his uncle's death. But his major work is the *Sturlunga Saga,* which is part of a larger work covering the period from the beginning of the twelfth century to the end of the Commonwealth. The objectivity of this work is really admirable, as it centres around the very struggles of Sturla's own family in which he himself had taken part. However, his painstaking truthfulness has a disadvantage: he crowds his narrative with names and incidents without much discrimination between what is important and unimportant, and this takes some of the life out of his admirable history. Yet he had obviously learned much from Snorri as well as from the *Sagas of Icelanders,* and some of the individual scenes are charged with dramatic intensity worthy of the best Sagas. This is the more laudable as Sturla's undertaking was more difficult than that of any other historian, for he was so clearly restricted by the closeness of the facts he was recording. This work is pure history and therefore only carries the name *Saga* in the very widest sense, which is the Icelandic sense.

We have referred to skaldic poetry several times, and some words about this branch of Icelandic literature are in place here. Skaldic poetry is quite different from Eddic poetry, which will be discussed in the next chapter. The skaldic poems were composed by a certain 'class' of people, *the skalds,* at a given moment in history, praising a king, commemorating a battle or expressing a deep personal feeling. They are not concerned with myth and legend as such, but derive from them images and symbols to illustrate or enliven a contemporary event. These poems are by no means simple or direct poetic expressions, as are most of the Eddic lays. The intricacies and artificiality of skaldic poetry are exasperating to all but the scholar and the crossword-puzzle-devotee. Sentences are hacked and dislocated, and metaphors far-fetched and obscure. These images, called *kennings,* are produced by naming a given object by means of two or three other objects. For instance, a shield becomes a 'field of spears', a ship becomes a 'steed of the sea', a head becomes a 'hill of the helmet', and so on. The effect of this playing with words and phrases is often quite sonorous and pleasing when the poems are read aloud, but their meaning is a matter of long and patient reconstruction, at least for a modern reader. In reality, skaldic poetry is more a matter of craftsmanship than a poetic genius, and some skalds achieved amazing mastery in it.

Many of the heroes of the *Sagas of Icelanders* were skalds, as we shall see, and some of them, like Egil Skallagrímsson, did combine form and feeling. Egil was a great innovator in Icelandic and

Nordic poetry and wrote some of the very finest skaldic verse ever written.

Unlike the authors of the Eddic poems and the Sagas, most of the skalds are known by name, because their calling was one which earned them great reputations, and the Icelanders soon came to monopolize skaldic poetry at all the Scandinavian courts, and even in the British Isles. Lee M. Hollander has written an excellent book, *The Skalds,* with translations which are probably the best available in English.

In conclusion we may name a few individuals who distinguished themselves in matters not directly related to literature. One of them is, indeed, not known by name, but he is included here for lack of a better place, and because he did an inestimable service to Icelandic letters. This individual is the author of *The First Grammatical Treatise* which is the earliest phonology in any Germanic language. This first phonetician of any modern language wrote a marvellously accurate and scholarly work on the phonetics of Icelandic, adapting the Latin alphabet to the vernacular and introducing all the necessary modifications. This pioneering work has been published in English. There were three other grammatical treatises, one of them written by the poet Ólaf Thórdarson, brother of Sturla Thórdarson, but the most valuable was obviously the work of the anonymous pioneer.

We have already mentioned the extensive travels of the medieval Icelanders. The most frequented places outside Northern and Western Europe were Rome, Constantinople and the Holy Land. The Sagas contain many informative descriptions of foreign parts. One of the skalds, Nikulás Bergsson (or Bergthórsson), made a trip to Rome and the Holy Land around 1150 and wrote an excellent account of his travels through Germany, Switzerland, Italy, Sicily, and Palestine. Nikulás was an abbot and probably wrote his *Guide* around 1159. Another travel book by Gizur Hallsson (*d.* 1206) is lost.

In mathematics there were some notable achievements. We are told that already in the tenth century people noticed irregularity in the calendar, and the ingenious Thorstein Surt corrected it by inserting seven days every sixth year. This week was called the *summer addition.* This shows that the seven-day week was already established, in place of the older five-day week. Arabic numbers were not introduced until the thirteenth century.

Astronomy was of vital importance to the Norse navigators, and we have evidence of great interest in these matters. One of the outstanding men in this field was 'Star'-Oddi Helgason, a man of lowly origins, who lived in the twelfth century. He made more accurate observations of the variations in the altitude of the sun from day to day throughout the year, and fixed the time of the solstices more precisely than any contemporary European astronomer. He is also supposed to have played a major role in the successful reconciliation of the old Icelandic year-reckoning with the Julian calendar. 'Star'-Oddi and Bjarni the Mathematician are considered the founders of later Icelandic calendrical computations.

Thus we know the names of a number of individuals in ancient Iceland who distinguished themselves as historians, skalds and scholars, but the great works of art in Icelandic literature, the *Poetic Edda* and the *Sagas of Icelanders*, are anonymous with the sole exception of *Egil's Saga*. Although they are undoubtedly to a greater or lesser degree the creations of individuals, they now belong to that large group of national epics which include the *Mahabharata*, the *Ramayana*, *The Old Testament*, *The Gilgamesh Epic*, *The Romance of Sinuhe*, *The Legend of Keret*, *The Song of Roland*, *Beowulf*, *The Cuchullin Cycle*, *The Cid*, the *Nibelungenlied*, *Tristan and Iseult*, and the *Kalevala*.

Notes

1. G. Turville-Petre, *Origins of Icelandic Literature*, Oxford 1953, Chapter IV.
2. Ibid., p. 90.
3. Sigurdur Nordal, *Snorri Sturluson*, Reykjavík 1920, Chapters 5 and 6.
4. Snorri Sturluson, *The Prose Edda*, translated by Jean I. Young, Cambridge 1954, pp. 23-5.

3. Myth and Legend

The records of mankind are preserved or destroyed according to the caprice of fate. But for a series of apparent 'accidents', the entire pre-Christian history of the Germanic peoples—that is to say the Scandinavians, the German-speakers and the Anglo-Saxons—would be almost entirely lost to us. We should know next to nothing about their daily life, their religion, customs, preoccupations and values.

The first of these 'accidents' was the settlement of Iceland in the ninth century—the moving away of a segment of the continental population of Europe to a remote and comparatively secluded island. There can be little doubt that one of the principal reasons for the literary activities of the Icelanders was the wish of the noble chieftains to preserve their family traditions and keep a record of the deeds of their ancestors. These people had been uprooted from their old country and settled in a new and in many ways strange environment. They were bent on preserving in poems and prose narratives their links with a glorious past.

The second 'accident' was the adoption of Christianity in Iceland—again a shift from one tradition to another, but with a difference, since the change of religion paradoxically led to the preservation of the old heathen tradition by committing it to vellum.

Still, we might know less of the unique Old Icelandic literature than we do, but for a third significant 'accident' which occurred much later and involved a paradoxical change of locality in that the literature was bodily transferred to another country.

During the centuries after the collapse of the Icelandic Commonwealth in 1264 there was a gradual decline in the life of the nation, both culturally and economically. The literary output became markedly inferior in quality as well as quantity. During those centuries, however, the Icelanders performed an important work both for themselves and the world at large. They were untiring in copying the manuscripts of the best literary works from the Golden Age. These became the possession of the people as a whole, both rich and poor, and they were instrumental in preserving the language in scattered communities through the succeeding centuries. These works actually became the life nerve of the race during the dark ages of foreign domination.

Nevertheless, as the lot of the population progressively deteriorated, many of the precious manuscripts, written as they were mostly on the hides of cows and calves, were taken and used for 'practical' purposes, such as clothing and footwear. Some of the works were saved for a time by paper-copies which in turn would be damaged or destroyed by damp, fire or other calamities. At present it is impossible to evaluate how much of the old literary treasures perished in this way, but the quantity was certainly enormous.

At the crucial moment, however, when much had been lost but much was still to be rescued, there appeared on the scene Árni Magnússon (1663-1730), who may properly be called the 'saviour' of Old Icelandic literature, even though many other devoted individuals had a hand in the miraculous deliverance. He was a brilliant scholar and had been appointed Professor at the University of Copenhagen at an early age. He made it his life's mission to save what was still extant of the ancient literary treasures of his country and bring them to safety in the University of Copenhagen which at the time was also the Icelandic univeristy, Iceland having come under Danish rule along with Norway in 1380.

For ten years Árni Magnússon travelled all over Iceland collecting manuscripts, haggling and purchasing wherever he went, buying them from anyone at almost any price. In 1720 fifty-five cases of manuscripts were taken to Copenhagen where Árni Magnússon set up a special collection to which he gradually added manuscripts acquired from other collectors. There were quite a number of these at the time and there are records of large collections sinking to the bottom of the ocean when the ships carrying them to Copenhagen foundered in the storms of the North Atlantic.

On 20 October 1728, Copenhagen caught fire, and a day later the fire reached the collection. Heroic efforts fell short of saving the printed books but perhaps one-third of the library survived according to the estimate of a contemporary who helped rescue the manuscripts. Fortunately, these were the oldest manuscripts. 'Here have gone writings which are nowhere else to be found in the wide world,' was Árni Magnússon's comment on a misfortune from which he never recovered. He is the hero of Halldór Laxness's novel *The Bell of Iceland*.

Despite this irremediable disaster, much of what we now call Old Icelandic (or Old Norse) literature was preserved in manuscripts collected by Árni Magnússon. During the last two centuries scholars all over Northern and Western Europe and North America have been studying, editing and translating them into their languages. In Iceland these works can still be read in the original by every child who has learned to read, so slight are the changes in the language during the past one thousand years. It is the oldest living literary language of Europe. Even the language of Shakespeare in England and that of Luther in Germany sound relatively archaic to modern English and German readers, whereas the genuine language of the Sagas has been employed by modern Icelandic novelists, such as Laxness.

A happy conclusion to the long and tumultuous history of the Icelandic manuscripts came in the spring of 1965 when the Danish parliament passed a hotly contested resolution to return the bulk of the manuscripts to Iceland where a special institution for their perusal has been set up.

Old Icelandic literature falls into two main categories, poetry and prose. The poetry is largely divided into two distinct classes, Eddic poetry and skaldic poetry. The latter has been briefly discussed in the previous chapter. Skaldic poems have a certain historical importance, since they describe contemporary events and were recited in the presence of people who had witnessed or taken part in those events.

Eddic poetry is quite distinct from skaldic poetry in that it is direct, dramatic, and impersonal. It avoids description of battles or other events, but makes extensive use of dialogue. Elaborate imagery is almost totally absent, and the poets make their points with stark simplicity. None of the authors is known by name.

One of the most important manuscripts of Snorri Sturluson's *Prose Edda*, a parchment from about 1320, is prefaced by this statement: 'This book is called *Edda*; Snorri Sturluson wrote it in the same order in which it is set out here.' When the manuscript of the *Poetic* or *Elder Edda* was discovered in 1643, the scholar-bishop Brynjólf Sveinsson made the assumption that he had found the source of Snorri's work and that this work had been written by Saemund Sigfússon the Wise of Oddi. He therefore called it *Edda Saemundii multiscii*, and this name has stuck to the book for better or for worse.

What the name 'Edda' denotes has never been established. Of the three principal theories, one is that it derives from the Icelandic word *ódr* (poem, poetry), and simply means 'Poetics'. That would fit some parts of Snorri's *Edda*, but recent scholarship has tended to discount this theory.[1] A second theory is that it comes from Oddi, and therefore means 'The Book of Oddi'. This would be in accordance with Icelandic customs of naming books, and is philologically plausible. Moreover, Snorri spent his youth at Oddi, and probably acquired much of his knowledge there. It is not at all impossible that a collection of mythological poems was in the library at Oddi, and thus it may well be justified to apply the name also to the mythological and legendary poetry. The third theory is that the name simply comes from *Rígsthula's* 'edda', great-grandmother or ancestress. Whatever its true origin, the name now denotes a certain kind of Icelandic poetry.

This poetry is virtually the only pre-Christian Germanic literature now extant. Much of what we know of the beliefs, cosmology, customs, and outlook of our pagan ancestors is preserved in the *Poetic Edda*, which we shall henceforth refer to simply as *Edda*. The poems in this collection were committed to writing as late as *ca.* 1200, but they still have much more of the heroic pagan spirit than for instance *Beowulf* which is several centuries older, not to speak of the Austrian *Nibelungenlied* which is permeated by the Christian spirit of chivalry. In Germany and England the conversion to Christianity led to a radical change in the literary tradition, resulting in new subjects and new ideas, which for many centuries proved refractory material to handle. In Denmark, Norway and Sweden the conversion resulted in the quenching of literature for several centuries. Of all the Germanic countries only Iceland preserved a continuity with the past.

There is no knowing how many of the original mythical and heroic poems current in ancient Iceland were lost, but thirty-five of them have been preserved and make up the *Edda*. This is by no means a homogeneous group of poems, although some of them are clearly interconnected. Each of them is an independent creation, treating one incident or a group of incidents in a mythical or heroic cycle. Thus the *Edda* is a collection not properly of myths and legends but of independent artistic expressions of some aspects of known myths and legends. An Eddic poem may well be compared to a Greek tragedy. It dramatizes certain events from the world of myth or from prehistoric times and gives them an independent existence. On the whole, the Eddic poems have close connections with drama. Many of them consist of dialogues and monologues, and some of them reveal deep psychological penetration and great dramatic tension. One is tempted to think that these poems may have had some connection with the ritual enactment of the various myths, which would bring them still closer to Greek tragedy.

Bertha S. Phillpotts makes this point in her suggestive book *The Elder Edda and Ancient Scandinavian Drama,* and sees vestiges of old ritualistic drama most fully exemplified in a drama about the fertility god Frey, *Skírnismál.* Frey falls in love with Gerd by seeing her from a distance, sends his messenger Skírnir to get her, sacrificing his good sword, and the messenger finally secures her promise by threat of magic curses. Lord Raglan, in his *The Hero*, also makes suggestions worthy of consideration, even if he goes far beyond the available evidence in his conclusions. First, he points out the predominance of dialogue in the Eddic poems, which is indeed striking, for some of them read exactly like scripts of modern plays without stage directions. Prophecies are another important part of ritual drama, and they figure prominently in the Eddic poems. Characteristically, they do not serve as warnings to the characters involved, for they are never heeded, but they are indications to the audience as to what will happen in the play. An interesting feature in drama as well as in heroic poetry is that the characters do not age with the passing of time. Clothes and ornaments are, along with dialogue, the most conspicuous features of the Eddic poems, and this again points to dramatic origin. In ritual the dressing of the principal actors is an essential factor, a remnant of which we still have in our church services. In one of the Eddic poems Óðin appears as an old one-eyed man, barefooted, with tight linen breeches, a cloak, and a slouch-hat. The goddess Hel is described as being 'half blue-black and half flesh-colour', which might be taken as a stage direction. Would she require recognition except on the stage? The setting of many of the poems also suggests the stage. Lord Raglan points out that the usual setting for ritual drama is a doorway or a gateway. The entrance to the shrine is the place where sacredness can be combined with visibility. This is true of Attic tragedy and we find it too in *Beowulf*. In some of the Eddic poems the setting is similar, for instance in *Fjölsvinnsmál* where Svipdag comes to a mysterious castle and has a debate with the giant guarding the gate, and also in *Atlamál* where the battle takes place at the entrance to the house.

Shape-shifting is a very common feature in Eddic poetry and even more common in the ritual. As Lord Raglan points out, persons disguised or partly disguised as animals are an almost universal feature of ritual and ritual drama. We find it with the Egyptians, the Indians, the Geeks, the Africans, and even the Christians when Christ is represented as a lamb. In the *Edda* there is the account in *Reginsmál* of the gods catching a dwarf who is in the form of a pike, and Loki's slaying Otter, son of the rich and mighty Hreidmar, in the shape of an otter. Fáfnir, Otter's brother, takes the form of a dragon who is killed by Sigurd. This, Raglan suggests, may originally have been an account of a king-killing which was eventually dramatized.

In ritual drama the chief part is played by a king or a priest, or actor representing him. It is noteworthy that all the characters in heroic Eddic poetry are royalty. This is especially noteworthy as there was no actual royalty in Iceland. These royal heroes invariably engage in contests of various kinds, and whenever the hero is represented as fighting, it is always evident that the combat is staged and not real. The only function of the combatants, if they appear on the scene at all, is to fall in heaps before the hero's all-conquering sword. We have various examples of this in the

Edda. In the famous *Ragnarök* ('Doom of the Gods') each god is assigned a certain adversary, a monster with whom he must try conclusions.(Says Lord Raglan: 'It would seem that there was a procession of men dressed as the gods, and then a battle between them and men in animal masks.'[2])

Another feature of ritual drama is what Raglan calls the *Spielman* who in all probability spoke but did not act, whereas the other characters acted but did not speak. He was the leader or 'director' of the drama. This is still in existence in Java in the so-called *tópeng.* We recognize the Spielman in various roles, for instance as Mephistopheles in *Faust,* as Merlin in the Arthurian legend, and especially as Athena in the *Odyssey.* For the Icelandic example we quote Vilhelm Grönbech:

Among the gods Loki occupies a place of his own. His place in the sacred drama is that of the plotter who sets the conflict in motion and leads the giants on to the assault that entails their defeat. His origin and *raison d'être* are purely dramatic; like his confrères in other rituals and mythologies he is a child of the 'games', and herein lies the cause of his double nature. As the wily father of artifice whose office is to drag the demonical powers into the play and effect their downfall, he comes very near representing evil ... but as the sacred actor who performs the necessary part in the great redemptory work of the *blot* [sacrifice], he, i.e. his human impersonation, is a god among gods, beneficient and inviolable.[3]

In the heroic poems of the *Edda,* as distinct from the mythological ones, it is Óðin rather than Loki who plays the Spielman's role, but he rarely meddles in human affairs.

We have cited Lord Raglan at some length, for many of his observations are suggestive, even if on the whole he shows only a sketchy knowledge of Icelandic literature. His suggestion that many of the dramatic conventions mentioned above also found their way into the Sagas is quite probable, if not obvious.

Bertha Phillpotts says that some of the Eddic poems 'bear the unmistakable stamp of dramatic origin.... Yet these poems are not the remains of folk-drama in the modern sense of the word. Modern folk-drama is a degenerate descendant of the ancient religious drama, whereas these poems are the actual shattered remains of ancient religious drama.'[4]

The Eddic poems can hardly be properly termed epic, even though they possess many of the qualities of epic literature. As W. P. Ker says in *Epic and Romance,* they are too hurried, and lack 'the classical breadth and ease of narrative'.[5]

But on the other hand, there pervades Eddic poetry that heroic outlook, that abhorrence of mystery and romantic fantasy which is the hallmark of all epic literature, as distinguished from romances and ballads. One belongs to a heroic age, the other to an age of chivalry. Epic poetry takes in all of life, the common as well as the elevated aspects, but it does so with dignity, never with sentimentality or rhetoric. It centres around character and action, courage and pride. It does not rely on history, even when it treats historical events. In that sense the Eddic poems are epic.

Heroic literature demands a certain kind of society in order to thrive. There must be definite standards, accepted codes of behaviour and at the same time freedom for the individual to assert himself and choose the roles he wishes to play. There must be room for the clash of strong wills, but also adherence to well-defined ideals. W. P. Ker remarks: 'The most perfect heroic literature of the Northern nations is to be found in the country where the heroic polity and society had most room and leisure; and in Iceland the heroic ideals of life had conditions more favourable than are to be discovered anywhere else in history.'[6]

About the date, authorship and birthplace of the Eddic poems there has been long and heated controversy, and a solution to the problem is unlikely to be found. Most of the poems dealing with mythology have been taken to antedate the year 1000 in their present form, as most of them are so clearly untouched by Christian ideas, but this assumption is open to question. A rough guess would be that the Eddic poems in their present form were composed in *ca.* 800–1200, but this does not exclude the possibility that portions of them are much older, even dating back to the sixth century. Again some of them probably existed in different forms earlier, since many of the heroes in the legendary poems lived as early as the fourth century A.D. Poems about them probably came into being shortly after their death and then travelled among the Germanic tribes on the continent of Europe, became connected with poems about other heroes of different times and finally reached Iceland where they were written down and sometimes modified in accordance with local needs and customs.

Of the thirty-five Eddic poems, fourteen deal with mythological subjects and twenty-one with legendary heroes. There is a marked difference between these two groups in so far as mortals rarely intrude into the mythological realm, and conversely the legendary world is peculiarly 'realistic', that is to say the gods rarely interfere in human affairs. In this respect Nordic mythology stands out in bold contrast to the Greek and Hindu, where gods and mortals move around and aid each other without the slightest discomfort. Curious as it may seem, the Norsemen seem to have been more rationalistic than the Greeks when dealing with their myths and legends. Even in Greek drama the gods make their appearance among mortals in a much more conspicuous manner than in the dramatic Eddic poems.

The heroic Eddic poems can be divided into three main groups. The oldest one has as subject-matter events as far back as the Migration Period in Europe (*ca.* A.D. 300-500). There are poems about three historical kings, Attila the Hun, the Ostrogoth monarch Ermanaric whose kingdom was conquered by the Huns in 375, and the Burgundian king Gundicarius (called in German Gunther, in Icelandic Gunnar) who was defeated by the Huns *ca.* A.D. 437. The second group deals with the famous heroes, Helgi and Sigurd (Siegfried). There are three poems devoted to each of them, poems of great tragic intensity. The third group consists of heroic elegies dealing with the death of Sigurd and the fates of the two women who loved him, Brynhild and Gudrún. Both are heroic women of the highest order who face their grim fate with a tragic majesty which has few counterparts in world literature, except possibly in some of the Greek tragedies.

As an example of how the Eddic poets treated historical events we may look briefly at Ermanaric. According to a contemporary historian, he was a wise and noble ruler whom distress over the fate of his people under the Huns drove to take his life. By the sixth century his suicide was forgotten and more dramatic motifs had replaced it. When the Huns invaded his territory, Ermanaric was lying wounded. The reason for his wounds was that, angered by a treacherous attack by a chieftain of the Rosomoni, probably a subject tribe, Ermanaric had caused this chieftain's wife, Sunilda (Svanhild), to be torn to pieces by wild horses. In revenge, her brothers, Ammius and Sarus, attacked him and left him mortally wounded. The names of these brothers have tempted scholars to associate them with the Old Icelandic word *hamr* (skin covering or guise) and the Old English *searu* (armour), especially as in later versions the brothers wear magic armour which cannot be pierced by steel. The personal name Sarus is, however, known to have been borne by a Gothic nobleman in the early fifth century.

Thenceforward Ermanaric lived in legend as a mighty but cruel and sometimes cunning tyrant. Sympathy shifts from him to the beautiful Svanhild whom he tortured, and her fearless brothers who in the Icelandic tradition are called Hamdir and Sörli. Svanhild is now the wife not of a neighbouring chieftain but of Ermanaric himself. He caused her to be trampled to death because he believed—wrongly—that she had committed adultery with his son Randvér; Randvér himself was hanged. The brothers attacked the emperor and wounded him, but lost their own lives in the act of doing so.

The story of Ermanaric is told in the *Lay of Hamdir,* one of the most forceful heroic poems in the *Edda,* even though it has come down to us in rather bad shape. It expresses more clearly than any other early source the truly heroic spirit, without pathos or psychological interest in feminine emotions, which is prominent in some other poems. Heroism, as the author of this poem saw it, implied willingness to face predestined death not only with resignation but with joy.

It is interesting to see how the legends of Ermanaric spread among the peoples of Western Europe and Scandinavia and how they were linked with various other cycles of legends. In the North the legends of Ermanaric were associated chiefly with two other cycles, that of the Burgundians and that of Sigurd (Siegfried). The most famous of the Burgundian heroes was Gundicarius (Gunnar). The tribe of which he was king inhabited the middle Rhine in the early fifth century. In 437 the Burgundians were assailed by a force of Huns, their kingdom was destroyed and Gundicarius lost his life. Like Ermanaric, Gundicarius's career suffered so great a change in the imagination of the poets that his historical basis is barely recognizable.

The oldest extent poem about Gundicarius, or Gunnar as we had better call him, is probably *The Lay of Atli* (Attila), one of the finest pieces in the *Edda,* even if the text is one of the worst preserved. Here there is no battle between Burgundians and Huns, but instead there is a family quarrel between Gunnar and Atli—who are made brothers-in-law as Atli is married to Gudrún, Gunnar's sister. In history Attila is not at all associated with Gundicarius and did not even take part in the war against the Burgundians. This war had political causes, but in the poem the quarrel was due to the avarice of Atli, who coveted the gold possessed by Gunnar and his brothers.

According to *The Lay of Atli,* the Hunnish king met his own death after he had tortured Gunnar to death in a snake-pit. His wife Gudrún took revenge for her brother Gunnar: she slaughtered the sons she had borne to Atli and served him with their hearts. Later, when he was drunk, she murdered Atli in his bed, and his blood flowed into the bedding. This Nordic story has similarities with the Greek stories of Atreus, Medea, and especially Procne and Philomela.

Actually there is a grain of historical truth in the story of Atli's death. According to historians of his own age, Attila had married a new wife Ildico (suggesting German origins). During the wedding feast he drank deep and, going to bed, he bled from the nose and was so drunk that he suffocated in his sleep. Soon the story began to circulate that Ildico had murdered him, which would not be too far-fetched had she been German. The name Gudrún in the Icelandic tradition is evidently meant to emphasize her relationship with Gunnar, since the names alliterate.

In the *Edda* the legends of the Burgundians are linked with another group, those of Sigurd and Brynhild. These figures are hard to recognize in history, but they most probably were Franks. Sigurd has been identified with Sigebert, King of Metz (d. 575), and Brynhild with Brunehild (d. 613), the wife of this Sigebert.

In *The Lay of Atli*, the oldest poem about the Burgundian legend, there is no reference to Sigurd or Brynhild, but in the *Fragment of a Sigurd Lay*, a comparatively old poem, the two legends are treated as one. Sigurd is murdered by his brothers-in-law, Högni and Guttorm and Gunnar, at the instigation of Brynhild, who is the wife of Gunnar.

In the Icelandic tradition the Ermanaric legend is related to those of Sigurd and Gunnar by making Svanhild the daughter of Sigurd and Gudrún, and Hamdir and Sörli are said to be Gudrún's sons by a third husband. Some poets also said that Brynhild was the daughter of the Hunnish king Budli and therefore the sister of Atli. These close family relationships between the heroes and heroines of the Eddic poems obviously give their conflicts an intense tragic aspect.

The outline of the Nibelung story in the *Edda* is as follows, ignoring certain inconsistencies and contradictions due to differing versions:

Sigurd (having killed the dragon Fáfnir and won its hoard of treasure) comes as an honoured guest to the court of King Gjúki. He marries Gjúki's daughter Gudrún, and swears oaths of brotherhood with her two brothers, Gunnar and Högni (the Gjúkungs).

Gunnar sets out to win Brynhild, who is surrounded by a wall of flames and has vowed only to marry the man who rides through it. Gunnar fails to do so, but Sigurd takes on his likeness, penetrates the flames and woos Brynhild on Gunnar's behalf. He shares her bed, but lays his naked sword between them. Brynhild marries Gunnar, believing him to have duly won her. Later, in a dispute with Gudrún, Sigurd's wife, over which of them has married the nobler hero, Gudrún betrays the truth. Brynhild thereupon incites Gunnar to kill Sigurd. Gunnar and Högni persuade their younger brother, Guttorm, to perform the deed, as he is not bound by the oaths of brotherhood. Guttorm falls unawares on Sigurd and kills him, but is himself killed by his victim.

After Sigurd's death, Gudrún is persuaded to marry Atli, King of the Huns (in the later poems Atli is made Brynhild's brother). Atli invites Gudrún's brothers, Gunnar and Högni, to a banquet and treacherously kills them. Gudrún, in vengeance for her brothers, kills her two young sons by Atli, serves up their hearts to him at a meal, which she then reveals to him; later she stabs him in his bed and burns the hall and everyone in it.

The story is told in a number of Eddic poems, often in widely divergent versions, one stressing this and another that aspect of each incident. Sometimes there is a certain kind of continuity: *The Lay of Regin* telling of Sigurd's stay with the smith, *The Lay of Fáfnir* telling of the fight with the dragon, *The Lay of Sigrdrífa* telling of the hero's visit to the Valkyrie. But more often there are parallel poems treating the same material in different ways, for instance the two Atli lays.

What is perhaps strangest in many of the Eddic poems in the Nibelung cycle is the concern with the heroines Brynhild and Gudrún, rather than with the heroes Sigurd and Gunnar. The interest of the poets seems to centre mainly around a psychological approach to the feelings of the women who play such a tragic part in the life of Sigurd. How could Brynhild, who really loved Sigurd, send him to his death? What did Gudrún feel when her husband was stabbed beside her? These and similar questions give rise to long monologues or heroic elegies in which the woman lays bare her heart. The style of these poems is no longer as hard as the old ore of heroic song, such as *The Lay of Hamdir, The Lay of Atli* or even the *Fragment of a Sigurd Lay*. It is softer and more sensitive, closer to medieval knightly ballads.

Brynhild's side of the story is told in *The Short Lay of Sigurd* and in *Brynhild's Ride to Hel.* Gudrún's case is elaborated in three lays of Gudrún, *The Greenlandic Lay of Atli,* and *Gudrún's Lament.*

The elegiac tone of these poems seems neither to fit the old heroic spirit nor the famous style of the Icelandic Sagas, but Bertha S. Phillpotts has pointed out:

If we must look for a period in which a literary tradition like that in the Edda poems could have established itself, it would rather be in the Germanic societies described by Caesar and Tacitus, who say that among the Germanic peoples women were held in great veneration, and were thought to be the possessors of prophetic gifts—as in these poems. In the Iceland of the Sagas the persons with outstanding prophetic gifts are usually men, and men also are the usual interpreters of dreams. In only one of the Eddic poems does a man prophesy—and it is significant that it is in the late Icelandic *Prophecy of Gripir*. All the other prophecies are uttered by women, and all the interpretation of dreams too is by women, until we come to the late *Greenlandic Atli Lay*. It certainly looks as if the poems were reflecting some non-Icelandic tradition.[7]

We have devoted considerable space to the Southern legends in the *Edda*, but there is also a Northern cycle worthy of attention, although much briefer: the three so-called Helgi lays. Obviously there were a great number of poems current in the North which dealt with native Scandinavian heroes, some of them have been reproduced by other sources. Apparently the Eddic collector was only interested in such native Scandinavian material as could be linked with the Nibelung story. Two Northern heroes were connected with that cycle, both of them named Helgi: one the son of Hjörvard, the other called the slayer of Hunding. Late Northern genealogies had made Helgi the Hunding-Slayer into a son of Sigmund, Sigurd's father, by a previous wife, so that he was the half-brother of Sigurd, born before Sigmund went to the land of the Franks. Thus two lays on Helgi the Hunding-Slayer were included in the *Edda*. *The Lay of Helgi Hjörvardsson* was also included, probably because its lovers, Helgi and Sváva, are reborn in Helgi the Hunding-Slayer and Sigrún.

Some of the place names in these poems point to the Baltic (North German) coast, others to East Götland in Sweden. The names Helgi and Hjörvard are those of the Scylding dynasty of *Beowulf,* and Helgi's adversaries, Hunding and Hödbrodd, may be paralleled by the Hundings and the Heado-Beardan in *Widsith-Beowulf,* another proof of their fifth-century provenance.

The story of Helgi and Sváva covers a large period of time, although the actual remnants of the story are small. It is a tragedy beginning with the wooing of the hero's father and mother. The hero is dumb and nameless from his birth until the Valkyrie Sváva meets him and gives him his name, Helgi, and tells him of a magic sword, on an island that will bring him victory. The tragedy is brought about by a witch who drives Hedin, the brother of Helgi, to make a foolish boast—an oath on the boar's head that he will wed his brother's bride. Hedin confesses his vanity to Helgi and is forgiven, Helgi saying: 'Taunt thee no more, for true will come/thy vow on beaker, for both of us:/ on holm I was bidden by hero bold;/in three days' time we there shall meet.' Helgi is mortally wounded, sends a message to Sváva to come to him, and asks her to take Hedin for her lord after he himself is gone. The poem ends with two short energetic speeches: by Sváva refusing any love but Helgi's; and of Hedin taking leave of Sváva as he goes to make amends and avenge his brother.

The First Lay of Helgi the Hunding-Slayer is a skaldic eulogy of the young hero who is victorious both in avenging his father and winning his bride, the Valkyrie Sigrún, who in turn, riding through the sky, gives him magical help in battle. Sigrún has summoned Helgi to help her against her father, Högni, who has betrothed her against her will to Hödbrodd, son of Granmar. Helgi then summons his men to save her from the marriage. Tragedy comes in the second lay which partly tells the same story, but adds the important detail that Helgi has to kill Sigrún's brothers and father to win her hand. When the surviving brother, with Odin's help, kills Helgi, Sigrún curses her brother and goes to Helgi's burial mound, but for one night only, for after that he does not return and she dies from grief. This lay is the most dramatic of all the heroic love stories.[8]

There are a number of other poems in the legendary part of the *Edda,* but they are of less importance, even if some of them are not uninteresting.

This leads us to the mythological part of the *Edda,* the first fourteen poems of the collection dealing with the heathen gods and their exploits. These poems, along with Snorri Sturluson's *Prose Edda,* are our chief source of information concerning the ancient Germanic religion. The variety in form, content and approach in the mythological poems is indeed striking. There are poems dealing with the gods and their doings in deadly serious manner interspersed with biting satire on their immoral and inefficient behaviour, calling to mind some of the Hindu Vedic hymns in the same vein. There are down-to-earth didactic poems dealing with the everday life of the poor and wretched farmer, exhibiting much common sense and psychological insight, and there are magnificent visionary poems like *the Song of the Sybil* (*Völuspá*) revealing in a series of swiftly changing scenes the course of the world from its chaotic beginnings, through the creation of the gods, earth and men, to its and their ultimate doom and destruction in fire and water, out of which a new earth will arise in which gods and men will live in family unity and happiness.

The myths as we find them in the *Edda* had reached a stage where the phenomena of nature had been personalized and there were many humanized gods, each of whom had his own department and was worshipped accordingly. Still, there are traces of these myths of their earliest childhood, for instance in their peculiar mixture of small and great. They tell us at once why the whole world shakes with the writhings of the fettered Loki—and why the salmon is narrow at the tail. Also their whole group of ideas is a reflection of a primitive social structure. The gods constitute a petty tribe which aims to get the better of another tribe, the giants, by means of combat or (more often) cunning. They steal women or chattels from each other and get them back by conquest. They fight for precedence at river fords and harry each other's lands very much as two savage tribes might do. This division is of course also found in Greek mythology.

Many of the individual myths are a heritage from remote ancestors, as for instance the myth of the stolen drink. Many primitive tribes have tales concerning a great frog or serpent who has swallowed all the water and withholds it from other creatures until forced by some cunning hero to yield it up again. The animal is later developed into a monster who keeps the water vessel in his cave. But in the course of time this tale begins to be regarded as childish. The water is then transformed into the divine mead which a god in the disguise of a falcon has dragged forth from the giant's glen. This is the form in which the myth appears in the Hindu Vedic lays as well as in the Northern myths concerning the skald's mead.

One must always keep in mind that the myths and legends in their present form are the result of a thousand years of story-telling, in which the tales were passed orally. Every age has added to them, reinterpreted them, putting into them something of its own spirit. Consequently, no single explanation will open the gate to all the myths.

We can see this transformation in the fact that what was once a natural phenomenon manifested in a divinity later appears changed into a characterization of the individual god, either physically or spiritually. Thór no longer drives a chariot in his combat with the giants, but fights standing up. His hammer is less often hurled as a thunderbolt than used for dealing direct blows. Odin who was originally associated with a natural phenomenon (the roaring nocturnal rout through desolate plains) no doubt retains his spear, his retinue of wolves and his swift eight-footed steed, but these things are now merely his stage properties, when he appears at Valhall, while his cloak and his low-hanging hat are transformed into the disguise he wears when he travels among men.

But the mythological poetry of the *Edda,* with its wealth of sharply defined individual characters and its rapid succession of splendid scenes, has also evolved a unified conception of the world-order, a definite philosophy. The world holds nothing that can be enjoyed without a struggle between the gods and the giants—not an indiscriminate struggle of all against all, but a combat between the forces that would preserve human life and all that is of value to it and those that would destroy these things. In reality, the struggle between the gods and the giants is the dominant theme for the poets of the Eddic lays. The world is maintained only by means of a struggle in which the power and ingenuity of the gods is constantly put to the test. Thór is engaged in repeated journeys in search of aid to match against the numerical superiority of the giants. Odin travels around disguised in order to trap the cunning giant Vafthrúdnir and to acquire by secret means the clever devices that will give him strength. He learns wisdom from one; he entices the maid who guards the mead of Suttung to deliver it to him; he obtains by stealth the love from which an avenger will spring; he engages in a life-and-death contest with a giant; or he summons the dead Wise Woman of the giants from the grave and forces the prophecies from her lips.

This 'philosophy' is perhaps best expressed in the image of the world-ash tree, *Yggdrasil*: existence is a continuity, an organism. Its living force is concentrated in Yggdrasil. The crown of the tree is the sky; of its three roots one is among the gods, one among the giants and one in Niflheim, realm of the dead. The dew that drips from it supports the life of nature, but the tree is also the scene of the councils of the gods, and at its base flows the spring of Urd, whence emerge the three wise maidens, the Norns:

> *They laws did make,*   *they lives did choose:*
> *For the children of men*   *they marked their fates.*

The three are Urd (the Past), Verdandi (the Present) and Skuld (the Future). The idea of a tree is found in the myths of other races. Homer sings of the human race as a tree whose leaves are steadily falling but are constantly replenished. The Eddic world-tree also involves the idea of suffering and striving: a hart eats from its crown, on one side it decays, and the serpent Nídhögg gnaws its roots. But the Norns water it from the spring, and it 'stands ever green over Urd's well'.

The great energy released in this eternal struggle corresponds to something in the character of the Scandinavian—perhaps in the whole Germanic race: a tendency to dualism, often with a distinct ethical emphasis. These contrasts are clearly expressed in the myths about the end of the world, the *Ragnarök* or ultimate doom of the gods; about belief in a *Fimbul* Winter (three winters without a summer) or in the sinking of lands into the sea, in the swallowing of the sun by the constantly pursuing wolf, and the tremendous approaching battle between gods and giants, which the great and hallowed gods will finally lose. But they will not die unavenged, for that is something the Northern warrior could hardly have imagined. Vídar, the young son of Ódin, tears apart the jaws of the Fenris-Wolf, and makes possible the beginning of a new race of gods and men who will continue the forms of life. The life force is only just rescued from destruction, and that only after a desperate struggle. To what extent these ideas have been shaped by Christianity is hard to say, but obviously we must accept a certain Christian influence.

The world-struggle between gods and giants is by no means an exclusive Nordic theme. It is common among most Indo-European peoples, and it is also found in the Judeo-Christian tradition in a modified form. The Celts have a story of a single tremendous battle of the gods which has something of the same tragic element as the Nordic version. The Greeks and the Hindus do indeed abandon the tragic concept, by reason of a joy in life or a renunciation of life, but the Eddic poets carry it to the ultimate consequences. The closest parallel to the Eddic idea is probably to be found among the ancient Persians, who imagined a constant struggle between good spirits and monsters. But this very similarity also underlines the difference. Based on the contrast between fruitfulness and drought and always engaging human beings as active participants, the Persian myth is a religion that has arisen among people who guard their flocks and till their soil. The world-combat of the *Edda* is the outcome partly of war and partly of melancholy brooding over the human condition. The role played by men in the drama is very insignificant: living men do not participate in the *Ragnarök* battle, but only the warriors who have been gathered to Valhall after death. The Persian version has something of the cheerful faith of the toiling man that his efforts will prevail, while the Eddic poems reveal the melancholic's dream that all will be destroyed.

The Eddic poems are coloured by this mood of gloom. In the midst of brilliant scenes we often hear the undertones of *Ragnarök*, a reminder of the hour when Ódin will meet the wolf, and the sons of Múspell will ride through the dark forest. This may be partly due to the art of the poet who wants the gay scenes of the myths to appear against the dark background, a tendency we also see in the heroic lays. But side by side with myths concerning the great world drama there are other myths, not associated with it but nevertheless allowing their characters to be tried in conflicts and situations of the most varied kind—though with a happy outcome. Thus Thór shatters the stone-head of the giant Hrungnir with his hammer Mjöllnir. Or disguised as a bride, he recovers his lost hammer from the king of a giant tribe. One of the favourite myths of the ancient poets was the account of how Thór with his fish-hook drew the Midgard-Worm (the earth-girdling Serpent) itself out of the ocean, how the spotted venomous creature stared with hatred in its eyes at its mortal enemy while heavy blows were showered upon its head. This myth was the great expression of the struggle between the destructive and constructive forces.

The first poem of the *Edda* is unique in that it tries to shape the entire mythology into a connected action, the drama of the gods in which the *Ragnarök* becomes the centre of gravity of the whole. The author of this magnificent poem is unknown, but most authorities consider him to have been an Icelander living around the year 1000. He was without a doubt the greatest poetic genius of the North during the Middle Ages. He was a man with a large view of life and great experience. He had most probably heard the Christian songs of the West about God's might, the destruction of the world and its resurrection, but he was also closely attached to the world of the heathen gods and their life-struggle. His desire was to understand existence as a whole and reconcile the new with the old. In this respect he had affinities with the anonymous author of *Njál's Saga*, the great swansong of the classical Icelandic Sagas.

No pagan poet before him had attempted to present so vast a subject as the entire course of the world. The other mythical poems in the *Edda* constitute not whole pictures but individual and immediate observations, now humorous, now solemn, but never on a grand scale. The poet of the *Song of the Sybil (Völuspá)* did the revolutionary thing: he reviewed the entire world of the old heathen order and made of it an organic and continuous whole. The poem expounds the interrelation of the various myths but, like Homer, the poet seems concerned to polish the crude old myths and make them conform to the taste of a new and more rationalistic generation. He exhibits a daring sweep of the imagination and his mastery of the verse is equally unmistakable. The poem tells of the creation of the world by the gods and the first happy age, the fall from grace succeeded by a period of struggle and misfortune, the gradual oncoming of *Ragnarök,* and finally the rebirth to a life free from all distress, with a new earth and a *Gimli* thatched with gold. This poet is the only one in the *Edda* to expect the same ethical standard from the gods as from human beings, and here, as in the heroic poems, disaster becomes the ultimate test of character.

The bulk of the mythological poems can be roughly divided into two categories: incident poems and conversation poems. Of the former there are four, the most accomplished of which is *The Lay of Skírnir,* a humorous poem in dialogue form about the god Frey, sick with desire for the giant's daughter Gerd, despatching his messenger Skírnir to plead with her for her favours. Skírnir's perilous journey is described, and then follows his colloquy with Gerd, whose reluctance he overcomes with dire threats. He returns and reports his success to Frey, who answers by bewailing the nine nights that will separate him from his heart's desire. This poem has been taken by some authorities to indicate the dramatic origins of some of the Eddic lays, as we have seen earlier in this chapter. There is more action in *The Lay of Skírnir* than in any other extant mythological dialogue-poem.

The Lay of Thrym is another incident poem, in dialogue and narrative verses, a rollicking account of how Thór awoke one morning and found his hammer missing. Loki borrowed the goddess Freya's feather-coat and flew to Jötunheim, abode of the giants, where he questioned the giant Thrym, who admitted that he had the hammer and would only return it if Freya would become his wife. Thór and Loki try to persuade Freya to attire herself as a bride, but she refuses in a terrible rage. The gods and goddesses hold a council, and Loki proposes that Thór himself should dress up as Freya and go to Jötunheim accompanied by Loki disguised as a maid. Thór agrees grudgingly to this and there is a delightful scene where Thór's appetite nearly betrays him at the wedding feast, but Loki saves the situation, and the scene closes with Thór regaining the hammer and beating up his hosts, crippling all the giants.

The Lay of Hymir rather clumsily combines a number of myths, using skaldic *kennings* in profusion (a boat is called 'swine of the surf', 'sea-goat' and 'stallion of the rollers', the beard is called 'chin-forest', etc.), but the verve of the poem is undeniable and many of its scenes remarkably vivid, as for instance Thór carrying the giants' cauldron on his head, its handles clanking around his heels, and his fishing of the terrible earth-encircling Midgard Serpent.

The fourth incident poem, *The Song of Ríg,* is a somewhat unusual commingling of Celtic and Nordic elements. In one sense it belongs to Celtic as much as Norse mythology, since Ríg is the ancient great king (Rig-Mor) of the Irish, the god Dadge, who is the source of all human wisdom and ingenuity and also the originator of the three traditional classes of society.

Some of the elements in this poem are clearly Irish, such as the contest of wisdom with a subsequent change of name, a tradition which has found its way into other Eddic lays. Similarly, the double paternity—an earthly and a heavenly father—was a common theme in Irish heroic poetry.

But the human characters in the *Song of Ríg* are Nordic, and the whole outlook of the poem is clearly Germanic. The division into social classes is the same as in other Icelandic lays: the nobleman, the peasant and the slave. These are called in the poem *Jarl* (earl), *Karl* (franklin) and *Thrall.* They are of the same father, Ríg, but have different mothers and are therefore half-brothers. The three social classes are in reality conceived of as three different races, and the classes are therefore divine institutions. This calls to mind the caste system set up by the ancient Aryans in India.

The lay tells of Ríg's travels to three different houses, in each of which he leaves offspring. The door of the first house is closed, and inside Ríg finds Ai (great-grandfather) and Edda (great-grandmother), 'two hoary ones by the hearth there sat', who have nothing to give him but a loaf of coarse bread and a bowl of broth. The son begotten with Edda was sprinkled with water (an ancient Germanic custom) and named Thrall. He was wrinkled, rough-handed, ugly and twisted. But he was strong and diligent, and worked from morning to evening. Then one day a bow-legged woman came to his hut. She was sunburned and flatnosed, and her name was Thir (female thrall). They chatted and whispered and prepared to go to bed. They had many children, all of whom carried names with overtones of insult or derision. This was the race of slaves.

Next Ríg comes to a prosperous house where the door is ajar—an invitation to the traveller. Here live Afi (grandfather) and

Amma (grandmother) who own the house. Afi's beard is trimmed and his clothes fit him well. He is planing wood for the weaver's beam, and his wife is working at the spinning-wheel. She is well dressed and ornamented, and sets vessels full of the best food before the guest. The son begotten with her is named Karl, and is the ancester of the race of franklins. He is ruddy of face, and his eyes sparkle. He cultivates the soil, tames oxen, and builds wagons, houses and barns. A girl clad in goatskin and carrying keys is brought to Karl. They exchange rings and form a household, and their children's names convey the honourable qualities and occupations of a proud class.

The third house Ríg enters is a mansion. The doors are open and face the sunny south. There is a ring on the doorpost, and the floor is strewn. The occupants, Fadir (father) and Módir (mother), sit playing with each other's fingers and gazing in one another's eyes. Fadir's occupations are winding bow-strings, shaping bows and fashioning arrows. The lady of the house looks at her arms, smooths her veil, arranges her sleeves, and adjusts her headgear. She is richly dressed, a clasp on her breast, her gown blue with a broad train. She is beautiful, her brow bright, her breast shining, her neck whiter than new-fallen snow. She covers the table with an embroidered cloth and serves cakes of snow-white wheat, game, pork, roasted birds in dishes, cups and pitchers richly ornamented. The son begotten with her is named *Jarl,* the ancestor of the nobility. He has light hair, bright cheeks, and eyes as piercing as those of a young serpent. He grew up at home and learned to handle all kinds of weapons, to ride horses, to swim, etc. Ríg taught him runes (secrets), gave him his own name, declared him his own son, and bade him hold his heritage and his ancient home. Jarl became a ruler and a warrior, waged wars, reddened the fields, and won lands. He distributed gold and rich treasures and had many palaces. He sent a messenger to find him a wife, and he found a fair and rich lady, whom he brought back with him. Jarl and Erna were wedded and lived happily, blessed with many children whose names do not denote any occupation but are terms of endearment and honour. Their lives were spent at sports and plays.

But one of Jarl's sons, Kon the Young ('noble descendant'; *konung,* the Norse word for king), learned to use the everlasting runes of life. He could dull the swordblade, still the sea, lessen flames, understand birds, quiet minds, clam sorrows. His wisdom became greater than that of his father, and he won the right to be called Ríg (*ri* or *rig* is the Old Irish word for king). Once on a journey through a forest *Kon* was asked by a crow, sitting on a bough: 'Why, Kon, do you lure the birds to come? You would do better to go forth on your horse and kill the enemy.' After some further admonition from the crow the poem breaks off suddenly, and the conclusion is lost. But we are to understand that Kon is actually the first king. This indicates that the poem was composed outside Iceland, perhaps in the Norse colonies in the British Isles. It is interesting to note that according to the *Song of Ríg* the race of slaves was the first to come into being, and the race of kings the last.

The *Song of Ríg* gives us an informative account of the social classes and their status in ancient Germanic societies. In this sense it is a Norse poem. But it is unique among the Eddic lays and has distinct traces of Celtic influences, in regard both to its literary nature and to some of the words used. The racial distinctions in the poem should not lead us to think that all slaves in Scandinavia were considered to be of a race different from that of free men. Those captured in warfare, which had been the fate of most of the Irish slaves in Iceland, could be of any 'race', and often were of royal stock. Nevertheless, the division into three social classes (slaves, peasants and chieftains) was probably still in existence during the first years of the Commonwealth, even if in a somewhat modified form.

The *Lay of Grímnir* is mid-way between a poem of incident and one of conversation. A prose introduction tells how Ódin and his wife Frigg quarrelled about the character of a certain king, whom Ódin decided to visit in disguise under the name of Grímnir (the Hooded One). Frigg sends a message to the king, Geirröd, to warn him of the coming of a wizard who might destroy him. The king takes the vagrant blue-mantled Ódin for his enemy and tortures him to make him speak by setting him between two fires, where he sits for eight nights, until the king's ten-year-old son Agnar takes pity on him and offers him a drink. Having drunk, Ódin starts his monologue, all in verse, which is a summary of mythology, describing all the worlds, the homes of gods and men, ending with a revelation of Ódin himself and of all his various names, among them 'Masked', 'Truth-seeking', 'Fickle', 'Bale-working', 'Lord of Cargoes'. The poem includes a description of the world-tree Yggdrasil, more detailed than in *Völuspá*. Discovering the true identity of his guest, the king leaps up, says the prose ending of the poem, stumbles on his drawn sword and dies. This poem is the only one in the *Edda* where the action takes place in both the world of the gods and that of men.

The *Lay of Vafthrúdnir* tells of a match of wit and knowledge between Ódin and the wise giant Vafthrúdnir. Ódin is disguised under the name Gagnrád ('Giving Good Counsel', i.e. for victory), and the giant questions him about various mythological names, the creation and the end of the world, and other such matters. The myths retailed by the giant are the main ingredients in the cosmogony of the heathen religion, to which we shall return. As was to be expected, the giant loses his life in this contest of knowledge.

In *The Lay of Allwise* the parties in the dialogue are Thór and the dwarf Allwise, who has come to claim Thór's daughter as his bride. Thór holds him in conversation until daybreak and then tells him that he is lost and beguiled: the sun shines into the hall and the dwarf is turned into stone. The learning of Allwise is not strictly mythological but rhetorical: he gives Thór the names for things which are called one thing by men and another by gods. This has a parallel in Homer, for instance, where he says that the river Skamandros is called by the gods Xanthos, 'the Pale One'.

Balder's Dreams, a short poem purporting to be a supplement to *Völuspá,* tells how Ódin rides to the gateway of Hel to discover why Balder is afflicted with heavy dreams. By his spells he summons a seeress from the grave, who tells him that Balder will be slain. Most scholars consider this poem to be the work of a skilful imitator of the ancient manner—perhaps writing in the twelfth century.

Two of the conversation poems in the *Edda* are so-called 'flytings'. *The Lay of Hárbard* confronts the two main deities of the North in something like a 'matching of men'. Thór summons a ferryman and asks him to ferry him across a sound. The ferryman, Hárbard ('Hoar-beard'), is Ódin in disguise, who proceeds to twit Thór, telling him he is instructed only to ferry over respectable persons, and Thór looks like a beggar. The match consists mostly of Thór's boasting of his victories over giants, and Ódin's boasting of his love affairs. Thór loses out when his slow wits are pitted against the superior irony and smooth readiness of speech of the god of runic wisdom.

The Taunting of Loki is the product of a witty and clever poet who conceived the idea of showing up the seamier side of the solemn and glorious gods. In many ways it calls to mind Lucian's famous and amusing *Assembly of the Gods.* The Mephistophelian Loki thrusts himself into a banquet of the gods and engages each of them in a 'flyting' or running dialogue of vituperation, often in quite a spicy manner, where every god and goddess gets his or her share of defamation, until the disturber of the peace is finally put to flight when Thór appears on the scene and threatens him with violence. Interludes of the same comic and racy manner are also found in the heroic Helgi Lays.

From the mythical poems of the *Edda* we are able to piece together the cosmology of the heathen religion, the gaps being filled by Snorri Sturluson's *Prose Edda* and by references in skaldic poetry. Our ancestors imagined the infinity of space to be a yawning gap, to the north of which lay the icy world of frosts and mists, Niflheim, while to the south lay the torrid region of Múspellsheim, the land of fire. As the ice of Niflheim gradually melted away under the fiery clouds of Múspellsheim, there flowed forth from Niflheim into the yawning gap chill streams of venom, and yet the animating beams from Múspellsheim called the first living beings to life: an enormous giant called Ýmir or Aurgelmir, and the cow Audhumla, from whose milk he drew sustenance. From Ýmir sprang other giants and so he became the progenitor of that evil race. The cow Audhumla also brought about life by licking the icebound boulders of salt. Thus Búri, the progenitor of the gods, came into being: his son Bur or Valtam, with Bestla daughter of the giant Bolthorn, had three sons named Ódin, Vili and Vé, good and fair to look at.

When the race of Ýmir multiplied beyond number the sons of Bur put Ýmir to death; in his blood all the giants were drowned except Bergelmir, who with his wife saved himself in a boat. His descendants grew to a mighty host and persisted in their evil courses. Ódin and his two brothers made from the body of Ýmir earth, sky and sea, the earth from his body, the sea from his blood, the heavens from his skull. His bones became mountains and stones, his hair became trees and grass, his brain became clouds, and the maggots in his body became small dwarfs who lived below the earth's surface and in rocks, and who were on better terms with the giants than with the gods.

Ódin, Vili and Vé were at first the only gods, but they were not content with creating inanimate nature and therefore brought to life sentient beings also, both men and animals. The first human couple, Ask and Embla, were created from trees. Ódin gave them breath, Vili gave them soul and understanding, and Vé gave them bodily warmth and colour. From Ask and Embla sprang the entire race of men. The three brothers also created the celestial bodies by taking the sparks from Múspellsheim and placing them in the sky as the sun, moon, and stars. The sun and the moon were placed each on its wain, and each wain was drawn by two horses; the horses of the sun were named Árvak and Alsvinn ('Early Awake' and 'Very Swift'). Before the sun stands the shield Svalin ('Cooling'), without which all life on earth would be scorched.

The giants were so ill-disposed toward mankind that the gods felt themselves compelled to build from the eyebrows of Ýmir a great defensive wall or fortress encompassing the midmost region of earth where men lived. The space within was called Midgard. Beyond its confines lay Jötunheim where the giants lived. In the centre of the universe the gods established their own glorious dwelling, Ásgard.

A wonderous ash-tree, Yggdrasil, supported the universe,

striking its roots through the worlds. It had three roots, one among the gods, another among the giants, a third in the depths of Niflheim. Beside the root in Niflheim there was a fearsome well and a dreadful serpent Nídhögg, which, together with a great number of other serpents, constantly gnawed at the root of the tree, threatening to destroy it. One day they would succeed in killing the tree, and the universe would come crashing down. Beside the root that rested with the giants there was also a well belonging to the wise Mímir; in it lay hidden the highest wisdom, and from it Mímir drank every day. To secure knowledge from that well Ódin sacrificed one of his eyes. Beside the third root, stretching to the gods, there was a third well, called Urd's Well, guarded by the three Norns (see p. 57). It was here that the gods held their assemblies every day, passing over the quivering Rainbow Bridge (Bifröst), to pass judgment on the deeds of men.

In one of his historical works, *Ynglingatal* ('Enumeration of the Yngling Kings'), the first section of *Heimskringla*, Snorri Sturluson offers an euhemeristic explanation of the origin of the Norse gods:

Far to the east of the river Don in Asia was a land called Ásaland or Ásaheim, whose chief city was called Ásgard. In that city was a chief called Ódin. It was a great centre for sacrifice. Twelve priests of the temple, according to custom, directed the sacrifices and judged between men. They were called gods (*díar* an Irish loan-word) or lords (*drótnar*); everyone paid them service and veneration.

Snorri goes on to say that Ódin was so wise in counsel and skilled in magic that people began to call his name in trouble, and after his death worshipped him as god. He relates how the tribe of Ódin travelled north across the continent of Europe, finally settling in Sigtuna in Sweden, where he allotted different dwellings to his temple priests. Thus Ódin became the progenitor of the Yngling dynasty. In the *Gylfaginning*, the first part of his *Prose Edda*, which is an exposition of the traditional Icelandic myths, Snorri states that there are twelve divine gods, and then proceeds to list thirteen: Ódin, Thór, Balder, Njörd, Frey, Týr, Bragi, Heimdall, Höd, Vídar, Váli, Ull and Forseti. Ódin had two brothers, Vili and Vé, who qualify as gods, and there is also Aegir, god of the sea. There are a number of goddesses, but the only ones playing significant roles in surviving myths are Freya, daughter of Njörd and sister of Frey; Frigg, Ódin's wife, whose name and function suggest that she was originally the same goddess as Freya; and Idun, Bragi's wife and guardian of the magic apples which restore youth to the gods. Snorri adds that Loki is also sometimes counted among the gods, for he is friend and companion of Thór and, strangely, foster brother to Ódin, though both his parents were giants. Bud Ódin and Thór had at least one giant parent as well.

Of the thirteen principal gods in Ásgard, Ódin was the foremost. He was the preserver of all things, and therefore he was called All-Father. Some of his many other names were: High One, Father of the Slain and the Hooded One. The last appellation refers to his many disguises on his journeys through the worlds to learn of the fates of the gods. Ódin is a strange and solemn figure, always aloof, and the inevitable fate of the gods weighs heavily upon him. Even when he sits at the feasts of the gods in his golden palace Gladsheim, or with his heroes in Valhall, he eats nothing—but does take a drink. The food set before him he gives to the two wolves crouching at his feet. On his shoulders perch two ravens who fly each day through the world and bring him news of all that men do. They are called Hugin (Thought) and Munin (Memory). While the other gods feast, Ódin ponders what Thought and Memory teach him. Ódin had the responsibility, more than all the other gods together, of postponing as long as possible the inevitable doom, and for this purpose he was constantly in search of new insight and more wisdom. He paid with one of his eyes for a draught from the Well of Wisdom; he also won the knowledge of the runes by suffering. The runes were magic inscriptions, immensely powerful for him who could inscribe them on anything, wood, metal, stone. Ódin learned them at the cost of a mysterious pain, hanging nine nights on a windy tree, wounded with a spear. He passed the hard-won knowledge on to men. They, too, were able to use the runes to protect themselves. He imperilled his life again to take away from the giants the *skald's mead* which made anyone who tasted it a poet. This good gift he bestowed upon men as well as upon the gods. Ódin was the god of poetry and ecstacy, of wisdom and magic, of war and the battle-dead. Hence he was master of the *Valkyries* (Choosers of the Slain) who brought to Valhall (Hall of the Slain) heroes Ódin had designated to die on the battlefield. They also waited on the table in Ásgard and kept the drinking horns full. Ódin was principally the god of kings, earls, chieftains, magicians and poets. He was deceptive and an oath-breaker; it is said that his breaking of oaths sworn to the giants brings about the wars leading to the gods' final destruction. Thus Ódin stands out as a very complex character, magnificent, dominating, demonic and sadistic.

If Ódin is the god of the aristocrat, Thór is the god of the common man. The son of Ódin and Earth, Thór held sway over air and climate, over rain and harvest. He guarded men and their labours from the wild forces of nature, personified as giants. He was strength incarnate and performed many a mighty deed to save the gods from disasters, but was on the other hand lamentably slow-witted, even if on one occasion, in an ironic inversion of roles, he defeated the dwarf Allwise in a battle of wits. There are striking similarities between the Nordic Thór and the Greek Heracles of myth and comedy. Both were killers of many giants; both were constantly disappearing on some perilous adventures; both visited the realm of the dead; both fought Old Age; both were gigantic eaters and drinkers; both were ribald and quick-tempered, but also easily pacified. Both had marked humorous traits incompatible with their heroic stature. Thór was not only the protector of the gods against all their enemies—specifically dwarves, elves, giants, trolls and the Midgard-Serpent—but also the strong and faithful protector of the peasant and human kind in general. When he raced across the clouds with his team of he-goats, it thundered; when he went forth with his hammer Mjöllnir in his hand, he was irresistible. The Northerners invented many vivid stories of his exploits, bearing witness to their appreciation of this benevolent deity, of whom it was impossible to say evil things.

Njörd and Frey are not properly *Aesir* (divine gods), but *Vanir*, who had come to Ásgard as hostages after a war between the *Aesir* and *Vanir* over the question of which of the two races should demand worship. Njörd is the male counterpart of the Germanic goddess Nerthus, mentioned by Tacitus in the first century A.D. as the object of fertility rites on an island in the north. His role in the Norse pantheon is rather similar to that of his son Frey, one of the three principal gods (with Ódin and Thór) in the religious cults of Scandinavia as well as in the poetry, for all the extant mythological poems feature one of these three gods. Frey was the god of fertility whose idol at Uppsala in Sweden was distinguished by a gigantic phallus. He seems to have been especially popular in certain valleys and plains in Iceland which were considered to be particularly propitious, though his popularity was greatest in Sweden. In Iceland he was sometimes called 'the Swedish god'. The single myth about him in the *Edda, The Lay of Skírnir,* may easily be interpreted as an allegory of the impregnation of the earth with fertile grain. Njörd as well as Frey governed sea and fire, and gave good fortune at sea and in the chase. At the ancient sacrificial feasts men drank to Njörd and Frey next after Ódin, and from an early formulary for taking oaths it is clear that oaths were sworn by Njörd, Frey and by the 'Almighty God' (presumably Týr).

Týr is a deity less clearly defined than most of the other gods. He is the god of battle, brave and virtuous, and sacrifices his hand when the Fenris-Wolf is fettered. At Ragnarök he fights with Garm, the hound of the goddess Hel (Death). Our sources tell little more about him, except that he took pleasure in creating strife and did nothing for the promotion of concord; he gave men courage and heroism in battle. It may, however, be surmised by his name that he was in reality an archaic, later dethroned, King of Heaven. His Norse name Týr, Tír or Tí is cognate with the Latin Jupiter, the Greek Zeus and the Indian Dyaus. The Germanic peoples called days of the week after their principal gods: Tuesday (Týr), Wednesday (Ódin: the Southern form of the name was Woden), Thursday (Thór), and Friday (Frey).

Balder, the son of Ódin and his wife Frigg, was the most beloved of all the gods, on earth as well as in Ásgard. He was the pure and white god, symbol of innocence and piety. He was also wise, eloquent, gentle and lenient, and so righteous that his judgments always stand unshaken. Every living thing, with the sole exception of the mistletoe, had sworn not to harm him. His death was the first of the disasters which befell the gods. The story of his death is most moving and tragic, and perhaps gives us the best example of the inability of the gods to avert fate. Frazer devoted a whole volume of *The Golden Bough* to the Balder myth.

Heimdall, sometimes called Ódin's son, was the warder of Bifröst, the luminous Rainbow Bridge between Ásgard and Midgard (Earth). The sound of his immense horn was heard in all the worlds. By night or by day his vision spanned hundreds of miles; he was able to hear the grass coming up out of the earth and wool growing on the backs of sheep. The *Song of the Sybil* calls human beings 'Heimdall's sons', Heimdall being the wandering god who, in the *Lay of Ríg,* creates the three classes of society. He and Loki, old enemies, kill one another in Ragnarök.

The god of hunting was Ull who excelled at archery and skiing. Men did well to summon him to their aid when they engaged in single combat. He was the son of Sif and the stepson of Thór. Höd, the son of Ódin, was blind but vigorous. He unwittingly brought about the death of Balder, being duped by Loki into throwing the mistletoe at him. He is subsequently killed by Váli, the son of Ódin and Rind, a bold warrior and good archer, who swears neither to wash nor clip his hair until he has avenged the death of Balder. He will survive the destruction of the universe. Vídar, too, shall return after Ragnarök. The son of Ódin and the giantess Gríd, he is next to Thór in strength and is called the God of Few Words. Bragi, son of Ódin, is the god of eloquence and poetry, whom our ancestors imagined as a venerable man with a long beard. According to Snorri Sturluson, minstrelsy of every kind is given the title *bragur* (still used in Icelandic) after him. His wife is Idun, keeper of the marvellous apples. Forseti (literally 'President'), the son of Balder and Nanna, was the god of justice and conciliation: those who refer their disputes to him never go away unreconciled.

The Satan of Norse mythology is Loki, next to Ódin the most singular and strange deity. He is the offspring of a giant and in many ways a split personality; he is allowed free entrance to

Ásgard because for some reason, never explained, Ódin had sworn brotherhood to him. He continually involves the gods in difficulties and dangers, even if at times he seems to solve their minor problems, and he is one of their fatal opponents in the great final battle, with his terrible progeny the Fenris-Wolf, the venom-spewing Midgard-Serpent, and the horrible hag Hel who reigns supreme in Niflheim, the pale world of the shadowy dead, to which go all who die of illness or old age, whether men or other creatures on earth. Some authorities have seen in the story of Loki similarities to that of the Caucasian Prometheus, especially in the account of his punishment after he has caused the death of Balder. He tries to escape by changing himself into a salmon, but the Aesir capture him and fetter him to a rock underneath a serpent dripping poison. His second wife Sigyn manages to catch the venom into a bowl, but whenever she misses a drop his trembling makes the earth quake. This will be his fate until Ragnarök, when he will join forces with the giants. Although Loki has been compared to Satan and Prometheus, he has none of the fallen Lucifer's longings nor the splendid defiance of Prometheus. He is evil incarnate, exclusively self-interested, incapable of friendship, deceitful, cunning, without humour, but relishing satire. Loki is a much younger figure than Ódin, Thór and Týr, not to mention the *Vanir*. He is not really a god at all, in the sense of inspiring worship, but rather as one author has aptly put it, the product of mythological speculation.[9]

Goddesses are not prominent in Norse mythology. Ódin's favourite wife Frigg was reputedly very wise, but she was also very silent and told no one, not even Ódin, what she knew. She is a rather vague figure, usually sitting at the spinning-wheel, where the threads she spins are golden but why she spins them is a secret.

Freya was the goddess of love and beauty, the sister of Frey, but half of those slain in battle were hers (Ódin's Valkyries could carry only half to Valhall); she herself rode to the battlefield and claimed her share of the dead, and to the Eddic poets that seems to have been a perfectly natural task for the goddess of beauty. There were two other goddesses of love, Sjöfn and Lofn, one of whom kindled love between men and women, while the other helped those who loved but had difficulties in winning the beloved.

There were a host of other minor deities and supernatural beings, such as dwarfs, various kinds of elves, trolls, familiar spirits, attendant spirits, sprites, forces of nature, etc.

Obviously the cosmology outlined here is that of the Eddic period, i.e. the Viking Age. We know little about actual religious practices during the period, but from older sources, scanty though they are, we may infer that the heathen religion had been greatly modified through the preceding centuries. The religion that we have in the *Edda* is the expression of the Viking Age and has become to a great extent a religion for warriors, worked over by poets who found in the mythology material suitable for great poetry with tragi-heroic implications.

Before leaving the *Edda* we should consider the longest poem in the collection, *Hávamál* ('The Sayings of the High One'), which comes after the *Song of the Sybil* in the mythological section, although it deals mainly with mundane affairs. It was probably included among the mythical poems because the sayings purport to be the utterances of Ódin, but actually only about half the stanzas are connected with him. The poem is largely didactic, presenting us with that homely wisdom, that sternly realistic view of life, those not ignoble ethical conceptions, which are given such classic illustration in the Icelandic Sagas. It is a humanistic piece of literature, unique in content, dealing directly with daily life, behaviour, social ideals, expounding a deep knowledge of human nature in aphorisms and proverbs which bear comparison with those of the Sophists of Greece or the Preacher in Jerusalem.

At least five separate sections can be made out in the poem. The first, consisting of seventy-nine stanzas, might be called Wisdom for Wanderers and Counsel for Guests. Here we are presented with the common situations of life and told how they should be dealt with. The emphasis is on the laws of hospitality, decent conduct, circumspection in one's dealings with men, the need for moderation in eating, drinking and all the acts of life, and the vanity of mere wealth compared with true merit. All this is expounded with austere dignity and strength, sometimes with terse humour, which gives a distinct character to the moralistic verse.

Some of the stanzas reflect the sentiments of the peasant and farmer who has to be content with his lot in life:[10]

It is better to live   than to lie a corpse,
   The live man catches the cow;
I saw flames rise   for the rich man's pyre,
   And before his door he lay dead.

The lame rides a horse,   the handless is herdsman,
   The deaf in battle is bold;
The blind man is better   than one that is burned,
   No good can come from a corpse.

But there are also stanzas expressing the true heroic spirit of the Viking, who looks with disdain on death, striving only for that which will survive man's death—his fame:

Cattle die,   and kinsmen die,
   And so one dies one's self;
One thing I know   that never dies,

The fame of a dead man's deeds.

The second section of *Hávamál* deals in a frankly cynical way with man's relations to woman, in particular with woman's inconstancy and treachery, but also with her gullibility and the ruthlessness of men in love, as exemplified by the two love affairs of Ódin, told in the first person:

> *A man shall trust not   the oath of a maid*
> *Nor the word a woman speaks;*
> *For their hearts on a whirling   wheel were fashioned,*
> *And fickle their breasts were formed.*

> *Clear now will I speak   for I know them both,*
> *Men false to women are found;*
> *When fairest we speak,   then falsest we think,*
> *Against wisdom we work with deceit.*

Then there follows the *Lay of Loddfáfnir*, containing miscellaneous counsel on such subjects as love and friendship, supposedly given to the bard Loddfáfnir when he acted as an eavesdropper at *Urd's Well* overhearing Ódin's utterances. Example:

> *Mingled is love   when a man can speak*
> *To another all his thought;*
> *Nought is so bad   as false to be,*
> *No friend speaks only fair.*

The fourth section, the so-called *Rune Poem*, deals obscurely with runic wisdom as acquired and taught by Ódin. Here he relates how he hung nine nights in a tree, stabbed with a spear, himself offered to himself. Scholars used to regard it as showing Christian influence but, as was later pointed out, various scraps of evidence indicated that in prehistoric times in the North the dead were hung in trees before being burnt. If this is correct, it suggests that Ódin won the knowledge of the runes by penetrating the world of the newly dead, which calls to mind the journey of Odysseus to the land of the dead in order to seek knowledge for his homeward journey, and there are such other parallels as Aeneas, Christ, Dante and even St Paul according to one tradition.

The final section of *Hávamál* tells of eighteen magic charms, efficient in dulling the blades of swords, curing disease, to calming the sea, and performing other useful services, if used with proper runes.

The poems of *Hávamál* were probably composed in the early tenth century. Their place of origin is not known, but some of them seem to hail from Norway rather than Iceland; a number of beautiful nature passages point unmistakably to the former. The poems probably lived orally among the Icelanders before they were committed to writing, and may have suffered from omissions or accretions.

The first and by far the longest section of *Hávamál* is well preserved. It is rich in wisdom, expressing mostly the outlook of a cosmopolitan who has travelled widely, met different people, and acquired a wide horizon. It is put into a poetic framework. A stranger, perhaps Ódin in disguise, comes to a house. Neither guest nor host knows anything of the other, and neither is given a name. We are actually not clear as to who is speaking when, and some think of a third person advising the other two. It seems likely, however, that the guest is the one who speaks. He talks of how a guest and a host should behave, stressing always the guest. Then he goes farther afield and discusses the home, friendship and other boons of life. The gods are not mentioned at all, not even their relations with men. Nor is there mention of king or slave.

The whole poem deals with the relations of free men, and it has a peculiarly modern outlook. Family relations are rarely alluded to, but friendship is stressed emphatically. There is no trace of Christian influence. Everything is seen in terms of this present life. The whole poem is permeated by a pagan liberalism and scepticism.

First we are informed what is most essential to a traveller in foreign parts. At home everything is known and easy, and therefore not conducive to thinking or observation. A man's wisdom and common sense is first tested when he comes into unknown situations. Habit will not help him then—he has to be wide awake and aware of everything. The more wisdom he has, the easier it is for him to adapt himself to new circumstances. Here we have keen psychological insight which is in agreement with those modern psychologists who consider intelligence to be the ability to adapt oneself to new circumstances or solve new problems with the help of experience. The poem is concerned throughout with one aspect of new circumstances, namely the human: the relations of people, the social aspect of human existence, which after all is the most difficult aspect.

According to *Hávamál,* the value of a man consists in his wisdom, in all the ramifications of the quality. Wisdom is partly innate, but what matters is to apply it correctly. You use your wisdom to deal with the problems of life, to govern your instincts and temper when dealing with other men. A wise man is not ill-tempered. This is in agreement with the ancient Greek philosophers and later thinkers like Descartes: It is not sufficient to have a good intelligence; what is important is to apply it well. You can, in other words, cultivate your wisdom.

Wisdom also implies a sense of value. Some things are worth thinking about, others not:

> *The witless man   is awake all night,*
> *Thinking of many things;*
> *Care-worn he is   when the morning comes,*
> *And his woe is just as it was.*

The wise man seeks facts that have value for him, and these then become part of his experience.

Hávamál also stresses knowledge of oneself and others; these two are interdependent. One only has the measure of one's own strength and value when it is compared to that of others:

> *The man who is prudent   a measured use*
> *Of the might he has will make; .*
> *He finds when among   the brave he fares*
> *That the boldest he may not be.*

Introspection and extraspection are mutually dependent and must both be present, if we want a clear view of ourselves and of others. Hence social life is very important to one's spiritual development.

The main emphasis in *Hávamál* is on restraint, care, temperance. But one should not overdo it: 'I bid thee be wary, but be not fearful.' Life would indeed be burdensome if one were always on guard, and therefore the wise man knows to choose: when to trust, when to be wary. Also too much wisdom is not desirable:

> *A measure of wisdom   each man shall have,*
> *But never too much let him know;*
> *For the wise man's heart   is seldom happy,*
> *If wisdom too great he has won.*

Compare this to Solomon's dictum in *Ecclesiastes* 1.18.

The wise man is also curious. He takes interest in others and in human affairs generally:

> *To question and answer   must all be ready*
> *Who wish to be known as wise;*
> *Tell one thy thoughts,   but beware of two,—*
> *All know what is known to three.*

The wise man is a faithful friend, who talks openly to his friends and frequents their homes:

> *If a friend thou hast   whom thou fully wilt trust,*
> *Then fare to find him oft;*
> *For brambles grow   and waving grass*
> *On a rarely trodden road.*

> *Be never the first   to break with thy friend*
> *The bond that holds you both;*
> *Care eats the heart   if thou canst not speak*
> *To another all thy thoughts.*

On the matter of wealth and poverty *Hávamál* takes a balanced view. Wealth is a means, not an end. It is not always ennobling, but neither is there virtue in poverty. A man should be judged by what he is, not by what he has:

> *A man knows not,   if nothing he knows,*
>   *That gold often apes begets;*
> *One man is wealthy   and one is poor,*
>   *Yet scorn for him none should know.*

One should spend one's wealth for the enjoyment of oneself and one's friends, for wealth left behind at death may often go to the wrong hands.

The ethical view of *Hávamál* is not based on any particular religion or belief in the hereafter, but stresses our behaviour here and now in our dealings with others. The value of a man lies in his renown: his life becomes a force in the lives of later generations. This is a high ideal. It is not supported by any belief in reward or punishment. Our life carries its own reward. Man has eternal life through the influence his life will exert on later generations. This view is indeed one of the principal contributions of Nordic thought toward the understanding of the value of human life.

Thus we may once again reiterate that the *Edda* as a whole expresses unequivocally the twofold Nordic ideal of the heroic warrior and the wise man, which we shall find again in new contexts in the *Sagas of Icelanders*.

Notes

1. Einar Ól. Sveinsson, *Íslenzkar bókmenntir í fornöld*, Reykjavík 1962, p. 177.

2. Lord Raglan, *The Hero*, London 1949, p. 272.

3. V. Grønbech, *The Culture of the Teutons*, London-Copenhagen 1931, p. 255.

4. Bertha S. Phillpotts, *The Elder Edda and Ancient Scandinavian Drama*, Cambridge 1920, p. 114.

5. W. P. Ker, *Epic and Romance*, London 1922, p. 120.

6. Ibid., p. 60.

7. Bertha S. Phillpotts, *Edda and Saga*, New York 1931, pp. 65-6.

8. See ibid., pp. 85-6.

9. Johannes Brønsted, *The Vikings*, London 1965, p. 282.

10. *The Poetic Edda* (*Hávamál* 139), translated by Henry Adams Bellows, New York 1957, p. 60. All the translations quoted here are from this volume.

4. The Icelandic Sagas

If the *Edda* constitutes a priceless contribution to the heroic and mythical store of world literature, throwing unique light on the prehistory and religion of the whole Germanic race, the so-called *Sagas of Icelanders (Íslendingasögur)* are unparalleled in medieval literature and may best be compared with the great novels of the nineteenth and early twentieth centuries in regard to style, psychological depth, character portrayal and scope. They were composed mostly in the thirteenth century by anonymous masters who have been placed beside the great authors of all time for their creative genius and literary craftsmanship. The tradition lasted for more than a century, and its production within this short span of time is remarkable both for the variety, quantity and quality. We are indeed reminded of the short but brilliant periods of Greek and Elizabethan tragedy.

The *Sagas of Icelanders* were the first prose novels of Europe, written in the vernacular when the rest of Europe was priest- and caste-ridden, dominated by Latin and religious preoccupations. They deal with the everyday life of the great families and individuals in Iceland in the tenth and eleventh centuries, in a manner at once heroic and realistic. W. H. Auden and other modern writers have pointed to the extraordinary modernity of the Icelandic Sagas, both in style, technique and subject matter. It has even been suggested that the famous matter-of-fact camera-eye style of Hemingway must have been derived, directly or indirectly, from the Icelandic Sagas.[1] This is inferred from the fact that both the Saga-writers and Hemingway stress the depiction of external facts and observable reactions, and make extensive use of dialogue, often in short utterances and cutting repartee. But in reality the lucid and perfectly natural style of the Sagas is a far cry from the elaborate mannerisms of Hemingway and his school. A comparison has also been made between the Saga-writers and William Faulkner in regard to themes and intent, and there are indeed striking similarities.[2]

The *Sagas of Icelanders* were written mainly in the thirteenth century, an age of moral and social dissolution, somewhat reminiscent of the late Renaissance, and may be said to represent a nostalgic reconstruction of a lost 'Golden Age'. They were perhaps, as Sigurdur Nordal has suggested, an attempt to embody and preserve the concepts of human dignity and individuality in a period of savage internecine warfare waged by ruthless chieftains greedy for wealth and power. At the same time they demonstrated, paradoxically, how the heroic ethos of the 'Golden Age' carried within it the seeds of self-destruction. The rigidity of the moral code, the principle of equal revenge, the demand of one life for another—these had to culminate sooner or later in a collapse of the order it strove to preserve.

The word *Saga* means etymologically 'something said' and is related to the Old English 'saw', but it came to have the special significance of 'prose narrative'. It has roughly the same meaning as the Latin *historia,* which appears in English both as 'story' and 'history'. In its most comprehensive use the term includes history, biography, legend and story, but the *Sagas of Icelanders* refer to the group of Sagas dealing with persons who lived in Iceland between about A.D. 870 and 1030.

There has been endless controversy over the question to what degree the Sagas were actually composed by the men who penned them. Behind most of them there was probably an oral tradition, but as they have come down to us they are clearly the works of conscious artists who made use of any material at hand, whether written or oral, to fashion complete and unified historical novels. Their historicity is spurious, especially when we come to the later ones. We are strictly not dealing with historical writings. The Sagas have their basis in actual history: most of the individuals and families mentioned existed, many of the events actually occurred, and most of the places are authentic. But that is as far as we can go. Their historicity is incidental and subordinate to the artistic aims of the writer, who does as he pleases with the materials he has the good fortune to find.

These materials were generally of three kinds. First, there was oral tradition, the stories transmitted by word of mouth from generation to generation. Secondly, there were written sources, 'authorities' as they might be called. Thirdly, there were poems and verses, usually contemporary with the events described, which were incorporated in the Sagas to lend credence to the narrative. No doubt the oral traditions and the verses, where they appear, are the core of each Saga, but it has proved a tricky business to determine which verses are genuine, and especially which Sagas are closest to oral tradition. This was dramatically illustrated in the case of *Hrafnkel's Saga,* a masterpiece among the shorter Sagas, which was generally believed to be historically quite reliable and very close to oral tradition, until Sigurdur Nordal demonstrated in 1940 that it is purely fictitious and one of the later *Sagas of Icelanders.*

We know for certain that the Icelanders early gained a reputation as good story-tellers and reliable recorders of past events. The special conditions prevailing in the Commonwealth were especially favourable for the development of story-telling. There was a great deal of movement and social intercourse within the country, and a relatively large number of Icelanders travelled abroad. People were eager to hear reports from foreign parts, as was quite natural in a remote island, and the annual assemblies, both in the districts and at Thingvellir, provided ample opportunities for the spreading of news and the exercise of story-telling. We have in the Sagas many accounts of such incidents: a good story-teller attracting a large crowd of eager listeners. There is a famous episode which throws light on this national pastime of the Icelanders and the high degree of excellence it reached. A young Icelander came to the court of King Harald Hardruler of Norway in the autumn (about 1050) and offered to entertain the court with his stories or 'Sagas'. All went well until Yuletide (Christmas), when the young story-teller seemed to be losing heart. When the king noticed this and asked him whether his stories were running low, he admitted that they were. He had, he said, only one story left and did not dare to tell it, since it was the Saga of the king's own exploits as a Varangian chief in Byzantium and around the Mediterranean. 'But that is the very story I want to hear,' the king declared and arranged for the youth to tell it all during the twelve days of Yule. The king would not show whether he liked it or not. But when the tale was finished he was greatly impressed by the fact that the extensive report was correct in every detail, and he asked the young man where he had learned the story. The Icelander declared that he had learned it bit by bit at the Althing during several summers, listening to Halldór Snorrason telling it, Halldór having been a close friend of the king who had accompanied him on his expeditions.

There can be no doubt that this anecdote gives us a clue to the making of the Sagas, their inception and first stage of development. There are a number of stereotyped phrases and conventions in the extant Sagas pointing to their oral origins, but when they came to be written down in the thirteenth century they had reached a new stage, that of *literary* works, where a number of traditions had been fused. Nordal's observation is apposite in this context: 'The Icelanders succeeded—thanks both to their knowledge of the Latin literary language and translations of it from about 1100 onwards—in creating for themselves a saga style from these two contrasts, and in uniting much of the simplicity of colloquial speech with the richness of the language of books.' The contrasts he refers to are the relatively primitive oral narration and the foreign ecclesiastical style found in the numerous translations he mentions.

The Sagas are at once contrasts and counterparts of the heroic

Eddic poetry. The main contrast consists in the different environment. The Saga heroes are not foreigners like their Eddic counterparts; they are an integral part of a larger whole, a heroic society which plays almost as prominent a part in the action of the Sagas as the chief characters.

On the other hand, the similarity between the Eddic poems and the Sagas is striking in regard to conception of character and action. Right conduct, the core of the heroic way of life, is the overriding principle. Destiny had to be faced squarely, without regard for the consequences, however dreadful. Conduct was far more important in itself than any consequences. It was not a question of right or wrong in the ethical sense, but of *right action* in a given circumstance, where there was only a choice of two evils. The circumstances might be trivial, as they frequently were—such as quarrels over women, horses, sheep, hay or merchandise—but the matter in dispute was subordinate to what the characters chose to make of it in the story. Its value only depended on the persons and their reactions. This whole outlook is closely related to the concern for 'renown' after death, which was so deeply ingrained in the ancient Icelanders. Only such conduct as was in accordance with the heroic ideals made a person worthy to be remembered and told about in a Saga, no matter what were his origins.

Fate is the great protagonist in many of the best Sagas, appearing in many guises, sometimes with primitive symbolism such as the fatal gold of the Nibelungs in the *Edda*. There are fatal swords in *The Saga of Gisli* and *Laxdaela Saga*. Sometimes fate appears in dreams foreshadowing the whole course of events, as in *Laxdaela Saga* and *Gunnlaug's Saga*, or foretelling certain events, like in *Droplaugarsona Saga* and especially *The Saga of Gisli*, where dreams play an uncommonly dominant, and unique role in that they reflect also the psychological condition of the great outlaw, the struggle within his soul between hope and fear. But in its most commanding and imposing aspect, fate becomes a mover and manipulator of events which bring about the conflict and resolution of each Saga. The role of the individual is to face his destiny and resolve the tragic dilemma into which fate has thrust him. This is familiar from Greek tragedy. As a matter of fact, heroic society and heroic literature are unthinkable without a strong sense of the inexorable and all-pervading power of fate.

The tragic dilemma is found in many variations in the Sagas, sometimes calling to mind the heroic lays of the *Edda*. In *Njál's Saga* one of the most striking cases of the tragic dilemma is that of Flosi who burns Njál and his sons (and incidentally an old woman and child) alive, not because he wants to, for he hates the task, but because fate has put him in a position where it is the only thing he can do. In *The Saga of Gisli* the hero, who is 'a wise man, and one who had prophetic dreams', has to make up his mind whether not to avenge his wife's brother or to kill his sister's husband. He takes the latter choice. The sister then decides to avenge her husband, outlawing her brother and causing his death, but later she wants her brother's killers destroyed. Here we have an interesting parallel to Gudrún's plight in the *Edda*.

In *The Saga of Gisli* there is also a striking instance of the heroic spirit among the common people. A chieftain threatens his humble tenant Ingjald with death because he has sheltered the great outlaw. The tenant's answer is: 'My clothes are threadbare, and it is all the same to me if I don't have to wear them into rags.' From the *Saga of Eirik the Red* we know the name Bjarni Grímólfsson, not so much because he sailed to America as because he gave up his place in a boat to a man more concerned to live than he. Certain death was the price of this gesture, but the name of the survivor was not worth remembering; he was only the occasion of Bjarni's moment of destiny.[3] The modern reader is sometimes struck by the similarity between this ancient ethos and the existentialist outlook of modern times.

Even though the *Sagas of Icelanders* do by no means form a uniform group they reveal a good deal of homogeneity with regard to composition, style and general tone and outlook. Aside from the traditional and often rather tiring genealogies given whenever a character is introduced, there is a peculiarly modern taste to these narratives. One of the outstanding characteristics is the emphasis on realism in the presentation. Nothing is related which could not have been told by the characters themselves or observed by a third person or group of people. The reader is made to *see* the course of events, and the art of the Saga-writer shows in his skill to select relevant events and action. He thoroughly rejects the technique of those modern novelists who presume to be all-seeing and all-knowing. He will only tell what the watching countryside could have known, and his use of this chorus-like 'countryside' is one of the fine touches by which he avoids direct comment or moral judgment. There is created an illusion of complete objectivity, and it is up to the reader to draw his own conclusions—sometimes, it is true, with the aid of what 'people said' or what 'was rumoured'.

Two famous passages from the Sagas will illustrate this method. One is from the less well-known *Droplaugarsona Saga*. Droplaug, a widow, has married again, somewhat beneath her, and against the wishes of her son Helgi:

Some seasons later Helgi Droplaug's son came down from the autumn Thing to the Lower Vidivellir, to Hallstein his stepfather and his mother Droplaug, and he had not been there before since she was married. Droplaug said to her husband Hallstein that he ought to ask Helgi to stay there for the winter. He says: 'I am not much inclined to do that. I would rather give him a present, oxen or horses.' But at her urging he invited Helgi to be there, and he accepted.

Hallstein had a thrall called Thorgils. It was a fortnight later that those three had a long talk together, Helgi and Droplaug and Thorgils, Hallstein's thrall, and other folk did not know what their talk was about. Thorgils looked after the sheep during the winter in a fenced field south of the homestead, and was good at his work. A great deal of hay was carried to the field. One day Thorgils came to Hallstein and asked him to come and see his hay and the sheep. He came, and went into the barn and began to go out by the upper hatchway. Thereupon Thorgils struck at him with an axe which belonged to Helgi Droplaug's son, and no second blow was needed to end Hallstein. Helgi was coming down the slope from seeing to his horses, and saw that Hallstein was slain. Forthwith he killed the thrall. He went back to the house and told his mother the news; she was sitting by the fire and the women-folk with her. A little while later the home-folk at Vidivellir began to gossip about how Helgi and Droplaug and Thorgils had talked for a long while the day before Hallstein was killed, and this slaying became very unpopular.... (Chap. 7).[4]

In this passage there are a number of facts that have to be inferred from the way the story is told. It is not directly stated that the mother and son agreed to have Hallstein killed and to make use of the thrall for the purpose, destroying the evidence afterwards, but it is obviously so. Neither does the author pass any judgment on the deed, but uses the 'neighbourhood' as a moral commentator: 'This slaying became very unpopular.'

A more famous passage is the charming and vivid scene in *Egil's Saga* where Thorgerd, the daughter of Egil, induces him to come out of his lock-closet, where he has locked himself up for three days, without food or drink, wishing only to die after his son has been drowned. When Thorgerd arrives her mother asks her whether she has eaten supper:

'No supper have I had,' Thorgerd answered loudly, 'and none will I, till I am with Freyja [i.e. dead]. I know of no better plan for me than my father. I don't want to live after my father and brother.' She went to the lock-closet, and 'Father,' she called, 'open the door. I want us both to go the same road.'

Egil shot back the bolt, and Thorgerd went up into the bed-closet and had the door fastened behind her. She lay down in a second bed which was there.

'You do well, daughter,' said Egil, 'when you want to keep your father company. Great love have you shown me. What hope is there that I will want to live after this sorrow?'

Next they were silent for a while. Then, 'What is now, daughter?' Egil asked. 'Are you chewing something?'

'I am chewing seaweed,' she replied, 'for I believe it will then go worse with me than before. Otherwise I fear I shall live too long.'

'Is it bad for a man?' asked Egil.

'Very bad,' she assured him. 'You would like some to eat?'

'What difference will it make?' he said.

Some time later she called out, asking them to give her something to drink. She was now given water to drink. 'So it goes if one eats seaweed,' said Egil. 'One grows thirstier all the time.'

'You would like to drink, father?' she asked.

He took hold and swallowed deeply. It was a horn. 'We have been tricked!' cried Thorgerd then. 'This is milk!' At these words Egil bit a notch in the horn, as big as his teeth could fasten on, and afterwards dashed the horn down.

The scene goes on to describe how Thorgerd goads her father into prolonging his life and composing a funeral-ode about his son, after which she says, they can die if they think it fit. This led to Egil's composing *Sonatorrek (The Terrible Loss of My Sons)*, a poem famous in the annals of Germanic literature, since it is generally regarded as the first great expression in the North of the emotional life of an individual. It was composed around 960.[5]

This strictly objective method of relating a story demands much greater attention to detail and especially to the sequence of events than the modern reader is accustomed to pay. The Saga method implies a relation of cause and effect between two events by the order in which they are told. This is one reason why the Sagas often introduce incidents a long way back, for which the reason only later becomes apparent, and then only to the reader who is aware of the chronological relation of cause and effect.[6]

The most salient trait of the *Sagas of Icelanders* is undoubtedly their character portrayal, which is all the more admirable considering the stylistic restrictions under which their authors worked. Characters in the Sagas are mainly described by their action and interaction with other characters, sometimes with vivid sketches of their facial expressions and demeanour. Often they are revealed through their speeches, which are usually charged with great weight and sharpness. Finally they may be elucidated through other people's comments or countryside gossip.

Two much-quoted passages, each from one of the two greatest Sagas, will give an idea of two ways in which character could be portrayed. The first is from *Njál's Saga*, where the famous hero Gunnar is defending his life against overwhelming odds. Just before he meets his end at his farm, where he has been taken by surprise by a large band of enemies, one of them succeeds in cutting the string of Gunnar's bow, and his chances of keeping up the defence are greatly diminished. He turns to his wife:

'Take two strands of your hair,' he said to Hallgerd, 'and you and mother twist it into a bowstring for me.'

'Does it mean much to you?' asked Hallgerd.

'It means my life,' he replied. 'Because they will never get at me as long as I can use my bow.'

'In that case,' she said, 'I'll remind you of the slap in the face you gave me, and I don't care whether you hold out long or not.'

'Everyone has his own way of gaining fame,' said Gunnar. 'I won't ask this of you again.'

'You are acting shamefully,' said Rannveig [Gunnar's mother], 'and your disgrace will long be remembered' (Chap. 77).

This celebrated passage gives us in a nutshell the two memorable characters, Gunnar and Hallgerd, while at the same time summing up some of the essential themes of the Sagas, the hurt pride and the overwhelming desire for revenge, the self-control of the hero in his hour of destiny, coupled with biting sarcasm, and finally the Icelanders' perennial concern for posthumous renown, indicated by the words of both Gunnar and his mother.[7]

The second passage is in *Egil's Saga*. It is introduced at the point where Egil emerges as the chief character of the Saga: we see him in the hall of King Athelstan in England after the battle in which his beloved older brother Thorolf was killed:

Next Egil went with his troop to find King Athelstan, and at once went into the king's presence as he sat at the drinking. There was a great noise and rejoicing there. Once the king could see Egil had come inside, he ordered that the lower dais should be cleared for them, saying that Egil should sit there in the high-seat opposite the king. Egil sat down there and drew his shield in front of his legs. He wore helm on his head and set his sword across his knees, and from time to time slid it halfway out and then slammed it home into the scabbard. He sat upright, but his head was deeply bowed. Egil had strongly marked features, was broad of forehead, heavy-browed; the nose not long but very thick, his lips wide and long, the chin notably broad and so throughout the jaw, thick-necked and big-shouldered, so that in that respect he surpassed what other men were: hard-faced and forbidding to look on when he was angered. He was powerfully built and taller than any man else, the hair wolfgray and thickset, and he had become bald early. And while he sat as has already been described, he was twitching one eyebrow down on his cheek and the other up into his hair-roots. Egil was black-eyed and with brows of dark brown. He would drink nothing, though drink was fetched him, but twitched his eyebrows up and down, now this way, now that (Chap. 55).[8]

The Saga then goes on to tell how King Athelstan first gave Egil a fine big gold ring from his arm with great ceremony, after which Egil's eyebrows fell into line: he now drank his full share and conversed with other men. Later the king had two large chests full of silver brought in, and soon Egil began to grow cheerful. This passage gives a very graphic description of Egil's physical appearance and of his moodiness, but it also underlines one of his most pronounced characteristics: avarice.

In spite of his great economy in presenting characters it is truly amazing how deeply a Saga-writer can delve into the psychology of his subjects, and what extraordinary variety of distinct and memorable individuals is to be found in Saga literature. A large number of these characters have through the centuries been familiar figures in the homes of Icelanders of all classes, and they have been more real to the people in every epoch than the contemporary leaders of the nation. It is not at all uncommon to read in the newspapers long and perspicacious articles, written by farmers, artisans or fishermen, about the Saga heroes and their motivations.

The Sagas are written in a style at once factual, non-lyrical and completely without inessential epithets. As the Swiss scholar Andreas Heusler has pointed out, it would grate upon one to read in a Saga such a sentence as 'He drew his *sharp* sword'. In Saga-style it would have to be 'He drew his sword; it was a sharp weapon'. The second sentence is strictly objective, without poetic or emotional stress. The Saga-writers strove for swift, lucid and dramatic narrative, rarely allowing themselves digressions that were not absolutely necessary for the story. Descriptions of nature are extremely rare, and where they occur they are important components of the action, as in *Njál's Saga* when Gunnar rides away from home with his brother, intending to leave the country for three years, since he has been outlawed, but his horse stumbles and he falls off: as he looks up toward his farmstead he utters the famous and fateful words: 'Fair is the hillside, fairer it seems than I have ever seen it before, with whitening grain and the home-field mown; and I will ride back home and not go abroad at all.' The same is true of *The Saga of Grettir the Strong* in the dramatic description of the hero's nocturnal struggle against the fearful ghost Glám: 'There was bright moonlight outside, and heavy clouds with rifts in them. Sometimes the clouds drifted over the moon, and sometimes the moon shone forth. Now at the very moment in which Glám fell, the clouds drifted away, and Glám stared piercingly up at Grettir. And Grettir himself said that this was the only sight he had ever seen which frightened him' (Chap. 35). Here the description of nature is used to intensify the terror.

Such episodes are rare in the Sagas, and where they appear they are used with typical restraint. In most of the Sagas understatement or litotes is one of the most striking characteristics. In *Sworn Brothers' Saga* Thorgeir, then fifteen years old, comes home to his mother late at night having just avenged the slaying of his father. His mother asks him if anything new has happened. He answers: 'A man was injured at Seljabrekka this evening.' What has happened is that Thorgeir thrust his spear through the farmer on his own farm. In *The Saga of Gisli* the outlawed hero slays one of two men pursuing him in a forest. The other pursuer turns back to his companions and greets them with the comment that the going in the forest is rather difficult. Sometimes this strong tendency to understatement is carried almost to excess, as in *Eyrbyggja Saga* when the crew of a fleet sent out by King Harald Finehair to subdue the Western Islands report to him on their return 'that they had not observed that Ketil [their admiral] was furthering the power of King Harald in those parts', meaning of course the exact opposite!

In the Sagas the expression of deep emotion was not achieved by speech. It could be expressed through physical demeanour, but the best and most common mode of expressing deep feeling was by composing a verse or a poem in skaldic metre. This versifying, a national pastime of the Icelanders down to the modern age—is an important ingredient of the Sagas, as has already been shown, and in the scattered verses or poems we often find the most telling clues to the actual feelings of the characters. For instance in *Egil's Saga* the portrayal of the hero would be very much duller and shallower without his own verses which give us the clues to his deepest self. The same is true of most of the poets appearing in the Sagas—and there were quite a number of them.

The *Sagas of Icelanders* comprise a considerable bulk of literature. In a complete Icelandic edition (1946-9) they fill twelve volumes. Even if a number of late efforts in Saga style, printed in this edition, are omitted, there remain eleven volumes of 450-500 pages each. Included in this edition are a large number of *novellas* or short episodes, but the Sagas proper are about forty in number. They vary greatly in length. The longest, *Njál's Saga*, is over 400 pages, followed closely by *Egil's Saga* and *The Saga of Grettir the Strong*. The shortest Saga may run to only 10-20 pages.

The earliest *Sagas of Icelanders* date from the first three decades of the thirteenth century. They include *The Saga of the Heath Slayings, Björn's Saga, Hallfred's Saga, Kormák's Saga* and *Egil's Saga*. Snorri Sturluson is by most authorities considered to be the author of *Egil's Saga* (which is enacted in the district of Borgarfjord in Western Iceland) and this may explain the high literary quality of such an early Saga. In the fifty-year period beginning around 1230 at least twelve Sagas were composed. In the West there were *Laxdaela Saga, Eyrbyggja Saga, Sworn Brothers' Saga, The Saga of Gisli, The Saga of Eirik the Red,* and *Graenlendinga Saga*. In the North-east there is *Vatnsdaela Saga*. In the North-west there are *Víga-Glúm's Saga, Reykdaela Saga* and *Ljósvetninga Saga*. In the East there are *Droplaugarasona Saga* and *Vopnfirdinga Saga*. During this intermediate period of Saga writing the greatest works were composed in the West, and it would not be unreasonable to seek an explanation of this fact in the example and influence of Snorri Sturluson. But the zenith in Saga writing was reached in the last quarter of the thirteenth century with such works as *Njál's Saga* in the South, *Gunnlaug's Saga* and *Hen-Thórir's Saga* in the West, *The Saga of the Confederates* in the North-west, and *Hrafnkel's Saga* in the East. In these Sagas there is a stronger element of fiction than in the earlier ones and on the whole a surer artistic grasp of composition.

With the beginning of the fourteenth century a certain decline set in with changing literary tastes, mainly caused by foreign romances. From this period we still have a number of good Sagas, by far the best being *The Saga of Grettir the Strong*, which has been designated the last of the classical *Sagas of Icelanders*.

Space only allows us to discuss briefly some of the more significant of these Sagas. As has already been noted the Icelanders seem to have had a special predilection for the warrior-poet or warrior-sage as Saga hero, either in a single character or two complementary ones. This is seen in the mythical poems of the *Edda* by Odin and Thór, but it is even more prominent in the Sagas, a considerable number of which have warrior-poets as central characters: *Egil's Saga, The Saga of Gisli, Gunnlaug's Saga, Björn's Saga, Sworn Brothers' Saga, Kormák's Saga, Hallfred's Saga*. In others Sagas, where poets do not play a conspicuous role, there seems to be a tendency to confront warriors and sages, and work out the conflict between the heroic spirit and the wise counsels of far-sighted individuals. This is quite obvious in *Njál's Saga*, but it plays a part too in *Laxdaela Saga, Eyrbyggja Saga, Vopnfirdinga Saga, Vatnsdaela Saga*, and a number of other more or less significant Sagas. In *The Saga of Grettir the Strong* the theme is played in a slightly different key in that the hero is a man of good mental and physical endowments, but harassed by his ill fortune which drives him to violence and finally to disaster, although he is both wise and exceedingly strong.

Egil's Saga is in certain respects unique among the Sagas. It deals with the entire life, from the age of three to his death around 990, of a great warrior who at the same time was one of the truly great poets of Scandinavia during the Viking Age, and an innovator in poetic technique. But it also relates the story of his immediate ancestors, how they clashed with King Harald Finehair in Norway and were compelled to move to Iceland and settle there. This account is the most dramatic in the Saga and takes up about one-third of it.

The lucidity of style and firmness of construction of *Egil's Saga* places it among the very best Sagas, probably the second greatest,

after *Njál's Saga*. The portrayal of Egil Skallagrímsson is unequal-
led in other Sagas. He confronts the reader as an exceedingly
complex character, and the violent contrasts in his psychological
make-up are presented with extraordinary skill and deep knowledge of human nature. Strangely, this great hero does not strike
the reader as a particularly attractive individual; he is ugly in
appearance, cruel, avaricious, coarse and mean; but his very
complexity is somehow endearing, for he also has redeeming traits,
such as moral and physical courage, unwavering fidelity to and
affection for his friends, a certain nobility of soul, and genuine
human feelings which he expresses in a masterly manner in his
poems and verses, particularly his great lament *Sonatorrek*.

There are many splendid scenes in *Egil's Saga*, both from
Iceland and from foreign parts, some of which have already been
quoted, showing the author's thorough knowledge of all aspects of
his subject, the topographical no less than the historical. The
continuous controversy of Egil's family with the Norwegian royal
house runs like a scarlet thread through this hero's colourful life.
He engages in many plundering expeditions as a Viking abroad
and has various adventures in Scandinavia and the British Isles,
before finally settling down on the family estate Borg in
Borgarfjord. All this is told with the true storyteller's relish and a
clear eye for detail as well as for the larger coherence of the
narrative. But perhaps the master-stroke of the Saga is the account
of Egil's old age which is in violent contrast to his former prowess
and recklessness. We see this one-time friend and foe of mighty
kings blind and stumbling, and being driven from the fireside by a
sharp-tongued woman servant, but the blind and deaf Viking is
still his old self, the lover of strife for its own sake. He wants to be
taken to the Althing, and when his stepdaughter coaxes him to tell
her the reason, he confides his plan to her. He wants to take the
two chests of silver which King Athelstan gave him—one of which
he failed to hand over to his father as prescribed—and scatter the
coins over the Assembly: 'I plan there should be kicking then and
clouting, or it might even turn out at last that the whole Assembly
are at one another's throats' (Chap. 85). When his wish is denied
him, Egil still has the last word. He buries the treasure, sacrificing
the lives of two thralls to ensure secrecy, and dies soon afterwards.

In the early nineteenth century the Danish scholar Grundtvig
proposed that Snorri Sturluson, the renowned descendant of Egil,
had written *Egil's Saga*. There has been long and heated
controversy over the issue, but Sigurdur Nordal, the foremost
expert on both Snorri and *Egil's Saga*, has demonstrated with
convincing evidence that Snorri should be regarded as the author,
making him the only known author of any of the *Sagas of
Icelanders*.

The story of Egil's life is not tragic in any sense, but the prelude to his story, the strife of his grandfather and uncles with the king of Norway, contains tragic subject-matter and is one of the finest passages in Saga literature. *Laxdaela Saga,* another of the longer Sagas and also from the western part of Iceland, has the same general scheme as *Egil's Saga,* but with opposite proportions. Here the long prelude, taking up almost half of the book, only gradually leads up to the great central tragedy of Kjartan, Bolli, and Gudrún. The numerous colourful characters and fascinating episodes of the prelude are like vignettes which can be enjoyed in themselves, but they are also part and parcel of the whole action, laying the foundation for what is to come. The pace is slow, the links in the chain of action many, but the movement gains momentum step by step until the culmination is reached.

Laxdaela Saga is deservedly one of the most popular of the Sagas. In regard both to construction and style it is extremely well written; it has an organic unity, remarkably fine technique as regards recurring use of words, phrases and themes, and a scheme of composition which represents in symbolic form the rigidity of the moral code, the principle of equal revenge, and the inextricable entanglements that carry the dilemma onward to its ultimate conclusion.

The story is at once tragic-heroic, ironic and highly lyrical, which is a rather unusual combination. The lyrical quality stems from the fact that the Saga's author was strongly influenced by chivalric romances which began to be translated in Norway during his lifetime and became quite popular in Iceland. This influence is revealed in several ways, by the frequent use of non-Icelandic chivalric words, by the detailed descriptions of weapons, ornaments and splendid garments, and by a marked tendency to depict the male characters as romantic heroes rather than as realistically drawn 'round' characters. There is, as Einar Ólafur Sveinsson has pointed out, a strong feminine air about the whole Saga, reflected not only in the fondness for ornament, clothes, romantic exaggeration and idealized male characters, but also in the interesting fact that the women of the story, of whom there are quite a number, are both more individual and memorable than the men. There are the two dominating women, Unn the matriarch in the first part and Gudrún the tempestuous heroine of the main theme. The Saga begins and ends with pictures of these two great women in old age, Unn who does not want to be asked about her health, Gudrún living in solitude and piety, devoted to her granddaughter and finally throwing a light over the whole tragic story when she tells her son Bolli Bollason: 'To him I was worst whom I loved most.' Then there is Thorgerd, the daughter of Egil Skallagrímsson and mother of Kjartan, a chip off the old block who after Kjartan's death reminds his brothers of his unatoned slaying with burning sarcasm, and follows her sons on the expedition of vengeance to egg them on, despite their protests. There is Breeches-Aud, who goes about dressed in breeches like a man and who, sword in hand, personally takes vengeance on her husband who has divorced her. Another is Vigdís, the wife of Thórd Goddi, who divorces her husband for sheltering an outlaw. There is Melkorka, the mother of Ólaf Peacock and the paternal grandmother of Kjartan, a proud Irish princess who has been abducted from her home by pirates and sold to an Icelander who begets a child with her. She feigns dumbness until one day she is discovered conversing with her little son. There are Jórunn, Thórdís, Hrefna, Kjartan's wife, and a host of other memorable women. But it is Gudrún who dominates the whole Saga and who has become, in the mind of the Icelander, the prototype of the proud woman of violent emotions, whose demands, whether in love or hate, have to be satisfied.

One striking point about the characters in *Laxdaela Saga* is their similarity to the tragic heroes of the Eddic lays, Sigurd, Gunnar, Gudrún and Brynhild. The women of the Saga (Melkorka, Thorgerd, Hrefna, Gudrún) have strong affinities with the Eddic Brynhild and Gudrún. There are many thematic parallels (sometimes in the very wording) between Brynhild and Sigurd on the one hand and Gudrún and Kjartan on the other. But these obvious Eddic influences in no way detract from Saga's great artistic coherence and tragic force, for the ancient legend has been transposed into terms that suited a different time and environment.

Laxdaela Saga has been called a 'Volcanic Saga' because of the seething passions lying just below a surface of majestic calm. One example will have to suffice to indicate the quality of this tragic tale. This is the exchange between Gudrún and Bolli after his return from the slaying of Kjartan, his childhood friend and fosterbrother, but Gudrún's true love:

Then Gudrún said: 'The seeds of discontent have certainly borne great fruit—I have spun twelve ells of yarn, and you have killed Kjartan.' Bolli answered: 'It is going to take a long enough time for me to forget that mishap, without your having to remind me of it.' Gudrún said: 'Such a thing I would not count among mishaps. It seemed to me that you enjoyed greater esteem that winter when Kjartan was in Norway than afterwards when he returned to Iceland and trod you underfoot. And last but not least, what means the most to me is that Hrefna will not be laughing when she goes to bed tonight.' Then Bolli replied and was exceedingly wroth: 'I have my doubts that she will turn any more pale at these tidings than you, and I'm not so sure but that it would have been a lesser shock to you if we all were lying out on the battle ground and Kjartan had brought you the news.'

Eyrbyggja Saga (or *The Saga of the Ere-dwellers*), one of the five longer Sagas, also deals with events in Western Iceland, i.e. on the long peninsula Snaefellsnes. It is the most episodic of the longer Sagas; there is no 'plot', no unity, except a certain coherence of atmosphere and locality. The Saga centres around two holy places in the district where one of the two first local *Things* (Assemblies) in Iceland was established. It is the chronicle of a whole countryside and especially valuable for its wealth of information about the religious beliefs and practices, and the folkways, traditions and manners of the Icelanders of the tenth and eleventh centuries, even though some of the facts related may not stand close historical scrutiny. The author was clearly both historian and antiquarian, besides being a master of character depiction. He is scrupulously exact in his statements and shows great reserve in assertions; sometimes, as has already been pointed out, his tendency to understatement is carried almost to excess.

Like *Egil's Saga* this Saga begins by relating the fortunes of several generations, the early chapters telling how a Norwegian went to Iceland, taking with him the timber of Thór's temple which he rebuilt in his new home. In these chapters we have most of the extant information about the worship of Thór in Norway and Iceland, but it should be remembered that the Saga was written in the thirteenth century and reflects contemporary ideas about the heathen religion. For instance, it has been demonstrated that temples were not built or used for religious worship in pagan Iceland.[9] Then the Saga hastens on to the main narrative, centring around the chieftain Snorri Godi, who settled at Helgafell, a sacred hill, as a youth and slowly rose to power, not by physical prowess but by cunning and common sense. Snorri is also a character in *Laxdaela Saga* and plays a major part towards the end. He was a great friend of Gudrún, arranged her fourth marriage, and married his daughter Thórdís to Gudrún's son, Bolli Bollason.

It is interesting to note that both in *Egil's Saga* and *Eyrbyggja Saga* the main protagonists are presented in full-length portraits just at the time when they are about to assume their roles as the dominant characters in the action, although Snorri is much less a central character in the Saga than Egil is in his. Snorri is by no means an admirable character in *Eyrbyggja Saga*. He is a shrewd politician and diplomat who plays the role of peacemaker when it suits his purpose, but can be ruthless if that serves his designs better. Snorri figures in several other Sagas, and in some of them he attains a larger stature.

One of the peculiarities of *Eyrbyggja Saga* consists in the numerous stories of berserks and sorcery and hauntings, told quite realistically. The story of the Hebridean woman Thórgunna, her death and subsequent marvels, is filled with macabre and grisly details. It adds little to the Saga itself, but forms a powerful and terrifying passage in Saga literature. Robert Louis Stevenson based his tale *The Waif Woman* on these episodes. When the wonders at Fróðá got out of hand the revenants were finally evicted by a sort of juridical procedure of exorcism in the haunted farm, each individual ghost being summoned. Some commentators have seen in this curious episode a satire on the Icelanders' fondness for legal manipulations. Among the marvels at Fróðá was the eating of dried fish by the revenants, and strangely enough it was this same district which in the seventeenth century was haunted by a ghost which also ate dried fish, rending it with its teeth.

Stylistically *Eyrbyggja Saga* would seem to be rather old, but actually the author quotes *Laxdaela Saga,* so that it must have been written during or after the middle of the thirteenth century. Sigurdur Nordal believes that the author was in conscious rebellion against the new tastes and fashions of his time, most clearly demonstrated in *Laxdaela Saga.*

The three long Sagas already discussed are from the first two periods of Saga writing. Before dealing with shorter Sagas from the second and third period, we shall briefly discuss the two remaining long *Sagas of Icelanders,* one from the third period (i.e. last quarter of the thirteenth century), *Njál's Saga,* and the other from the first quarter of the fourteenth century, *The Saga of Grettir the Strong.*

Njál's Saga is decidedly the greatest of all the Sagas, even though it may not be the most perfectly constructed. It is practically the only Saga from the southern part of Iceland (there is one other, *Flóamanna Saga*). It is written in the form of a trilogy, very skilfully interwoven, the first part telling the tragic story of Gunnar, one of the noblest of Saga-heroes; and the second part centred around events which led to the burning of Njál and his sons, culminating in that 'irredeemable crime'; and the third part relating the vengeance exacted by Kári and the final reconciliation. Within this structure there are a number of shorter three-act dramas and contrasting and parallel episodes, all of them integral parts of the main action, making the Saga a complex and extremely powerful tragic tale with large vistas and a strong current. Some of the individual scenes in *Njál's Saga* are among the finest in Icelandic literature, such as Gunnar's falling off his horse and returning to his farm, and later his last defence against overwhelming odds (already quoted), or the burning of Njál's homestead, a magnificent scene where light and darkness have equal share in a truly dramatic episode.

No Saga has a greater wealth of significant detail and striking characters, both male and female. If the author of *Laxdaela Saga* was a keen observer of things, but tending to produce rather blurred and generalised character portrayals, the author of *Njál's*

Saga was the reverse: he was an indifferent observer of things as compared with his intense preoccupation with human nature and its many manifestations. Most of his characters are marvellously individual and varied.

Njál, the noble wizard, stands at the centre of the whole story, a complex and often ambiguous individual. Basically he is a man of peace and goodwill, but we sense in all his actions a constant concern for the welfare of his own family, a concern which in reality lies at the root of the tragedy. His wisdom and foresight do not suffice to avert inexorable fate, and finally he seems to realize the futility of all his efforts and to accept fate. This ambivalent character is one of the most real characters in the Saga, as is his sombre and demonic son Skarphédin, a strangely ambiguous and complex warrior type.

Gunnar, a close friend of Njál, is an impetuous but good-natured model hero, with few blemishes and rather lacking in colour, although he is a distinct individual. In a sense his very guilelessness and 'innocence' is his tragic flaw. Although he seems to be the man who best understands his friend Njál, he ignores his good advice at two crucial junctures, when he decides to marry Hallgerd and when he decides to remain in Iceland, thus propelling the tragic action.

Kári, the protagonist of the third part, is an even more idealized hero than Gunnar; he has few individual features except his unquenchable thirst for revenge. He is the old Viking incarnate, free from problems and characteristics, nationally rootless, cosmopolitan, the courtier *par excellence*. His role in the Saga is important, and he does add an interesting note to the symphony of *Njál's Saga*. The same is true of the almost saintly Höskuld, Njál's foster-son who is wantonly killed by Njál's sons and who by virtue of his very innocence becomes at once the victim of vicious slander and the cause of the central tragedy of *Njál's Saga*.

There are several villains in the Saga, such as the headstrong Thjóstólf, the bickering liar Skamkel, the contriving, smooth Mörd,and the insolent scoundrel Hrapp. These men are not types, but real individuals different from each other. They are not spared in description, but they also have their redeeming traits, for instance Thjóstólf's fidelity to Hallgerd, Hrapp's valour, Mörd's love for his wife, his intelligence and his influence over others. Most of the characters have vices and virtues in more or less equal measure, and one of them, Flosi, is *the* tragic hero of the Saga.

As in most other Sagas the characters in *Njál's Saga* play the complementary roles of warriors and wise men. This is evident in the case of Gunnar and Njál, but their enemies also have their adviser, Mörd (and his father Valgard). Before Njál appears on the scene there are other wise counsellors: Hrút, Thórarin Ragi's brother, Mörd Fiddle. Later in the Saga, with Flosi, we have Hall of Sída, who plays a dominant role in the last part. There we also meet wizards like Snorri Godi (the main character in *Eyrbyggja Saga*), Thórhall Ásgrímsson and Eyjólf Bölverksson. All these men are individualized and distinguished from one another, just like the warriors.

Women do not play so dominant a role in *Njál's Saga* as in *Laxdaela Saga,* but they are nonetheless outstanding and highly memorable. There is the weak and shallow Unn; the lustful and imperious Queen Gunnhild of Norway (also a prominent character in *Egil's Saga*); the single-minded and peremptory Hildigunn, whose passionate grief over the loss of her husband, Höskuld, instigates the burning of Njál; and especially the puzzling and highly complex Hallgerd, wife of Gunnar. The author is most harsh in his treatment of Hallgerd—sometimes dangerously so from the artistic point of view, but she is certainly a living and impressive character. She is not directly evil, but unstable, selfish, pleasure-loving—'mixed' as the Sagas have it. Almost all the women in *Njál's Saga* are large in stature and temperament, and they greatly affect the evolution of the action. They are definitely not gentle creatures, but passionate, unsettling guardians of the ancient concepts of pride and family honour.

No Saga conveys such a strong feeling of fatalism as *Njál's Saga.* Its action evolves inexorably; at first sight one is led to think that human will and interference is of no consequence. But on closer reading we realize that fate in this Saga is not so much a supernatural force as something residing in the characters themselves, a predisposition to accidents or misdeeds on the one hand, a propensity to good fortune and prosperity on the other.

Njál's Saga comes at the end of an era and, as in *Völuspá* earlier, it is the conflict between the old and the new which makes for its drama and deep insight into human nature. Christianity had been established in Iceland for close on three centuries, and the author had clearly been influenced by it. He had heard the southern Christian legends and listened to preaching by the priests, but at the same time the stories of former ages were alive, and they were connected with various known places and people. He saw those two contradictory worlds reflected in his own time, the savage Age of the Sturlungs, and he tried to bridge the gulf between the old indomitable heroic spirit and the new Christian spirit of goodwill and forbearance. He did not succeed, and this gives the story its inner struggle and dramatic tension. The Saga seems to be born out of an acute spiritual agony, and in this sense it is timeless, the problems it deals with being of perennial, if not always immediate, significance. This has been provocatively elaborated in an essay by the English author Nigel Balchin in *Fatal*

Fascination[10] where he discusses 'the irredeemable crime' of Njál's burning in terms of contemporary international politics.

The Saga of Grettir the Strong is the latest of the 'classical' Icelandic Sagas and one of the most tragic of all in theme and conception, even though in its style and construction cannot be compared with *Njál's Saga, Egil's Saga* or *Laxdaela Saga*. In its present form it was composed early in the fourteenth century and seems to be based on an older Saga, now lost, by the famous historian Sturla Thórdarson, nephew of Snorri Sturluson.

Grettir the Strong is the most renowned outlaw in Icelandic history, having spent nineteen years in banishment, wandering all over the country among the desolate mountains and uninhabited valleys, before he was finally killed on the island fastness of Drangey off Northern Iceland. Grettir is mentioned in a number of Sagas and other thirteenth-century works, all of them bearing witness to his legendary strength.

The author of this Saga has made copious use of existing sources about the hero, such as Sturla Thórdarson's *Book of Settlements* and Sagas like *Laxdaela Saga, Björn's Saga, Sworn Brothers' Saga,* and *The Saga of the Heath Slayings*. He has elaborated their anecdotes and fitted them into his chronology. He has enriched his story with foreign materials, for instance in the striking parallels to the account of Beowulf's fight with Grendel, given in the Old English epic composed five or six centuries earlier, while in the last portion of the Saga dealing with the vengeance that Grettir's brother exacted for him in Constantinople and the ensuing love affair he has drawn from the story of Tristram (translated in Norway in 1226).

The Saga of Grettir the Strong is unusually rich in graphic descriptions of everyday life in Iceland (daily work, horse fights, ball games, wrestling matches, etc.) and a veritable thesaurus of hardheaded peasant proverbs, mostly uttered by the hero. There is a quantity of broad humour, some of it rather spicy, and the Saga abounds in folklore—tales about ghosts, trolls, and half-trolls. Despite the great diversity of incident, realistic and supernatural, there is a distinct unity in the whole story, a naturalness flowing from the author's constant concern with tangible detail.

But the unity of the Saga is above all due to a central theme running like a red thread through the whole account. That theme is summed up by one of the characters in Chapter 34: 'Luck is one thing, brave deeds another.' Grettir is a man of immense strength, power of endurance and courage, quick-witted and essentially good-natured, though headstrong and impetuous. But he is haunted by ill-luck—which, however, is not primarily some caprice of supernatural fate, but rather a consequence of his character, his rash and uncontrollable temperament. Grettir is in effect a rare

Icelandic example of the classical tragic hero, richly endowed with good qualities, but having one fatal flaw.

Through the first half of the story Grettir gains increasing fame for his strength, but the success spells his doom, for he becomes 'so overweening that he thought nothing beyond his powers'. This tragic *hubris* underlies his misfortunes, or as one of the characters expresses it, 'great arrogance is in him now, and I have misgivings about his luck ...' It is the ancient Greek notion of 'nothing in excess' which is the *leitmotif* in Grettir's progress towards extinction.

The *peripeteia* or turning-point in his career comes at midpoint in the Saga when he has his fateful encounter with the malignant revenant Glám, whom he overcomes but whose spell starts his lifelong nightmare of fear of darkness— a common Icelandic malady. This central episode in the Saga is a masterpiece of narrative technique, one of the most vivid and impressive ghost stories in any medieval literature, and its function in the development of the story is brilliantly conceived.[11]

The character portrayal of Grettir, who is on the scene almost continuously, is another admirable feature of this great and moving Saga, which has enjoyed great popularity in Iceland mainly because the hero became the symbol for many centuries of his frustrated nation, whose bad luck was out of proportion with her good endowments.

Out of some thirty-five shorter *Sagas of Icelanders* only four will be briefly discussed here, one from the second period and three from the third and most artistic period of Saga writing. Of these the earliest is *The Saga of Gisli,* laid in the Western Fiords, the story of the tragic life of Iceland's second most famous outlaw, Gisli Súrsson. This Saga is modelled on the heroic poems of the *Edda* to an even greater extent than *Laxdaela Saga,* with which it also shares a pronounced interest in dreams. The dreams in *The Saga of Gisli* are unusually dominant, and are unique in that they both function as an instrument of fate, foretelling the future, and reflect the struggle within Gisli himself between hope and fear, personified in his two dream-women, one evil, the other, shining bright.

Of all the *Sagas of Icelanders* that of Gisli is 'the most self-conscious in its tragic aim'[12] and one of the most moving. Honour is naturally a keynote in the story, but there is also a unique emphasis on love between man and woman. The whole action is concentrated around two themes: personal and family honour, and personal and family love.[13] When Gisli's wife, Aud, has to choose between brother and husband, she chooses her husband. In the *Edda* Gudrún, when faced with the same choice, chose her brothers in true Old Germanic fashion. Gisli's sister, Thórdís, first avenges her husband by having her brother killed, and then tries to take vengeance on her brother's slayer.

Character portrayal in *The Saga of Gisli* is on a high level. Gisli and Aud stand out as great heroic figures, perhaps a little too idealistically drawn, but their individuality is memorable. Gisli's brother, Thorkel, and their sister, Thórdís, are more complex in character. Thorkel is an extremely 'mixed' man, his bad traits outweighing his redeeming ones. Thórdís (who incidentally was the mother of Snorri Godi, hero of *Eyrbyggja Saga* and a dominant figure in many other Sagas) is probably the most interesting of all the characters in the Saga, a truly tragic figure who faces her great dilemma with integrity and dignity.

The Saga of Gisli is well composed and closely knit, the action is swift and unified, and its most lasting impression is that of the hounded outlaw who after years of ceaseless pursuit and agony seems almost to welcome the peace of death, while he makes a courageous last stand against his pursuers on the ledge of a high cliff. In spite of the Saga's dark and tragic theme there are several humorous episodes for comic relief, and the whole account is coloured by the author's human warmth, most explicitly reflected in the relations between Gisli and his wife.

Although there are numerous satiric-comic passages and undignified characters in almost all the *Sagas of Icelanders,* there is among them only one full-length comedy, the satirical *Saga of the Confederates (Bandamanna Saga)* mocking at the powerful chieftains and deflating the ethos of the heroic age, thus calling to mind the flytings in *The Taunting of Loki* in the *Edda* and a famous passage in *Njál's Saga.*

The action of the story takes place after the actual Saga Age (930-1030), another unique characteristic, and it gives informative glimpses of life in Iceland during a comparatively peaceful period of the Commonwealth. It was written towards the end of the thirteenth century and may also be a reflection of the author's own time, when the Commonwealth crumbled and many of the chieftains were impoverished and ruthless in their financial dealings.[14]

The Saga is told from an unexpected point of view and gives a brilliant description of the very complex procedure of Icelandic lawsuits, pointing out the essential weakness in the strict formalism and blind adherence to the letter of the law. It relates how a gang of eight chieftains conspire to have a judgment pronounced against a young and very prosperous merchant, who is rather a simpleton, by making use of a procedural flaw in an otherwise just lawsuit with the intention of depriving him of all his possessions and dividing them among themselves. The young merchant, Odd, is completely at a loss when his estranged old father, Ófeig, comes to his aid, outwits the chieftains with liberal bribes and ingenuous stratagems, inducing several of them to deceive their colleagues at the crucial moment. The spectacle of the chieftains exposing each other in public is among the most dramatic in Saga literature. The characterization of the eight confederates is masterly and every detail in the highly diversified narrative is superbly rendered. The necessary contrast is also here: a tragic incident which gives the whole action a new dimension, imbues it with deeper human feeling.

The Saga of the Confederates has been dramatized by the modern author Gunnar Gunnarsson (1889-1975) in *Raevepelsene* (*The Foxes*, 1930).

The two other shorter Sagas from the same period are quite dissimilar except for their fine construction, scarcity of secondary characters and an almost total lack of humorous incidents.

Gunnlaug's Saga (or *The Saga of Gunnlaug Serpent-Tongue*) has been far more popular outside Iceland during the past century than any other Icelandic Saga. The reasons for its popularity would seem obvious. The Saga is short and simple in plot and outline, and the characters are comparatively few and not very complex. Most important, the story is romantic with chivalric, slightly sentimental overtones, uncharacteristic of true Saga-style, even though there is enough of the ancient spirit to lend it an appearance of genuine Saga.

The author of *Gunnlaug's Saga* was apparently a 'slick' writer who knew the tricks of his trade and put in all the ingredients necessary for a 'bestseller'. He has borrowed profusely and rather indiscriminately from other sources, such as *Egil's Saga, Eyrbyggja Saga, Laxdaela Saga,* and a number of other Sagas. There is a striking resemblance between the themes of *Gunnlaug's Saga* and both *Hallfred's Saga* and *Björn's Saga,* all of them dealing with poets and thwarted love. No doubt the author used both of them as models, though the treatment is different.

The theme of *Gunnlaug's Saga* also has some resemblance to *Laxdaela Saga* in the tragic fate of the lovers, Gunnlaug Serpent-Tongue and Helga the Fair: the true lover comes back too late, while the second lover wins his unwilling bride by spreading false reports. The symbolic dream in *Gunnlaug's Saga,* where a lovely swan sits on the roof-ridge of the farm as two eagles kill each other in a fight over her, after which a falcon takes her away—a dream foreshadowing the whole course of events—has a parallel in *Laxdaela Saga.* But there is a greater resemblance to Kriemhilt's dream in the Austrian *Nibelungenlied* and a striking parallel in a dream in *Trójumanna Saga* (the Icelandic *Tale of Troy*), which is followed by an order to expose a new-born child. However, the order is not carried out and the prophecy is fulfilled (a motif we also know from the Greek Oedipus cycle). This is precisely what happens in *Gunnlaug's Saga* and it strikes a discordant note, since the fatalism of the Saga Age was such that the Icelanders would make no effort to avert preordained destiny.

The man visited by the dream is Thorstein, son of Egil Skallagrímsson and father of Helga, who is the heroine of the Saga. But she is definitely not a chip off Egil's block, tender and sensitive though she is, finding solace in unravelling the precious cloak her true lover has given her, after her death. She is much more akin to Ophelia or Gretchen than to the heroic Saga-women. Gunnlaug the hero, for all his serpent-tongued repartee and warlike exploits at home and abroad, is the romantic Viking to whom love is more important than honour. He brings his dying opponent a drink, thus inviting a fatal blow, a singularly melodramatic incident without parallel in the genuine *Sagas of Icelanders.*

Gunnlaug's Saga, even though not the last of the *Sagas of Icelanders,* shows signs of the rapid decline of the classical Sagas at the end of the thirteenth century. It is an interesting experiment in uniting the objective realism of the native tradition and the idyllic sentiment of the foreign romantic stories, which gained in popularity among the Icelanders as the national culture decayed.[15]

Hrafnkel's Saga is one of the gems of Icelandic literature as regard composition, lucidity and character portrayal. Sigurdur Nordal has classified it as 'one of the most perfect short novels in world literature'. The whole action is centred around the eight main characters, while genealogies and minor characters hardly enter the picture. Owing to its conciseness, hard-headed realism and heroic outlook it was long believed to be among the oldest Sagas, written around 1200, but Sigurdur Nordal demonstrated in a brilliant essay in 1940 that it is almost entirely fictitious and was composed around 1300.

Hrafnkel's Saga is the story of a proud and overbearing chieftain, Hrafnkel the priest of Frey, who, after suffering great humiliation for his fateful arrogance, emerges a wiser and better man. Character development is not very common in the Sagas, and Hrafnkel is one of the noteworthy instances along with Njál, Gisli and Grettir.

Hrafnkel is a devout worshipper of Frey, with whom he shares equally his most precious possessions—among them a magnificent stallion, Freyfaxi. He has solemnly sworn to kill any man who rides his stallion without permission. His shepherd, Einar, ignores this once and is slain by his master. Einar's father proudly refuses Hrafnkel's offer of compensation and it is left to Sám, Einar's cousin, to bring suit against Hrafnkel at the Althing for the killing, although the prospects of winning such a suit are slim. When Sám is about to give up, two brothers from a distant part of the country come to his aid unexpectedly with a large body of followers. However, Hrafnkel is outlawed and driven away from his estate, where Sám now settles. The temple of Frey is burned down and the stallion Freyfaxi pushed off a cliff. Hrafnkel settles in a neighbouring district where he soon becomes powerful again. In due time he retaliates, killing Sám's innocent brother and chasing Sám from his old estate, where he settles again, spending his remaining years in peace and propserity.

The symmetry and brilliance of the Saga are admirable. It seems clear that the author was a well-educated man and a conscious artist bent on counteracting the romantic and fantastic stories, native and foreign, that were enjoying increasing vogue during his lifetime. He was peculiarly averse to descriptions of battle scenes and other spectacular events, concentrating on character and telling dialogue, of which there is proportionally more in *Hrafnkel's Saga* than in any other Saga (53 per cent).

Hrafnkel's Saga, The Saga of Gisli and *The Saga of the Confederates* have the greatest structural unity among the Sagas: there every detail contributes to the main action.

In the fourteenth century a number of *Sagas of Icelanders* were composed (a single work even as late as 1500), but in every respect they were inferior to the classical ones. The old spirit had given way to a new delight in fantastic tales and the exaggerations of romances and mythic-heroic stories of times long past. Even some of the older Sagas came to be rewritten in this new fashion with deplorable results.

The literary activities of the Icelanders during the twelfth, thirteenth and fourteenth centuries were far from confined to the *Sagas of Icelanders*. We have already (in Chapter 2) referred to the voluminous *Kings' Sagas*, written by various Icelandic historians, and the remarkable *Sturlunga Saga*, dealing with contemporary events in the thirteenth century. To these may be added quite a large body of so-called *Sagas of Ancient Times (Fornaldarsögur)*, more or less fantastic tales from prehistoric times in Scandinavia and on the Continent. These stories were from the beginning told for entertainment; they existed in oral form as early as the twelfth century and were probably not written down until late in the thirteenth century. There are thirty-five such Sagas of differing size, the most important being the *Völsunga Saga* which in the nineteenth century inspired both Richard Wagner and William Morris. It is largely based on the heroic Eddic poems and is especially valuable for having preserved in prose many of the lost poems of the heroic cycles.

Added to these were romances of chivalry which were

translated, adapted and concocted in enormous quantities from about the second quarter of the thirteenth century onwards. There are extant some 265 of these tales, varying greatly in length and subject-matter. There are French and Anglo-Saxon romances as well as Greek, Roman and Oriental tales.

Around the turn of the fourteenth century the Icelanders began to cultivate a verse form called *rímur,* a hybrid of ancient skaldic poetry and popular medieval European verse. The *rímur*-poets used alliteration and *kennings,* but added end-rhyme and kept to very rigid three- and four-line stanzas which in time became so elaborate that over 2,000 varieties have been recorded. The *rímur* are mainly narrative poems, often running into hundreds of stanzas, divided into groups or cantos, corresponding to chapters in prose. The subject-matter of the *rímur* was mostly the *Sagas of Ancient Times,* the chivalric romances. From before 1600 we have some 115 *rímur*-cycles and after 1600 about 900 *rímur*-cycles by nearly 330 known poets, so that the same tales were used many times by different verse-makers.

Before concluding this account of the literary activities of the ancient Icelanders mention should be made of the great bulk of religious literature from the twelfth century onwards, both homilies, miracle books, exempla, saints' lives, sacred poetry and biographies of renowned Icelandic bishops. Two sacred poems soar above the rest and rank among the great achievements of Icelandic literature for their visionary force and poetic brilliance. One is the anonymous *Sólarljóð* ('Song of the Sun') from about 1200, uniting some of the spirit of *Völuspá* and *Hávamál* in the *Edda* with that of the Catholic *exempla, visio* and allegory. Here a father, returned from death, relates to his surviving son the story of his erring but pleasant life, and the fate of evil or blundering men after death. This poem is thought by some scholars to reflect the troubled and crime-infested Age of the Sturlungs. The other poem, *Lilja (The Lily),* composed by the unruly monk Eystein Ásgrímsson about 1350, surveys the history of the world as understood by Western Christianity in 100 inspired stanzas, dwelling mainly on sin and grace. This brilliant poem was the envy of every verse-maker in Iceland for many centuries and found its first match in Hallgrím Pétursson's *Passion Hymns* in the seventeenth century.

However we look at it, we cannot help wondering at the marvel that this remote island in the North Atlantic, on the very verge of the habitable world, should have become one of the world's most prodigious workshops and storehouses of literature in the Middle Ages.

Notes

1. Sveinn Bergsveinsson, *Sagaen og den haardkogte Roman,* Edda 42 (1942), pp. 56-62.

2. Julia McGrew, 'Faulkner and the Icelanders', *Scandinavian Studies,* 31 (1959), pp. 1-14.

3. See Gwyn Jones, *Introduction* to *Eirik the Red and Other Icelandic Sagas,* London 1961, p. xiv.

4. Quoted from Bertha S. Phillpotts, *Edda and Saga,* pp. 172-3.

5. Peter Hallberg, *The Icelandic Saga,* Lincoln 1962, pp. 129-30.

6. *Edda and Saga,* pp. 165-6.

7. See *The Icelandic Saga,* p. 74.

8. The translator of *Egil's Saga,* Gwyn Jones, remarks on the author's sense of occasion in delaying his description of Egil until this dramatic moment.

9. Olaf Olsen, *Hørg, hov and kirke,* op. cit.

10. *Fatal Fascination: a Choice of Crime,* London 1964, pp. 9-57.

11. For a lucid discussion of this Saga see Peter Foote's Introduction to *The Saga of Grettir the Strong,* Everyman's Library (699), London 1965.

12. W. P. Ker, *Epic and Romance,* p. 197.

13. Peter Foote in his essay accompanying his translation of the Saga, gives an admirable exposition of the whole plot. *The Saga of Gisli,* new edition, London 1973.

14. See W. P. Ker, *Epic and Romance,* pp. 229-30.

15. See Peter Foote's Introduction to *The Saga of Gunnlaug Serpent-Tongue,* London 1957.

PART TWO

5. Foreign Domination and Natural Catastrophe

Granted that the heroic ethos of the Golden Age carried within it the seeds of self-destruction, there is still a violent contrast between the luminous social and intellectual life of the Commonwealth, unique in the medieval world, and the progressive deterioration and depressing misery of life in Iceland during the following centuries, culminating in the seventeenth and eighteenth centuries. This 'interlude' of more than six centuries, until Iceland regained its independence, was in many ways the dark night of the nation with only a few glimmers of light here and there. It was a period of terrifying waste of human energy which might well have resulted in the complete extinction of the people, as in the Greenland settlement. There were almost continuous natural catastrophes, recurring epidemics, frequent famines, widespread undernourishment and starvation, and general physical and spiritual exhaustion. But as it turned out the Icelanders, though vastly reduced in numbers, emerged from this terrible ordeal with a burning desire to redress their grievances and regain their status as an agile, enterprising and fully independent nation. The role of the ancient literary treasures in maintaining the will for survival among the harassed and impoverished inhabitants of this isolated island can not be overestimated.

By the end of the twelfth century the essential weakness of the political organization of the Commonwealth had become manifest, and during the first decades of the thirteenth century things went from bad to worse, reaching a climax in the savage feuds of the Sturlung Age which led to the Commonwealth's collapse in 1262-4. The principal cause of this sad development was the gradual disappearance of the equality and equilibrium between the chieftains. During the early centuries of the Commonwealth the power of the chieftains was largely limited to their own districts, although they might have adherents in other districts. If any chieftain sought to exert his power with impudence or injustice, other chieftains would curb him and put him in his place.

It so evolved that a handful of mighty chieftains took over most of the chieftaincies, even subjugating whole quarters and forcing less powerful chieftains to hand over their authority. By 1220 most of the power in Iceland was held by only six strong families. During the following forty years they fought it out using every means at their disposal: treachery, assassinations, burnings and mutilations as well as pitched battles. All these families in one way or another sought assistance from the Norwegian king, who was only too happy to encourage the internecine warfare within the country, since the royal house of Norway had long intended to arrogate Iceland to itself and had even made some unsuccessful attempts at doing so.

Simultaneous with the disturbance of the precarious power balance among the chieftains was a radical change in the relative wealth of chieftain and freeholder. Formerly the chieftains had not felt themselves to be above menial work. They went about their business in much the same way as other farmers. But now there emerged a class of lawless magnates who flouted all authority and even refused to abide by their own promises given under oath. They amassed fabulous wealth, seized at will the best estates of the country, and imposed their arbitrary demands on their followers by force or threats. The Sturlungs themselves were perhaps the most outstanding examples of this new breed, especially Snorri Sturluson, his brothers and nephews, though many of them had great intellectual gifts which in a way redeem their bad traits, while others were outright villains. The old bond of mutual confidence between chieftain and freeholder was gone for ever as a consequence of the vast powers and far-flung territory of each chieftain, and towards the end anarchy reigned supreme. Many of the chieftains of the thirteenth century (Sturlung Age) were much closer in behaviour and mentality to savage Vikings on the run or oriental warlords than to responsible rulers. They kept the farmers away from home for weeks or even months, sending them on military expeditions to distant regions or using them as body-guards. They took provisions at will from any farm without recompense, levied heavy taxes on their followers and exorbitant fines on those who, either by force or free will, joined other chieftains. The Althing was without power and the local assemblies were useless. The need for a strong governing authority was ever more urgent, but due to the very nature of the Commonwealth such authority could hardly be found within the country except through an all-out civil war. When the 'civil war' of the Sturlung

Age had reached an impasse the king of Norway was brought in as the only feasible alternative to complete chaos, and the people were finally relieved to accept him as their ruler so as to establish some kind of law and order in the country.

The cause of the Norwegian king had been supported by the various chieftains when it served their purposes, and it was staunchly and relentlessly upheld by the church, which now began a dramatic and forceful drive for ascendancy in Iceland. The first bishopric had been founded at Skálholt in South Iceland in 1056, the second at Hólar in North Iceland in 1106. These two seats played a dominant role in Icelandic history until the late eighteenth century. Up to 1237 only native bishops, elected by the Icelanders themselves, served in Skálholt and Hólar, probably accounting for the comparative autonomy of the Icelandic church. But in 1238 Norwegian bishops were simultaneously appointed to both bishoprics, the king and the archbishop of Norway (whose archdiocese included Iceland) disregarding the traditions and the wishes of the Icelanders. The influence of the foreign-born bishops in Iceland in the following decades played no small part in the political developments leading to the collapse of the Commonwealth.

Many able chieftains contended for the 'honour' of serving as the first Norwegian governor of Iceland, but by 1262 most of them had been killed off in the numerous and highly dramatic military encounters of the Sturlung Age, thus leaving the scene to one of the most cunning of them all, Gizur Thorvaldsson (*d.* 1268), who was appointed 'earl' or governor of the island, a title dropped after his death. Gizur Thorvaldsson had at one time been the son-in-law of Snorri Sturluson and organized his infamous killing in 1241.

The turbulent Sturlung Age is graphically described in the contemporary *Sturlunga Saga,* part of which was written by the renowned historian Sturla Thórdarson, nephew of Snorri Sturluson and first lawman in Iceland under the new order, a title replacing that of the 'earl'.

The agreement of 1262-4 by which Iceland was formally brought under Norwegian sway created only a confederate union and did not change the status of the chieftains within the country. They and the people of Iceland had sworn allegiance to the king of Norway, not to the Norwegian state. The king in his turn promised to maintain peace within the country, adhere to Icelandic laws, and send six ships to Iceland every summer during the next two years, after which the matter was to be arranged in a way that the king and the best men of the country deemed most advantageous for Iceland. The stipulation about the six ships indicates that the Icelanders were anxious to secure their sustenance, since shipbuilding and sailing had greatly declined within the country, as a consequence of which commerce was often dangerously slow and irregular.

In 1281 (barely twenty years after the first agreement) a new code of law, *Jónsbók,* was introduced by the king and reluctantly accepted by the Althing. It led to the abolition of the chieftaincies and the assumption of complete authority by the king who through his direct representatives took over the government of Iceland. The Althing was still in operation and continued to function more or less regularly until 1800 with steadily dwindling authority and significance. It continued to perform its judicial business in co-operation with the king's representatives, the lawmen, who acted as judges, while special governors held the highest authority. The latter were Icelanders until the fifteenth century; after which they were mostly Danes, Germans and Dutchmen.

The latter part of the thirteenth century and the fourteenth century were characterized by a savage struggle between the church and the native landowners, in which the church gained ground and gradually amassed great wealth and authority. It was supported by the king when his own interests were not jeopardized, and the result was a steadily growing oppression and financial extortion practised against the common people who suffered equally at the hands of king and church. With the growing power of the church came widespread corruption abetted by the odious practice of the Norwegian power, whether exercised by king or archbishop, of appointing foreigners (who frequently bought their offices) to the two Icelandic sees. In the period 1236-1465 thirteen of the bishops of Skálholt were foreigners, while only five were native Icelanders. As a matter of fact, many of the native bishops were just as greedy for wealth and power as their foreign counterparts—indeed it was a common characteristic of the Roman hierarchy everywhere at the time. The extravagance of the foreign upstarts, while the people were poverty-stricken and dying from starvation, created among the Icelanders a hostile opposition which time and again found expression in acts of violence, such as the killing of a Norwegian governor and his retinue in 1362, or tying up one of the foreign bishops of Skálholt, Jon Gerreksson, in a sack and drowning him in a nearby river in 1433. Such acts were not infrequent, but more often the Icelanders sent written protests to the king against foreign bishops and other public officials, and against excessive taxes and the practice of summoning Icelanders abroad for judgment. Most of these protests went unheeded while the royal authority became steadily more arbitrary. In 1354 the king began leasing the country for three-year periods to the highest bidding 'governor', who then paid an annual amount to the crown and was free to collect taxes in any way he deemed efficient. That obviously led to still greater excesses and brutality, besides giving rise to a trade monopoly which proved disastrous to the country's economy.

In the fourteenth century a series of great calamities befell the Icelanders such as had not been witnessed earlier, and these disasters were to increase in volume and extent in the centuries to come. Cattle diseases, famines and epidemics had indeed ravaged the country in the closing decades of the thirteenth century, but with the eruption of the great volcano Hekla in 1300, the fifth to be recorded, and the violent earthquakes that followed, the misfortunes started in earnest. The eruption and its aftermath destroyed many farms and killed both people and cattle. In 1341 and again in 1389 eruptions of Hekla caused continued havoc. Added to this, recurrent epidemics, mainly of smallpox, killed hundreds of people. In general bad weather, natural catastrophes and fatal epidemics, made the fourteenth century a harsh one for the Iceland

The Norwegian trade with Iceland was of great value in this distress. During the first half of the century it was brisk since the Hanseatic League had closed all other avenues to Norwegian merchants, thus in effect destroying Norwegian commerce. As Hanseatic merchants with their effective network of transport had created a widespread demand for dried codfish, Norwegian traders began to import it from Iceland early in the fourteenth century. This obviously stimulated commerce and increased the volume of imports to Iceland, at the same time increasing the importance of Icelandic fishing at the expense of agriculture. The annalists state that during the fifth decade of the century there were a dozen or more ships in Icelandic harbours every summer; in 1342-4 numerous shipwrecks are recorded. But the encouraging prospect for commerce in Iceland was abruptly destroyed by the Black Death in Norway in 1349, carrying away in a short time one-third of the entire population of the kingdom. The Norwegians never quite recovered from this terrible blow. Their spirit was somehow broken, the expeditions to Greenland ceased almost completely and the trade with Iceland was severely curtailed. In 1349 only one ship from Norway is mentioned in Icelandic annals, and in the following year there was none at all. During the remainder of the century far fewer ships seem to have reached Iceland than earlier, and not until 1383 are as many as eleven ships again mentioned in a single year.

This radical reduction in trade, coupled with the natural cataclysms, was of course disastrous to Iceland, added to which the crown was utterly indifferent to the people's welfare as long as the necessary revenues for the treasury could be secured.

In 1397 a new development began with the formal union of Norway, Sweden and Denmark under the Kalmar 'Act of Union'.

Actually Iceland had already come under Danish rule along with Norway, in 1380. With the new Danish rulers, who were of German extraction, things did not improve, as the new authorities were even more greedy and indifferent than their Norwegian predecessors had been. Taxes were increased; and so were constant provocations and injustice. The general government, however, was much the same. The effects of the union showed themselves gradually in the choice of Danes as bishops and higher officials, and the adoption of Danish commercial policy.

By 1400 much of the old culture and way of life was extinct in the daily life of the nation, even though it might linger on as a distant memory and a dream. Foreign rule was now an established fact and the church had a stranglehold on the people. Living conditions had greatly deteriorated and the Icelanders were entirely dependent upon foreign trade.

If the fourteenth century was bad for the Icelanders the fifteenth proved even more disastrous. It began with one of the most devastating calamities in Icelandic history, the Black Death, which ravaged the island in 1402-4. An old estimate that the epidemic killed off two-thirds of the population is surely an exaggeration, but scholars agree that at least one-third was lost. Many districts were almost totally depopulated. Fifteen people might attend a funeral and only four or five would return. Whole families died out, farms lay idle, and almost all activity came to a standstill. The effects of this disaster were, for instance, the disappearance of any kind of history-writing, the accumulation of great wealth by the few survivors of big and well-to-do families, a great increase in church property and riches through votive offerings, a lack of manpower resulting in wage increases, reduced crops and catches leading to diminished trade, etc.

After the ravages of the Black Death economic life in Iceland was almost paralysed and the need for imports became more acute than ever. As it happened a new party entered the scene at this crucial juncture and virtually revolutionized the Icelandic economy: English fishermen and traders. From the beginning of the settlement in the ninth century the Icelanders, though mainly occupied with farming and agriculture, had been in exclusive possession of their rich fisheries, and during the thirteenth and fourteenth centuries only Norwegian citizens had traded in Iceland. But from 1413 onwards, the English maintained an increasing intercourse with Iceland, sometimes with the permission of the king of Denmark, but more often without it. The English traders found ready supporters and even partners in the foreign bishops (one of them, in fact, was English) serving in Iceland, who were only too eager to augment their wealth. The price of dried cod almost doubled in a few years, suddenly making the sea the most important natural resource of Iceland. The people flocked to the fishing villages along the coast, especially in the west and south, where a few powerful families gained great wealth exploiting the readily available manpower. This turn of events gave the country's farming and agriculture a heavy blow, from which it never quite recovered. When the trade with the English proved both more profitable and popular than had been expected, the Danish crown tried to curb the merchants' activities, but the latter were loath to give up their lucrative haunt. The king's representatives did all they could to control the English trade, but the merchants retaliated, killing some of them and plundering various places around the coast. As an indication of the strength of the English presence in Iceland at the time, the annals tell us for instance that on 13 April 1419, twenty-five English ships were wrecked on the coast of Iceland in a single storm lasting only three hours.

Soon after the English started their commerce with Iceland the German traders of the Hanseatic League began competing with them, having secured the support of the Danish crown. They had for some time been all-powerful in Bergen, the principal Norwegian trading centre for Iceland, but now they turned their attention to the island itself in the hope of excluding the English from the market and establishing their own monopoly in dried codfish. The first German merchants were from Lübeck and Danzig, but in 1475 the Hamburgers entered the scene and soon outstripped their competitors. When their position had grown ominously strong, the Danish king tried in 1490 to limit their activities by allowing the English and Dutch to trade in Iceland. The Dutch never made use of this permission to any appreciable extent, and English traffic with Iceland declined rapidly after a century of very lively intercourse.

In spite of serious attempts by the Danish crown to curb their activities, the Hamburgers continued to increase their trade and influence in Iceland, even to the extent that they took part in deliberations of the Althing around 1530. But the English were still in evidence and prevented the Hamburgers from taking full control of the country. From 1486 till 1532 there were eight severe clashes between English and German traders in Iceland. This rivalry came to an end in 1547 when the king leased Iceland to the city council of Copenhagen for a fixed annual tax. This was an important step towards securing the entire Iceland trade for the Danes, and was a preparation for the final step, taken in 1602, when full Danish monopoly was established in Iceland, ushering in a century and a half of inhuman economic oppression and almost constant misery.

In ecclesiastical affairs there were ups and downs, and some irregularities owing to the practice of appointing uninterested foreigners to leading church positions. But by and large the church enlarged both its wealth and power. Many of the bishops were unsparing in using excommunication to extort possessions from wealthy landowners, either for the church itself or for their own private use. There were numerous lawsuits between bishops and secular leaders, some of them dramatic. In 1513 it had come to such a pass that most of the secular leaders in North and West Iceland felt compelled to unite against the excesses of bishops and priests.

In general one might say that the bishops and some of the higher secular officials continued to play the roles of the ancient chieftains right up to the Reformation in 1550, when the king finally took over full control of the country, reducing the church to a mere servant by arrogating most of its vast property. The chieftainly behaviour was perhaps most vividly and dramatically demonstrated by the last Roman-Catholic bishops of Skálholt and Hólar, both of them stubborn, self-willed and powerful leaders who were at odds with one another until the struggle against the Reformation began in earnest.

Bishop Ögmund Pálsson of Skálholt (1521–42), the older of the two, had tried to prevent the election of Jón Arason (bishop 1524–50) to Hólar. Ögmund, who combined the qualities of an able and energetic administrator with those of an arrogant and headstrong chieftain, was in effect the secular ruler as well as the bishop of his diocese. But his opponent, Jón Arason, had the chieftainly qualities in an even higher degree. He was a highly gifted man, dignified and charming, and resolute and hard as flint when dealing with his opponents—a born leader. He was also, incidentally, an accomplished poet. From his young days he lived in concubinage with a lady who bore him many children and turned out to be so prolific that most modern Icelanders can trace some branch of their ancestry to this last Roman-Catholic bishop of Iceland. Like so many other deviations the practice of concubinage seems to have been officially tolerated within the church of Iceland from the beginning.

Although the authority of the two bishops was limited to their two dioceses, they had a number of clashes. The most serious occurred at the Althing in 1526 where Ögmund arrived with an escort of 1300 men, but Jón brought 900. When an open conflict seemed inevitable it was arranged through the patient efforts of mediators that peace should be maintained on the condition that the controversy should be settled by a fight between two champions selected for the purpose. This duel, which actually was contrary to Icelandic civil law, was fought on the island in the

Öxará river where duels had taken place in the old days, before they were made illegal. Ögmund's champion succeeded in throwing his opponent after a long fight before the assembly and was declared the victor, but Jón and his group were not satisfied. Still, peace was preserved and a year later the two bishops were reconciled, no doubt partly due to the common enemy threatening their church and position. On the day following the famous duel the cathedral of Skálholt was destroyed by fire. The calamity sorely distressed Bishop Ögmund, who soon set to work with his customary energy to rebuild the church, a task he almost completed before his death.

Ögmund Pálsson and Jón Arason are among the most illustrious Icelanders of the sixteenth century. Both came to a cruel end, although in different ways, and may well be considered the last chieftains of Iceland, the residual champions of what little remained of Icelandic autonomy.

At Skálholt there were a few theologians who had come under the influence of Martin Luther and who secretly paved the way for the Reformation. Among those was Ögmund's special protégé, Gizur Einarsson, whose studies in Germany the bishop had financed. There was also Odd Gottskálksson, son of a former notorious bishop of Hólar. Odd first translated the New Testament into Icelandic, working on part of the translation in a cowshed at Skálholt, to avoid attention, but later moving away.

In the meantime a civil war in Denmark over the suitable heir to the throne had concluded with the fanatically pro-Lutheran monarch Christian III as the victor. In 1537 he established the new order in Denmark and Norway, ruthlessly crushing all opposition, and sent a delegate to Iceland with authority to establish the Lutheran church there. Both bishops resisted, and two years later royal emissaries started plundering the monasteries, beating monks and abusing sacred objects. On one of his plundering expeditions the royal emissary visited Skálholt with his escort and stayed there overnight. His insulting behaviour towards Bishop Ögmund, who was by then totally blind, so outraged the bishop's counsellor that he secretly sent word to the people of the district, telling them what was taking place at Skálholt. In no time an armed force of angry farmers assembled, surrounded the house and killed the royal emissary with all his followers (1539). The case was tried before a jury of twelve men and the farmers were acquitted, but the Danish governor blamed the old bishop for the episode, although he had tried to warn his guests.

Bishop Ögmund, who was now too old and disabled to attend to his duties, had the Althing elect as his successor Gizur Einarrsson, whom he still trusted although he knew his doctrinal leanings. Gizur's election was sanctioned by the king in 1540. He was at first quite careful not to offend the people or the clergy who welcomed him. The new church code sent to Iceland in 1538 was not adopted by the Althing until 1541 when a new Danish governor was sent to Iceland with two warships. But Jón Arason was not present at the session and refused to abide by the decision.

The leader of the Danish king's mission had a second task with which Bishop Gizur Einarsson had entrusted him. At the instigation of Bishop Gizur, he perfidiously seized the eighty-year-old Ögmund while he was visiting his sister far away from Skálholt, and took him aboard one of the warships. Having treacherously persuaded him to hand over all his silver and his fifty farms as ransom, the Danes carried him away to Denmark. Some sources say he died on the voyage, others that he reached Denmark and died there shortly afterwards.

A great obstacle had been removed by deporting Bishop Ögmund, but Bishop Jón Arason in the north proved a much more formidable adversary. For nine years he held out and came close to ruling the whole country. At first he maintained friendly relations with Bishop Gizur Einarsson, and seems to have paid the royal taxes levied on the bishopric of Hólar until 1545. In 1546 Luther died in Eisleben, and two years later Bishop Gizur died, having made a journey to remove one of the most sacred crosses of his diocese, an object of great veneration to which pilgrimages had been made from all over South Iceland. The prospects of Jón Arason were therefore encouraging, and on Gizur's death he announced that he would take charge of the Skálholt diocese. But he was not popular there and his son, Björn Jónsson, who wanted to become bishop, was still less so.

In June 1548 there was a 'general synod' at Skálholt where a Roman-Catholic abbot was elected bishop by twenty-four priests, and Jón Arason was simultaneously chosen 'administrator' of the Skálholt cathedral and diocese until the new bishop had been consecrated. But the Lutherans at the synod, also twenty-four in number, elected for their bishop Martein Einarsson (1549-56), a benevolent and pious man who was reluctant to accept the office and eventually resigned after seven years when he witnessed the outrageous behaviour of Danish officials in his country. Jón Arason had brought more than 100 men with him from the north, but the Lutherans at Skálholt had learned of his approach and gathered 300 men to defend the place. Jón Arason had to camp outside the premises of Skálholt with his retinue, but he seems to have had free access to the synod which soon divided into two opposing groups. The Catholic priests were more numerous and therefore the abbot was legally chosen, but of the twenty-four Lutherans who elected Martein Einarsson, only six or eight were fully ordained priests. The certificates of election for both the candidates were sent to the Danish king with a request that he confirm the election. Later the same summer both the candidates went to Copenhagen seeking confirmation from the king, who decided that Martein Einarsson should be consecrated bishop of Skálholt. The abbot died in Denmark in 1550.

After the Skálholt synod in June 1548 Bishop Jón Arason rode to the Althing and persuaded it to pass a resolution whereby he was put in charge of the Skálholt diocese until the new and legally elected bishop could assume his office. But the clergy who had been placed in authority by Martein Einarsson, while he was abroad seeking the king's sanction, refused to heed the Althing's decree.

In the summer of 1548 King Christian III sent two letters to Iceland, one addressed to Bishop Jón Arason, summoning him to Denmark and issuing him with safe-conduct, the other addressed to the clergy and secular leaders of the country, warning them not to aid the bishop if he should disobey royal orders. Both letters were read at the Althing in Jón's presence, but he was resolute, heeding the advice neither of his friends nor of his son Ari, the former lawman of North Iceland, who had now resigned. Ari reluctantly joined his father and his brother Björn, but another son of Jón, the priest Sigurd, took no part in the rebellion.

From the Althing Jón Arason returned to Hólar, put up fortifications and bided his time. He wrote a letter to the Pope pledging his allegiance to Rome, but the Holy See was not in a position to render any help. He is also said to have written a latter to Emperor Charles V, and we know from other sources that the emperor wrote letters to King Christian III on behalf of Jón Arason, but they went unheeded.

In the spring of 1549 Bishop Martein Einarsson returned to Iceland with royal letters declaring Jón Arason an outlaw to be arrested, failing which the king threatened to send a military force to Iceland. A letter from the Pope greatly encouraged Bishop Jón, who decided to fight to the bitter end, sacrificing his life if need be. He did not attend the Althing in 1549, but in the autumn he learned that Bishop Martein was travelling with a small retinue in the western districts, and sent his sons Ari and Björn with a hundred men to seize him. Bishop Martein and another bitter opponent among the clergy were brought to Hólar and kept in custody through the winter. Martein's brother-in-law, Dadi, a powerful man, had a narrow escape.

In the spring of 1550 a royal commandant arrived in Iceland with instructions to unfrock Bishop Jón and forbid all the clergy in his diocese to obey him. When Jón heard of the royal orders he decided to overwhelm his opponents. He rode to the Althing with his two sons and a force of 400 men. All resistance was in vain. Jón

Arason carried the day and made such decisions as he pleased. The lawman of the north was forced to resign and Ari was reinstated. Jón had himself declared in charge of the Skálholt diocese and was now resolved on restoring the old order in the country. From the Althing he marched to Skálholt with his whole force, bringing with him the captive Bishop Martein. The place was surrendered and Martein left there under guard, while Bishop Jón proceeded to some of the monasteries which had been taken over by the Danes, drove the Danish commandant and his officials on board their ships and rededicated the monasteries, installing the former abbots and their monks.

After these victories Jón Arason was close to being all-powerful in Iceland. There was only one dangerous opponent still at large, Bishop Martein's brother-in-law Dadi, with whom he hoped to be able to come to grips shortly. In the autumn he went to the western districts with a small force, against the advice of his cautious son Ari, hoping to gain support from the local population there. But Dadi, a cunning leader, attacked him unawares and seized him along with his two sons in a church where they had sought refuge. Dadi reported what had happened to Bessastadir, the residence of the royal governor (now the Icelandic President's residence), but there was at the time no high Danish official left in the country. The only official was a bailiff who, according to royal instructions was to keep the prisoners until the next Althing, assisted by the two lawmen and Bishop Martein, who was now released. Later a meeting was held at Skálholt, attended by a number of leading Icelanders, to discuss how to keep the prisoners safely through the winter. After long discussions the steward at Skálholt said one day at the breakfast table that he might not be very wise, but still he knew how the prisoners could be safely kept. When asked how, he replied that the axe and the earth would keep them best. At first there was considerable opposition to this lawless method, but the Danish bailiff gave his ardent support and persuaded Bishop Martein Einarsson to approve it. The matter was finally settled, and on 7 November 1550 Bishop Jón Arason and his two sons were beheaded at Skálholt in violation of all existing laws and customs.

This ghastly act was bitterly resented in North Iceland. When men from the north came south to take part in the winter fisheries a band of them killed the Danish bailiff, his son and a number of his Danish followers. In March the following year the three bodies were exhumed and brought to Hólar by Jón's son Sigurd and a group of thirty men. The funeral, as it passed through many districts was everywhere shown the greatest reverence and at Hólar the bodies were interred with deep veneration and many marks of honour.

Thus ended a phase of Icelandic history—with a cruel and lawless act, preceded by the most flagrant violations on the part of the king of all the agreements forming the bonds of union between Iceland and the Danish crown. The Icelanders had been treated as a conquered nation, all their legal rights being abused or disregarded.

Jón Arason has been a national hero in Iceland since his execution, and a number of literary works have been written about him, the most famous being the novel *Jón Arason* (1930) by Gunnar Gunnarsson.

The Reformation marks the beginning of a great economic and political decline in Iceland which was to continue for more than two centuries. The Danish crown appropriated almost all the vast property of the church along with many other annual emoluments attached to church and clergy. It has been estimated that one-fifth of all landed property in Iceland thus came into Danish possession, which was a tremendous blood-letting for the economy. In addition, the Danish crown took over all the ships of German traders in South Iceland and used them for fishing. The tenants of the royal farms and estates were forced to contribute free labour on these ships and on the estates directly run by Danish officials, and to provide the king's men with horses for journeys to the Althing. From 1550 a quarter of all the tithes payable to the church as well as fines imposed in lawsuits were also considered revenue destined directly for the royal purse. This led to all sorts of outrageous acts of injustice and persecution. In 1563 the king decreed that heresy should be considered a capital crime and the property of those found guilty be forfeited to the crown. In 1564 repeated adultery was likewise made a capital crime with dire consequences in a country where sexual morals had never been particularly strict. This last stipulation remained nominally in force until 1838. Those convicted were executed, the men being beheaded. the women drowned. Half their property was forfeited to the crown, while the other half was divided among needy relatives. At Thingvellir the traveller still sees a reminder of this barbarous practice in the 'Drowning Pool' beside the bridge over the Öxará river in Almannagjá. Thieves were to be hanged, flogged or branded, and even minor offences were punished by the pillory, flogging or heavy fines.

It would not be unreasonable to assume that foreign oppression, injustice and arbitrariness had now reached its peak, but this was not so. Worse was still to come with the Danish trade monopoly. Still, it can be argued that the long-term effects of the Reformation led to an improvement in the spiritual and cultural spheres. What was outwardly lost was in a sense inwardly gained. The Icelanders lost the last vestiges of their political, judicial and economic rights, but they compensated for their loss by intensifying their educational and spiritual activities. In 1552 Latin schools were established at both Skálholt and Hólar enabling increasing numbers of students to seek higher education at foreign universities. Thus many Icelandic students went to study at the universities of Copenhagen, Bremen and Rostock. Moreover, the introduction of printing made reasonably cheap books available in the home, which was of paramount importance for the general education of the people.

This development went hand in hand with the emergence of a handful of brilliant individuals each of whom contributed in his own way to the spiritual renaissance. Chief among these was Gudbrand Thorláksson who was bishop of the Hólar diocese for fifty-six years (1571-1627). He greatly improved the position of the clergy and was a prolific writer, translator and publisher. He bought the printing press which Bishop Jón Arason had brought to Iceland about 1530, and improved it in many ways, sent an Icelander to learn the printing trade in Copenhagen, hired a specialist from Hamburg to teach his countrymen book binding, and set out on his great publishing enterprise. He published the Bible, mostly in his own translation, in a magnificent edition (1584) which is still the pride of Icelandic book making. He had hymns and other Christian literature translated for publication and wrote highly interesting introductions to these volumes. He also published Icelandic poets in a famous anthology as well as numerous other useful books and booklets. Gudbrand Thorláksson was one of the great reanimators of both church and folk literature in Iceland. After 1572 Hólar remained an important seat of printing in the country until 1844 when the printing press was moved to Reykjavík.

Gudbrand Thorláksson's younger contemporary, Bishop Odd Einarsson (1589-1630) of Skálholt, who had for some time been a pupil of the Danish astronomer Tycho Brahe, was also a highly gifted man, an energetic administrator of his bishopric and a diligent scholar who did much to preserve ancient annals and to record what was of interest in his own age.

A first cousin of Gudbrand Thorláksson was Arngrím Jónsson (1568-1648), sometimes referred to as 'the wise'. He was headmaster of the Latin school at Hólar and a scholar of European reputation for his extensive writing in Latin about Icelandic history and geography. He was a diligent collector of old manuscripts and has been called 'the restorer of Icelandic learning'. In his wake came a number of other great scholars and manuscript collectors, to whom we shall return shortly.

During the latter part of the sixteenth century epidemics, volcanic eruptions and severe weather ravaged Iceland, and the seventeenth century began with the hardest winters ever recorded in Icelandic history. For four consecutive years there was no respite from the bitter cold with the result that large numbers of livestock succumbed and some 9,000 people starved to death, while thousands took to the road. All requests to the crown for assistance went unheeded.

As if the natural calamities were not enough, the king in 1602 clamped a monopoly on all trade in Iceland, giving a company of merchants in Copenhagen, Malmö and Elsinore exclusive rights to trade there for twelve years at a time. The consequences of this for the Icelanders were indescribable. The merchants broke all agreements, flouted all regulations, decided their own prices, which were usually exorbitant, and imported what they pleased, without regard to the needs or wishes of the people. Often their goods were rotten and wormeaten. One thing they never failed to import: alcohol. Now and again the king was forced to intervene and regulate the prices but to little avail, for in the long run the merchants had their way.

The seventeenth and eighteenth centuries, when the Danish trade monopoly was in force, were in effect an unrelieved record of disaster and misery. The seventeeth century saw repeated raids by English, Spanish and even Arab pirates. In one such raid in North-west Iceland, in 1615, three Spanish ships were wrecked and the crews, about 80 in number, had to seek refuge on shore where they went robbing and ill-treating the local population. About half the raiders were killed in two encounters, but the rest managed to survive through the winter and got away in spring with an English fishing vessel which they robbed.

But the most notorious pirate raid in Icelandic annals was that of the Algerians in 1627, when the east coast and especially the Westman Islands off the south coast were ravaged. On 16 July three ships from Algiers arrived in the islands with 300 men who divided into three bands and overran the large inhabited island of Heimaey, yelling and massacring the terror-stricken and helpless inhabitants. All the survivors were herded together into a large storehouse belonging to the Danish merchants, where the youngest and strongest, 242 in number, were selected and taken on board the ships. The rest were burned along with the building. The pastor, Jón Thorsteinsson, a well-known hymn writer, was struck dead while kneeling in prayer in a cave with his wife and children, who were driven on board the ships. The parish church was burned, and those who tried to escape were hunted down and killed. Having destroyed what they could not take away, the pirates sailed back to Algiers and sold the captives as slaves. Most of them soon died. The survivors wrote such touching letters to their people back home that money was finally collected both in Denmark and Iceland. Nine years after their seizure thirty-nine of them were ransomed, but only thirteen ever returned to the native land. One of these became the wife of Iceland's greatest and most beloved hymn writer, Hallgrím Pétursson (1614-74).

Cold winters, volcanic eruptions and severe epidemics continued to harry the country. In 1695 and 1696 the winters were so bad that not only did the rivers freeze where they had never been known to freeze before, but the sea all around Iceland became ice-bound. In 1784 and 1792 there were also notoriously hard winters. Earthquakes and volcanic eruptions were still more calamitous. In 1618-19 many farms were thus destroyed. In 1625 a volcanic eruption in East Iceland lasted for twelve days and was so violent that the ashes reached Norway. In 1636 the Hekla had its fifteenth recorded outbreak, lasting from 8 May until the following winter, spreading ash and pumice over large areas. In 1660 the volcano Katla destroyed many farms. In 1693 Hekla again had a violent eruption, its ashes spreading all over Iceland and reaching both Scotland and Norway. During the eighteenth century the havoc was even greater. In 1727 an eruption in the Öraefajökul glacier lasted almost a whole year, blotting out many farms and killing hundreds of sheep and horses. An earthquake in South Iceland in 1732 destroyed twelve farms, damaging another forty. In 1755 Katla erupted once more, destroying thirteen farms and covering a whole district with a deposit of ashes so deep that fifty farms had to be abandoned. In 1783 these natural catastrophes reached an all-time climax with the devastating Skaftá or Laki eruption which made two whole parishes uninhabitable for two years, wiped out twelve farms entirely and ruined twenty-nine more, poisoning the soil all over Iceland, spoiling the growth and killing the livestock. According to reliable sources the loss of animals during 1783-4 was as follows: 11,461 head of cattle (53 per cent), 190,448 sheep (83 per cent), and 28,013 horses (72 per cent). In 1784 an earthquate in South Iceland destroyed sixty-nine farms totally, wrecked sixty-four, and seriously damaged 372. Of houses 1,459 were levelled to the ground, 212 wrecked, and 333 badly damaged.

The most graphic description of these terrifying events was given by Jón Steingrímsson, a pastor, who played a dramatic role in the tragedy by gathering his parishioners for a service in the local church as one of the three main streams of red-hot lava was approaching, threatening to overrun the church and the parish. During the service the lava-stream suddenly stopped not far from the church and piled up instead of flowing on, thus saving the church and the parish. This was on 20 July, about six weeks after the eruption started, and was taken as a sign of divine protection.

Jón Steingrímsson's autobiography is one of the gems of Icelandic literature.

As to epidemics, the worst swept the country in 1707, when 18,000 people died from smallpox, or about one-third of the entire population. In 1757, 2,500 people died of hunger in the Skálholt diocese. The effects of the Skaftá eruption were still more serious, for it is estimated that in 1783-5 over 9,000 persons died in Iceland from hunger and attendant diseases. People fell dead from exhaustion as they went from one farm to another. Not a single member of many families survived.

The writer and educator Magnús Stephensen says of the eighteenth century: 'During this century Iceland experienced forty-three years of distress due to cold winters, ice-floes, failures of fisheries, shipwrecks, inundations, volcanic eruptions, earthquakes, epidemics and contagious diseases among men and animals, which often came separately, but often in connection with and as a result of one another.'

In the year 1100, as was stated in Chapter I, Iceland is believed to have had a population of about 70,000. In the following six centuries the population actually halved:

The following statistics show the depletion of herds in the eighteenth century:

POPULATION

1703	50,444
1708	34,000
1800	47,086
1877	72,000

SHEEP		CATTLE		HORSES	
1703	280,000	1703	35,800	1703	26,900
1760	357,000	1770	30,100	1760	32,200
1784	49,000	1784	9,800	1784	8,600
1800	307,000	1800	23,300	1800	28,300

Even though the seventeenth century was in many ways an age of great intellectual and poetical achievement in Iceland as in the rest of Europe, it was also haunted by the witchcraft craze troubling other European countries, though Iceland lagged far behind Europe in the witch hunts. The first person put to death for witchcraft in Iceland was burned in 1625, in accordance with Danish, not Icelandic, law. In the period 1630-90 twenty-two persons were burned for the same offence in Iceland. Many people were also flogged or banished. Curiously, the victims of this frenzy were men, only one woman being put to death in the witch hunts. They came to an end in 1690.

Danish rule in Iceland was further consolidated when in 1662, exactly 400 years after the collapse of the Commonwealth, King Frederik III had himself established an absolute hereditary monarch in Iceland, having attained the same status in Denmark and Norway. Previously the king had been placed on the throne through election by the Danish Estates, an arrangement which enabled the nobility to safeguard their privileges and exercise a dominant influence on the government. In 1662 the leading men in Iceland were summoned to the Althing to pledge their allegiance to the new régime. But since the Danish governor-general was too late for the meeting at Thingvellir, he had the men called to Kópavogur, near his residence at Bessastadir, where on 28 July the required oath was taken under threat from an armed force. The old lawman of South Iceland, Árni Oddsson (son of Bishop Odd Einarsson), was reluctant to attend the meeting and is said to have signed the pledge weeping, after which he resigned his post. The lawman of North Iceland had resigned when he heard the king's request. The establishment of absolutism may have curbed the excesses of the nobility in Denmark, but in Iceland it only served to make royal officials more despotic and arbitrary.

Among the individuals of note in the seventeenth century four have already been mentioned: Bishops Gudbrand Thorláksson and Odd Einarsson, the scholar Arngrím Jónsson, and the lawman Árni Oddsson.

Perhaps the most influential man in Iceland during the latter part of the seventeenth century was Bishop Brynjólf Sveinsson (1605-75) of Skálholt, who was in effect also the secular leader of the Icelanders after Árni Oddsson died in 1665. He was highly educated, well versed in classical languages and in the literature of his country, a keen collector of Old Icelandic manuscripts who spared neither time nor money in his efforts to create a valuable manuscript collection which included many of the best works. He had planned to settle down abroad but was persuaded to assume the bishop's office at Skálholt. He was a born leader, with a majestic appearance, and his management of church affairs was exemplary; he raised the educational and moral standard of the clergy. He also became wealthy and powerful, and was instrumental in averting many harmful speculations by the Danish merchants, since his advice carried great weight with the crown. His life was darkened in his later years by a family tragedy, for which he was not entirely without blame. He lost his two children and a grandson and died a lonely man. He is the hero of Gudmundur Kamban's great historical novel *Skálholt* (1930-5).

The name of Brynjólf Sveinsson is linked with Hallgrím Pétursson (1614-74), Iceland's greatest hymn writer, whom he met in Copenhagen working as a blacksmith, and persuaded to prepare for the ministry. Hallgrím Pétursson had to struggle with dire poverty all his life, and in his later years he was afflicted with leprosy. He was a good speaker and won great distinction as a poet even in his own lifetime. His principal work, *Fifty Passion Hymns,* ranks among the best of its kind in world literature and has been published more than sixty times since it appeared, which is a record in the annals of Icelandic publishing. It has also been translated into many languages all over the world, even into Chinese and Japanese. It took the poet ten years to compose the great hymns that are based on the Passion of Christ. They are at the same time an eloquent testimony to the predicament of his people during one of the most difficult periods of its history. Few other works have had such a profound and lasting influence on the nation as a whole. The hymns are read over the Icelandic radio during Lent every year, and no burial takes place without Hallgrím Pétursson's transcendent hymn *Allt eins og blómstrid eina* being sung. He also wrote secular poetry of rare poignancy and formal mastery.

Another accomplished poet of the seventeenth century was the Reverend Stefán Olafsson (*ca.* 1620–88), a nephew of Bishop Odd Einarsson. His secular poetry is extremely well written and natural in its delineation of human emotions, and his humorous poems have a special place in Icelandic literature. His diction is simple and direct, and his expression remarkably modern in tone.

A great ecclesiastical leader at the turn of the century was Bishop Jón Vídalín (1666–1720) of Skálholt, who is reputed to have been the most eloquent of Icelandic churchmen. He was grandson of the famous scholar Arngrím Jónsson, and was endowed with a keen intellect combined with religious zeal which made him one of the most influential preachers in Icelandic Christendom. Having finished his studies at the University of Copenhagen, he entered the Danish army hoping for quick promotion, but his hopes were in vain and in the end he had to be bought out of the service. He thereupon became a vicar at the cathedral of Skálholt and was strongly recommended by the old bishop on his deathbed as his successor. Jón Vídalín almost missed the office through the manoeuvres of one of the king's friends who wanted his Danish protégé to have the job, but in 1698 it was given to Jón Vídalín, probably through the intervention of the scholar and manuscript collector Árni Magnússon. Jón Vídalín was a superb administrator and great reformer who took the clergy to task for moral laxity and spiritual indifference. He was humble and kindly towards the common people, but proud and demanding when dealing with haughty officials and well-to-do farmers. He was a good poet in Latin, but his renown is based on his sermons, notably his very popular *Book of Family Sermons* which has appeared in fourteen editions and is regarded as the best Icelandic book of its kind. Except for Hallgrím Pétursson's *Fifty Passion Hymns* no other book has enjoyed such popularity in Iceland.

There were many outstanding scholars in the seventeenth century, two of whom have already been mentioned, Arngrím Jónsson and Árni Magnússon (1663-1730), who was briefly discussed at the beginning of Chapter 4. The third, Thormód Torfason, or Torfaeus (1636-1719), was a prolific historiographer who wrote histories of the Faroes (1697), Orkney (1697) and Greenland (1706), the story of the Norse discovery of America (1707), and a history of Norway up to 1387 in four large folio volumes (1711). All these works were written in Latin. Torfaeus was appointed royal historiographer in 1667 and was later sent as a royal official to Norway where he spent the rest of his life.

Living conditions in Iceland during these centuries were wretched. On top of the scarce and unwholesome food, housing was such that the peasants' hovels were a breeding-ground of all kinds of diseases which spread rapidly and further sapped the mental and physical energy of the people. The Icelandic historian Jón Adils gives the following descriptions of the general interior of the peasants' huts in the sixteenth century (and conditions later grew worse):

The *badstofa* [living room where people worked and slept] on the common peasant farmstead was usually not covered with boards on the inside. One could see between the rafters to the grass-covered roof, which soon looked like ordinary sod, and from which mildew and cobwebs were hanging. The floor was uncovered, consisting only of earth trampled hard. But during heavy rains when the roof was leaking water dripped down, and it soon became a pool of mud through which the people waded. The walls along which the besteads were nailed fast were covered with a grey coat of mildew, and green slime was constantly trickling down the walls, especially in winter. Bed clothes were very few among the poor people. Old hay, seaweed or twigs did service as mattress, and a few blankets constituted the covering. In some houses a little loft was built, the *pallr*, two or three feet from the ground, where the people of the household stayed. The dark room underneath the *pallr* was occupied by lambs and young calves which needed special care.... One trouble with all dwellings, though there might be considerable difference between them, was the want of light. In a house where there was no heating apparatus, as in the Icelandic *badstofa*, and in a climate as chilly as that in Iceland, it was necessary to preserve the heat as well as possible. The windows were, therefore, both few and small, and were usually placed in the roof above the bed. A window consisted of only one pane, and this was not of glass, but of a thin membrane [*líknarbelgr*] stretched upon a frame and placed in a hole in the roof. When the wind was strong, the windows would often break, and the women would have to mend them. It can readily be understood that these windows admitted so little light into the room that the people had to sit in continual darkness even in the middle of the day.[1]

Magnús Ólafsson, member of a royal commission, gives the following description of conditions in Iceland in the early eighteenth century:

One can understand how these miserably constructed houses of the poor contribute to the spread of all sorts of diseases, as the houses, especially the dwellings, are very low. There the people sit on a loft, and the air is so impure that a stranger who is not accustomed to it can scarcely endure it for an hour, as it is corrupred by the smoke of the train-oil lamps, and the respiration and perspiration of the people, of whom many are affected with scurvy and other diseases. When pregnant women and small children have to breathe this infected air, it is not strange that many even in their youth become affected with tuberculosis and spit blood when they move about rapidly.[2]

'One feature is still overlooked in these reports,' says Jón Adils, 'which did not improve the air in the *badstofa,* namely the fact that the men sat all day with their pipes in their mouths smoking, so that the smoke rolled out as from a factory chimney. The merchants had made them believe that if they only smoked a great deal no sickness would attack them.'[3]

These conditions prevailed more or less unchanged well into the nineteenth century, and the turf farm was the most common human dwelling in the countryside until about the First World War.

After a century and a half of the Danish trade monopoly, matters had reached such a pass, through repeated outrages and abuses of all existing rules and through ever-increasing oppression by the Danish traders, that drastic measures were called for. While people were dying in large numbers from famine, the merchants filled their measure of iniquity by shipping to Iceland putrid and wormy flour which the starving populace was compelled to buy.

At that critical juncture a man of great courage, vision and extraordinary enterprise entered the arena and did his utmost to raise the economic and spiritual level of his nation. Skúli Magnússon (1711–94) was, in 1749, the first Icelander to be appointed to the important office of *landfógeti* or royal superintendant and tax collector. He had his residence in the island of Videy, near Reykjavík, where he built a large stone house, which is still in existence, the oldest of its kind in Iceland and a beautiful building now in the care of the National Museum. Skúli Magnússon was by far the most energetic, persevering and influential Icelander of the eighteenth century. He succeeded in breaking the power of the

infamous Danish trading company and tried to create a new basis
for the economic life of Iceland. He urged that a stock company be
formed in order to improve farming and husbandry in the country,
but so far the foreign traders had controlled the fisheries and
exploited the manufacture of woollen goods Skúli Magnússon
drew up plans for the new company, got leading men of the
country to participate, and in 1752 secured royal support. A
woollen mill was built in Reykjavík, and German weavers were
brought to Iceland. Also a fulling-mill, a rope works and a tannery
were erected in Reykjavík. Farmers were sent from Denmark and
Norway to teach the Icelanders agriculture. Trees were imported
and planted, and fishing-smacks were purchased abroad. The
Icelandic fishermen were to be helped in constructing larger boats,
so that they could fish in the open sea, and the people were to
learn the best methods of salting meat and fish.

All this looked quite promising, but there were many obstacles,
the most formidable of which was the Danish trading company
which did everything in its power to hinder the new enterprise. The
merchants refused to handle the products of the new industrial
establishments. Skúli Magnússon turned to the government for aid,
and the Icelandic industries were granted permission to export
their goods from Iceland and import materials necessary for their
work. The Danish merchants persisted in their opposition, and
Skúli Magnússon brough suit against them for many wrongs
committed in Iceland. The ensuing legal battle was long and
complex. In 1757 the Danish company was dissolved, and until
1763 trade with Iceland was carried on directly by the government.
In that year a new Danish company was granted control of the
Icelandic enterprises, in spite of Skúli Magnússon's bitter protests.
This company adopted the policy of its predecessor, and Skúli
continued his legal fights. The industries were allowed to fall into
complete neglect. Thus, for a variety of reasons, the great
endeavours of Skúli Magnússon came to nothing.

In 1768 Skúli succeeded in having the Danish company heavily
fined for the outrage of importing mildewed, putrid and wormy
flour, disregarding a government order. In 1774 the company was
forced to surrender its charter and the trade was again conducted
by the government until 1787, when commerce with Iceland was
made free to all subjects of the Danish crown. The trade monopoly
had by then been in force for 185 years, and caused untold misery
and many deaths. No single man had done more to have this
infamy removed than Skúli Magnússon, but he had also enjoyed
the faithful support of his lifelong friend and confidant Jón
Eiríksson (1728–87), a highly respected and influential Icelandic
official in Copenhagen.

The effects of Skúli Magnússon's endeavours were many and

not all immediately obvious. His stock company was the first association of any kind to be founded in Iceland, and as such of immense importance: it demonstrated to the Icelanders what co-operation was capable of achieving. In 1771 a second association, the Icelandic Agricultural Company, was established, followed in the coming century by a number of more or less durable associations.

Even though there had been some wealth in individual families at the end of the sixteenth century, stemming from the fourteenth and fifteenth centuries, it had all but vanished in the seventeenth century. There was no longer any possibility of acquiring wealth, only varying degrees of poverty existed. Wealth in Iceland had mainly consisted of real estate, farms and lands, but in the eighteenth century the value of real estate declined by 40 per cent. What profit Iceland had to offer went abroad, to the royal treasury and the Danish merchants. Skúli Magnússon realized that there could be no hope of any progress within the country unless the trade came into native hands and the profits remained in Iceland. The so-called 'Free Trade' for Danish subjects, proclaimed in 1787, was an important step in the right direction and probably accounted for what little progress there was during the next forty years, but it had many shortcomings, especially as Icelandic ports were too small to support more than one merchant, so that the monopoly in effect got into the hands of individual local merchants, except in the larger ports in South-west Iceland. The greatest blow to the progressive efforts of the preceding decades were, however, the calamitous volcanic outbursts of 1783-4 which virtually laid the country waste.

Since the earthquake following the eruption in 1783 wrecked the buildings of Skálholt, steps were taken to remove the bishop's see and the Latin school to Reykjavík in 1785. In 1801 the Hólar bishopric was discontinued, and one diocese for the whole of Iceland was created, with Reykjavík as the bishop's see, an arrangement still in effect. The schools of Skálholt and Hólar were also united into one Latin school in Reykjavík. In 1798 the Althing assembled for the last time at Thingvellir, where it had met for 868 years. Only twelve representatives attended the session, eight of them government officials. The next session was held in Reykjavík, which was now the capital of Iceland, having received a charter as an independent township in 1786. On 11 July 1800 that Althing was permanently dissolved by royal order. It was replaced by a new High Court, consisting of a chief judge and two associate justices, which was to exercise the judicial powers hitherto vested in the Althing.

Thus all the institutions symbolizing ancient culture and national traditions were eclipsed at the close of the two worst centuries in Icelandic history. The individual who was mainly responsible for these radical changes was Magnús Stephensen (1762-1833) who was appointed the first chief judge of the High Court. He came from a distinguished family in Iceland, his father being the highest official of the country, and went to study in Copenhagen where he embraced the new Enlightenment and became the main proponent of rationalism and the cosmopolitan spirit of the age. He was a man of many interests, a prolific writer (although his command of the Icelandic language was lamentably poor) and great entrepreneur. In order to control the literary production he obtained possession of the two printing presses in Iceland and combined them into one printing establishment. He did not enjoy any particular popularity with his countrymen, even if he did effect many useful changes and publish many worthwhile books. His greatest blunder was probably a rationally revised church hymn book, which outraged the artistic as well as the religious sensibilities of the Icelanders. In a sense Magnús Stephensen cuts a strange figure in Icelandic history, even though he dominated the Icelandic scene for many decades: he was somehow 'alien' to the culture and traditions of his nation, his orientation being cosmopolitan and pragmatic, but it must be admitted that he was in many ways more of a realist than most of his contemporary fellow-countrymen and used his gifts to bring about necessary changes. The last twenty years of his life were spent in the island of Videy, where Skúli Magnússon had also resided.

The first decades of the nineteenth century were uneventful in Iceland, except for the distress brought by the Napoleonic Wars and for one strange tragi-comic incident which looms large in the annals of the country. The Wars gradually paralysed commerce and brought serious disturbance and sufferings, since Iceland for a number of years was entirely cut off from Danish trade. As a failure of crops further increased the Icelanders' economic difficulties, a shortage of daily necessities was keenly felt. Often the most important commodities like salt, iron, tar, lumber and staple articles of food were unobtainable. People tried to use sea water instead of salt. They made stirrups and horseshoes of horn and fishing-lines from rope, and buried their dead without coffins.

In 1807 Denmark was forced to enter the war, after the English had bombarded Copenhagen and made away with the Danish fleet. The war between England and Denmark lasted seven years. In the first summer nobody in Iceland knew about this, and both the Danish governor-general and the chief judge (Magnús Stephensen) were seized at sea by the English, but were later allowed to proceed to Copenhagen. But Magnús Stephensen, seeing what calamity would befall his country if commerce came to a standstill, prevailed on the English government to allow free intercourse with Iceland during the war. He also secured the release of other Icelandic captives in England. In these endeavours he was greatly aided by the renowned English naturalist, Sir Joseph Banks, with whom he had become acquainted while in captivity in Scotland. Sir Joseph had earlier travelled in Iceland and was a warm friend of the Icelanders.

The British privateers swarming the seas also visited Iceland. There were numerous plundering expeditions, one of them visiting the governor-general himself. But the most famous visit was that of the English merchant Samuel Phelps and his Danish interpreter, Jörgen Jörgensen (1780–1844), in the summer of 1809. Jörgensen was a restless adventurer who had been forced to leave the University of Copenhagen because of his reckless conduct, even though he was a gifted student. He spent several years partly as a whaler and partly as an explorer in the Pacific Ocean. In 1806 he returned home and became captain of a Danish privateer in the war with England in 1807. His ship was captured and brought to England where he was imprisoned, but he was soon released on condition that he did not leave the country. Then he entered the service of the English merchants and came with them to Iceland as interpreter.

Seeing that Iceland was entirely defenceless, Jörgen Jörgensen decided to free the Icelanders from Danish rule and establish his own authority in the country. With a small band of armed men he marched to the residence of the governor-general, took him prisoner and brought him on board the ship. He then posted signed proclamations in Reykjavík, stating that all Danish authority in Iceland had come to an end, and that he was 'protector of Iceland and commander on sea and land'. Anyone failing to obey his instructions would be court-martialled and, if found guilty, shot within two hours. All debts to Denmark or the Danish merchants should be cancelled, prices on grain lowered, taxes reduced by half, and a committee of seven Icelanders elected to provide the country with new laws. He promised to resign his powers as soon as the seven-man committee convened. Jörgen Jörgensen most likely acted as the agent of the English merchants, but as the Icelanders were unarmed and defenceless it was considered the most prudent course to await developments. Jögensen surrounded himself with a 'bodyguard' consisting of eight Icelandic vagrants, and imprisoned several leading officials. He declared that the country's flag should be three white codfish on a blue field and promised to defend it with his life and blood. Fortifications were constructed on the Arnarhól hill in Reykjavík, close to the harbour, where a few rusty guns were mounted.

Jörgensen rode to North Iceland with his armed followers to

seize the property of the Danish merchants, and met with no serious opposition. But the hostility of the people was apparent and he received threatening letters from officials in distant parts of the country, which made him exceedingly angry. Even so, a few influential and powerful Icelanders took his side against the Danish domination.

On 14 August the English man-of-war *Talbot,* commanded by Alexander Jones, arrived in Reykjavík. Magnús Stephensen and his brother entered into negotiations with the captain and the merchant Samuel Phelps, and on 22 August 1809 an agreement was made whereby all the doings of Jörgen Jörgensen were to be considered null and void, all property and valuables should be returned to their owners, and all former officials reinstated in their offices. The brothers Stephensen were to have temporary charge of all public affairs and the English merchants should have the right to trade and reside in Iceland, according to an earlier agreement.

Jörgen Jörgensen was taken back to England where he was thrown into prison for breaking his promise not to leave the country. In prison he made the acquaintance of criminals and became an incurable gambler. After many adventures he was deported to Australia where he spent his remaining years as a member of various exploring expeditions and as a policeman. He was also a diligent writer and left us many interesting accounts of his hazardous life. His autobiography has recently been published.

Thus ended one of the strangest episodes in Icelandic history, an episode which dramatically brought out the inner and outer weaknesses of the nation a few decades before the struggle for national independence began in earnest.

The first quarter of the nineteenth century was in many ways exceedingly hard for the Icelanders, mainly due to reduced foreign imports and the financial collapse of Denmark in the Napoleonic Wars. The free intercourse established by the English was of limited value, but without it Iceland would have been utterly isolated. After the war Magnús Stephensen tried to improve trade conditions by bringing before the Danish government in 1815 a proposal to establish free intercourse with Iceland. The government was reluctant to relinquish the valuable trade with Iceland, but in 1816 an 'agreement' was published providing for increased freedom of trade. Danish ships sailing to Iceland were allowed to carry Icelandic export articles directly to foreign harbours by paying an export duty. But foreign commerce with Iceland was severely restricted, and the few English traders who had settled in Reykjavík were ordered to sell their possessions and depart.

One positive result of the difficult war years was the marked progress in various productive occupations, especially vegetable gardening, which gradually became an important item in the economy. In 1800 there were only 283 gardens in Iceland. By 1810 the number had risen to 1,194, by 1831 to 2,977, and by 1861 to 6,749. There was a similar development in the population growth: in the eighteenth century the population of Iceland had been reduced by 6·35 per cent. It had been over 50,000 in 1703, but three times during the century it had fallen below 40,000: after the smallpox epidemic of 1707-9, after the great famine of 1752-7, and after the volcanic eruptions of 1783-4. During the first two decades of the nineteenth century the population only increased by 1,600, but after that the growth was more rapid; between 1820 and 1850 it rose by 10,000. The increase during the first half of the century, taken as a whole, amounted to 25·23 per cent.

This increase was of course closely linked to better living conditions and improved techniques in both agriculture and fishing. There were occasional bad years as before, but by and large Iceland was going through a complete, if very slow, revolution from about 1830 onwards.

By the Peace of Kiel in 1814 the king of Denmark had to cede Norway to Sweden, the latter having taken sides with the English in the Napoleonic Wars. By a strange misunderstanding Iceland, which had been united with Norway in 1262, was not included in the cession, but remained united with Denmark. In the subsequent struggle for independence the Icelanders had endless disputes with the Danes as to how the fundamental articles of the treaty of 1262 should be interpreted. The Icelanders maintained that Iceland and Norway had been united under one king, while the Danes contended that the treaty had brought about a material union of the two countries, and even that Iceland had been incorporated in the kingdom of Norway, having exactly the same status in the kingdom of Denmark. This dispute was not finally resolved until 1918.

The forces released by the rise of Romantic movement in Europe and by the July Revolution of 1830 in France had their reverberations in Iceland and shaped the struggle of the nineteenth century: on the one hand, the literary efforts to recreate the glorious past of the nation, to purify the language, and awaken the people to the natural beauty of their country, and on the other, the political endeavour to increase the national autonomy with a view to achieving full independence.

If the seventeenth century in Iceland was characterized by outstanding personalities and great poets, so to an even greater extent was the nineteenth century. Not since the thirteenth century had Iceland seen such an upsurge of fine literary production, and indeed this was very much inspired by the old literary master-pieces, notably the *Sagas of Icelanders* and the *Poetic Edda*.

A precursor to this development was the formation in 1816 of the Icelandic Literary Society by the Danish linguist Rasmus Christian Rask (1787-1832) in Reykjavík and Copenhagen, to preserve the Icelandic language and publish its literature, old and new. This society was later taken over by the Romantics and is still very much alive, its annual publication *Skírnir* being the oldest periodical in Scandinavia, founded under its present name in 1827, replacing an older publication which had begun ten years earlier. The interest in Old Icelandic literature also resulted in the foundation of the Society for Northern Antiquaries by Carl Christian Rafn (1795-1864) which published a series of Icelandic Sagas. Rafn also laid the foundation of the National Library of Iceland in 1818.

The great pioneer of Romanticism in Iceland was Bjarni Thorarensen (1786-1841), scion of a prominent family, brought up at Hlídarendi, the home of *Njál's Saga's* noble hero, Gunnar. He entered the University of Copenhagen at fifteen and completed his law studies at twenty. After serving in government offices in Copenhagen and at the High Court in Reykjavík, he was made governor of North and East Iceland in 1833, residing near Akureyri. While in Reykjavík he also served twice as a temporary governor of Iceland.

Bjarni Thorarensen embraced a Romanticism at an early age through the influence of the Danish poet Oehlenschläger and the philosopher Henrik Steffens. In Iceland he stood alone for a long time, clashing with the cosmopolitan, rationalistic and pedestrian Magnús Stephensen, who was his superior at the High Court. By contrast Thorarensen was nationalistic, orthodox and genial, a man of strong feelings and rare poetic talent, even though he was not very productive. He was a national conservative but joined hands with the young national liberals who in the 1830s began to demand an increased freedom and the resurrection of the Althing. He was steeped in Edda and Saga, as his poetry amply illustrates, and no poet of later generations has expressed the old heroic ideals of honour, endurance and iron will with such force as he did. He may well be ranked with such outstanding, if dissimilar, poets as Egil Skallagrímsson of the tenth century and Hallgrím Pétursson of the seventeenth century.

Bjarni Thorarensen's younger contemporary, Jónas Hallgrímsson (1807-45), is the most beloved of all Icelandic poets, a great formal master possessing delicate perception and keen observation. He has few equals in describing the Icelandic scenery or conjuring up episodes from the distant and resplendent Golden Age. His felicity of expression was coupled with intimate knowledge of history and nature (he travelled through Iceland as a natural scientist). Like Thorarensen he was deeply religious, but lacked the robust character of his older colleague.

Jónas Hallgrímsson descended from a family of poets and started composing verses as a child—some of which are still known to every Icelander. Before entering the University of Copenhagen he had been immersed in the classics—Latin, Greek and Old Icelandic—at the Latin school of Iceland, guided by the remarkable tutors there, especially Sveinbjörn Egilsson (1791-1852), the great translator of Homer, whose work was a landmark in Icelandic letters. In Copenhagen Jónas Hallgrímsson began with law, but soon turned to natural history and literature. In 1835 he joined forces with three of his schoolmates, the young patriotic leader Tómas Saemundsson (1807-41), the philologist Konráð Gíslason (1808-91), and the jurist Brynjólf Pétursson (1809-51), to publish the periodical *Fjölnir*, which became the rallying point and the organ of the new patriotic movement. Bjarni Thorarensen also assisted in the undertakings. Its aim was to reform Icelandic literature, purify the Icelandic language, cultivate the people's aesthetic sensibilities and arouse their patriotism and love of freedom by stimulating admiration for Iceland's ancient greatness,-her old institutions, language and literary treasures. *Fjölnir* (1835-47) was among the most influential publications in Iceland during the nineteenth century, although it was not received with particular enthusiasm at the outset. Before it appeared, a young and fiery intellectual, Baldvin Einarsson (1801-33), had published, also in Copenhagen, a progressive periodical, *Armann á Althingi* (1829-33), which aimed at improving the intellectual and economic life of the Icelandic nation; it had considerable success with the readers. Three of these five promising leaders died in their thirties, two from accidents in Copenhagen, while a fourth died at the age of forty-two.

In the wake of the great pioneers came many able writers who left their imprint on the development of their nation, directly or indirectly. Among these were the poets Hjálmar Jónsson (1796-1875), an unusually forceful and accomplished folk-poet who lived in total poverty all his life; Grím Thomsen (1820-96), a highly educated man of the world who returned to Iceland after a brilliant career in the Danish foreign service to write some outstanding poetry on ancient themes; Benedikt Gröndal (1826-1907), a versatile satirist and romantic poet in the grand manner; Pál Ólafsson (1827-1905), a fine peasant-poet; Steingrím Thorsteinsson (1831-1913), a lyric poet and outstanding translator; Matthías Jochumsson (1835-1920), who besides being a poet and dramatist was also a noteworthy translator (of Shakespeare, Byron, and German and Nordic poets).

In prose the most prominent name is Jón Thoroddsen

(1818-68), 'father' of the modern Icelandic novel, whose two books, *Lad and Lass* (1850) and *Man and Wife* (posthumous 1876), have long been regarded as classics.

During this great age of national awakening and intellectual activity there were distinguished men of letters at work in other fields as well. Jón Arnason (1819-88) and Magnús Grímsson (1825-60) collected Icelandic folk and fairy tales which were published in many large volumes. In philology many Icelanders won great distinction: in Denmark, Finnur Magnússon (1781-1847) and Konrád Gíslason, both professors at the University of Copenhagen; in England, Gudbrand Vigfússon (1827-89) at Oxford, and Eirík Magnússon (1833-1913) at Cambridge. Gudbrand Vigfússon completed and edited the monumental *Icelandic-English Dictionary*, edited almost the entire body of Old Icelandic poetry and prose in five huge collections, among them the *Corpus Poeticum Boreale* with English translations, and wrote much on Northern antiquities. Eirík Magnússon translated a selection of Jón Árnason's Icelandic folk tales into English and collaborated with William Morris in publishing the Sagas in English.

The literary renaissance in Iceland as well as the new revolutionary ideas in Europe quickened the patriotic and nationalistic sentiments of the people and gave substance to the long-dormant dream of a rehabilitated and independent Iceland. In the political field many able writers, such as Baldvin Einarsson and Tómas Saemundsson, rendered valuable service by publishing articles and exhorting the nation, but direct political action and the task of wrestling with the Danish government was left to the keenest political genius of the century, Jón Sigurdsson (1811-79), now the National Hero of Iceland, on whose birthday, 17 June, the Republic of Iceland was founded in 1944. His statue stands in front of the Althing in the old centre of Reykjavík.

After entering the University of Copenhagen in 1833 Jón Sigurdsson lived in that city till the end of his life. He was outstanding both as a philologist and as an historian, and made many lasting contributions in both fields. He published a large number of Icelandic Sagas and other ancient texts. His profound knowledge of the history of his country was of paramount importance in the long and complex political struggle he had to wage. Even though his scholarly activities alone would have sufficed to secure his reputation, it was his statesmanship which won him lasting renown. Most of the progress made by the Icelanders in the nineteenth century can be traced to him.

In 1841 he began, with a few friends, the publication of the periodical *Ný félagsrit*, which was published until 1873. In this organ all the important problems of the time (education, finance, trade and politics) were thoroughly discussed. Jón Sigurdsson wrote about two-thirds of its thirty volumes. He was a vivid writer and exerted a profound influence all over Iceland; but in Denmark he was also an indefatigable polemicist, writing with equal force in Danish and Icelandic.

Jón Sigurdsson was a clear-sighted realist and often clashed with the more romantic idealists who, for instance, wished to re-establish the Althing at Thingvellir. He wanted a popularly elected legislature along contemporary lines, which should assemble in the new capital, Reykjavík, that was rapidly becoming the centre of all national life. He also outlined all the main arguments to be used in the struggle for autonomy. His most important arguments were to the effect that in 1262 Iceland was united with Norway under an agreement which defined the rights and positions of the Icelanders. In 1662 they were persuaded to surrender many of their rights into the hands of the Danish king by swearing allegience to the hereditary monarchy. But when the king of Denmark renounced his absolute power in 1848 and took steps to establish constitutional government, the rights which the Icelanders had surrendered reverted to them. Their relation to the realm was now the same as under the only existing union agreement, that of 1262. He stressed the fact that the Icelanders were a distinct people with their own language and national culture, and therefore the re-established Althing should have the same power in dealing with Icelandic affairs as the Danish *Rigsdag* had in dealing with Danish affairs. He also wanted a viceroy or governor ro be appointed for Iceland who should be responsible to the Althing, a minister for Icelandic affairs in the king's cabinet, and a separation of Icelandic and Danish finances. These were some of the salient 'planks' in Jón Sigurdsson's 'platform', but there were many others as well, and for thirty years he expounded and elaborated his case with astounding perseverence. All his demands had the agreement of the great majority of his countrymen, and he was in effect the uncrowned king of the Icelanders for almost four decades.

Many decisive victories were won during that period. In 1843 the Althing was re-established by a royal decree of 8 March, and convened for the first time in the Latin school (the present Gymnasium) of Reykjavík in 1845. There were twenty representatives chosen by the people and six appointed by the king. Jón Sigurdsson was elected in his native district in Northwest Iceland, which he represented until his death. The new Althing was merely an advisory body with no power to enact laws. Little of any consequence happened in the first years, but after the February Revolution in Paris in 1848 and a change of monarch in Denmark the same year, which led to the abolition of the absolute monarchy, strong demands were voiced in Iceland for an autonomous home government. At that time Jón Sigurdsson published his important article on the status of Iceland *vis-á-vis* Denmark. But political complications in Denmark, arising from unrest in the duchies of Schleswig-Holstein, delayed action with regard to the Althing, whereas a new Danish constitution was adopted on 5 June 1849.

Public meetings were held throughout Iceland to discuss the questions pertaining to an Icelandic constitution and the status of the Althing in relation to the Danish Rigsdag. Many petitions were sent to Denmark. The most important meeting was held at Thingvellir in June 1851: 140 delegates from all over the country outlined the main features of a proposed Icelandic constitution to be discussed at a national convention, summoned by the king in Reykjavík om 4 July, 1851. There was a week's delay before the Danish draft was submitted, but when it appeared it explicitly stated that Iceland was a part of the Danish kingdom and that therefore the Danish constitution should also apply in Iceland. When the Icelandic delegates refused to accept the government proposals, the governor-general inexplicably stationed armed troops near the convention hall and without further ado adjourned the convention. This fantastic procedure created such indignation that when Jón Sigurdsson rose from his seat to protest against this unlawful act, the whole assembly arose and cried in chorus: 'We all protest!'

The following two decades brought little change in the political situation. But after many petitions and strong demands a law was finally passed on 15 April 1854 making Icelandic trade free to all nations, thus removing the economic yoke under which the people had suffered for two and a half centuries. Freedom of the press was also established in 1855, and a more liberal election law was published in 1857.

In 1871 the Danish Rigsdag passed a bill unilaterally declaring Iceland an inalienable part of the Danish kingdom, but with its own government in purely domestic affairs. The Danish Supreme Court was to be the highest judicial tribunal, but in other respects domestic suits should be separated from those of Denmark. This arbitrary measure was the subject of protest by the Althing, and only served to increase the bitterness of the struggle and strengthen the Icelandic opposition. At that time large-scale emigration to North America and Brazil started, and grew year by year until the turn of the century. There were of course climatic and economic as well as political reasons for that regrettable turn of events.

As the millennial festival commemorating the settlement of Iceland approached, there were mixed feelings among the Icelanders. Some proposed to make the occasion one of national mourning and farewell for an emigrating people, while others urged patience in the hope that the king might grant the long-awaited constitution in commemoration of this historic event. Meetings were held and petitions sent to Copenhagen, and on 5 June 1874 the king issued a constitution granting legislative power to the Althing and establishing self-government for Iceland in domestic affairs. The procedure was the same as in 1871, the Althing not being consulted over such an important matter, but at last some of the more urgent demands had been met, even if much was still wanting. The Icelanders were given control over their finances—a very important measure—and the number of representatives in the Althing was increased to thirty-six, of whom thirty were elected by the people and only six appointed by the king. The executive power in domestic affairs was vested in a governor, who was made responsible not to the Althing but to the minister of Icelandic affairs in Copenhagen. Iceland was not represented in the Rigsdag, had no voice in the general affairs of the kingdom, and paid no part of the national expenditures. The king had an absolute power of veto in legislation.

The celebrations in Reykjavík and at Thingvellir in August 1874 turned out to be a happy occasion. King Christian IX sailed to Iceland to take part in the festivities, the first reigning king ever to visit the island, and delegations from many other countries were present. On this occasion Iceland's present National Anthem, *Iceland's Thousand Years,* by the poet Matthías Jochumsson to a tune by Sveinbjörn Sveinbjörnsson (1847-1927), was sung for the first time. There was, however, one regrettable blunder: Jón Sigurdsson was not invited and could not rejoice with his countrymen on his native soil.

The great events of 1845, 1854 and 1874 were the landmarks in Iceland's political and economic development during the nineteenth century, but the spirit of enterprise and national self-assurance steadily grew, and economic conditions slowly improved, in spite of many obstacles and setbacks, caused mainly by earthquakes, volcanic outbreaks and extremely unfavourable weather during the last quarter of the century. The export and import trades took great strides forward. New fishing techniques came with the decked boats and later with the trawlers, and an increasing number of Icelanders made their living by the sea. From 1844 onwards new companies of various kinds were formed, and schools and cultural institutions were founded. One of the most important trading companies was founded in 1870, led by Tryggvi Gunnarsson (1835-1917), whose enterprise and versatility became legendary. He was a pioneer farmer, a builder of bridges, houses and ships, a writer, a photographer, a pioneer in fishing, and finally director of Iceland's first bank, the National Bank, which was founded in 1885. But the most lasting and beneficial contribution to Iceland's economic rehabilitation came in 1882 when its first co-operative society was founded in North-east Iceland, near Lake Mývatn. It was followed by many more in the following years. In 1902 these societies were united in the Federation of Iceland Co-operative Societies (*Samband*) which in time became one of the greatest enterprises in Iceland. From the very beginning the co-operative societies served the double role of selling agricultural produce for the farmers and providing their members with consumer goods. The first agricultural school in Iceland was founded in 1880, to be followed by a countryside agricultural society in 1899. A navigation college for all Iceland was established in 1891 (since 1852 there had been local navigation schools). The first newspaper (a weekly) was published in 1848. A theological school opened in 1847 and a medical school in 1876. The National Museum came into being in 1863 and the Museum of Natural History in 1889. The Reykjavík Theatre Company was founded in 1897. All at once it was as though the nation was waking from a deep slumber.

Jón Sigurdsson died in 1879, and the struggle for increased autonomy was continued by his able and eloquent lieutenant Benedikt Sveinsson (1826-99), at one time associate justice at the High Court, and later sheriff in North-east Iceland. He proposed in 1881 a revision of the constitution, calling for radical changes and more self-government. His proposal was submitted to every session of the Althing until 1895. It was twice passed by two successive Althings (1885 and 1886; 1893 and 1894), in accordance with the requirements of the constitution, but the king promptly vetoed it. In 1895 the majority of the Althing decided to drop the revision plan and request the Danish government to submit a plan for revision, but this was also rejected. There followed a deadlock in the Althing which was unexpectedly resolved in 1901 when a liberal government finally came to power in Denmark and appointed a Danish minister for Iceland. In 1903 a government proposal providing for an Icelandic minister to reside in Reykjavík was passed both by the whole electorate and the Althing.

On 1 February 1904 Iceland received home rule, according to the revised constitution, which stipulated that the minister should be able to speak and write Icelandic, should take part in the deliberations of the Althing, and should be responsible to it for all his official acts. From time to time he should go to Copenhagen to bring before the king in cabinet meetings bills and other important matters. The Althing was to assemble every second year and to consist of forty members, thirty-four elected by the people, and six, as before, appointed by the king. There were still to be two branches, an upper one with fourteen members, and a lower one with twenty-six.

The first Icelandic minister under home rule was Hannes Hafstein (1861-1922), a renowned poet and one of the early proponents of Realism in Icelandic literature. In statesmanship he was second only to Jón Sigurdsson in recent Icelandic history, an impressive personality with considerable charm, and an inspired leader with a keen sense of the practical. In his five-year reign he brought about much-needed improvements in education, health services, commerce and communications, inaugurating a telegraph and telephone service (1905) in the face of vehement opposition from his political adversaries.

The first decade of Icelandic home rule was characterized by regrettable political turmoil. There were many factions, ever-changing alliances and bitter feuds, bringing out the political immaturity and inexperience of many of the leaders as well as their personal ambitions, which often clashed with the country's true interests. In 1908 Hannes Hafstein and a committee of six other representatives, appointed by all the main parties in the Althing, went to Copenhagen to confer with a commission of thirteen parliamentary representatives with a view to drafting a law defining Iceland's position in the union. A satisfactory agreement was reached, giving Iceland much the same status as was finally attained in 1918. Only one of the Icelandic representatives refused at the last moment to sign the agreement. The news of this important event was followed by great political agitation in Iceland, with the result that in the general elections of September 1908, the first in Iceland in which the Australian system of secret ballot was used, the opponents of the proposed measure were victorious, gaining twenty-four seats in the Althing against ten for its supporters, while the six members appointed by the king were in agreement with the measure. Hannes Hafstein resigned in April 1909 (he served again briefly in 1918), but the ministers taking his place, one after the other, made no headway, and there the matter rested until 1918. In that year the international situation prevailing at the end of the Great War led the Danish government finally to settle the issue with the Icelanders to the satisfaction of both parties.

On 1 December 1918 Iceland became a sovereign state in personal union with Denmark, and received its own national flag, after a plebiscite in which 12,040 votes were cast in favour of the Act of union, and only 897 voted against. In the Althing two of the forty members voted against the Act. The two states, Iceland and Denmark, were to have a common king, and Denmark undertook the common defence as well as the handling of foreign affairs.

Citizens of the two states had equal rights in both countries. The Act was to be valid until the end of 1940, after which the Althing or the Rigsdag could ask for a revision. If a new agreement had not been reached within three years of that date, either party could by unilateral declaration make the Act of union void. This was the final step before full independence in 1944.

Meanwhile the University of Iceland had been established on Jón Sigurdsson's centenary, 17 June 1911, consisting of four faculties, three of which had already been in existence for some time (a school of jurisprudence since 1908). In 1914 another important step was taken with the formation of the Iceland Steamship Company, thus enabling the Icelanders to transport goods and people across the Atlantic independently. The Company's first vessel was the *Gullfoss*. A trade school had been founded in Reykjavík in 1904, a commercial college in 1905, a teachers' college in 1908 and a co-operative college in 1918. In the first quarter of the century great strides were taken in education, the number of schools of all kinds increasing rapidly. Since the eighteenth century, however, illiteracy had been non-existent in Iceland. A number of able scholars and scientists made their valuable contributions. Finnur Jónsson (1858-1919), Björn M. Ólsen (1850-1919), the first rector of the University of Iceland, and Sigurdur Nordal (1886-1974) were the outstanding philologists and literary historians (Old Icelandic), while Bjarni Saemundsson (1867-1940) and Stefán Stefánsson (1863-1921) wrote, respectively, important zoological and botanical works. Thorvaldur Thoroddsen (1855-1921) and Helgi Pétursson (1872-1949) were pioneers in Icelandic geological study, the latter also being Iceland's only truly original philosopher.

In literature Romanticism was for a while superseded by Realism, which first reached Iceland in 1882 through the annual *Verdandi*, published by a group of students in Copenhagen who had come under the spell of the literary historian Georg Brandes: Hannes Hafstein, Gestur Pálsson, Einar Kvaran and Bertil Thorleifsson (1857-60). Gestur Pálsson (1852-91) wrote some short stories concerned with social protest which have become classics. Einar Kvaran (1859-1938) was also active in politics and journalism.

Apart from the *Verdandi* group, there were several authors in Iceland writing in more or less the same vein, without adhering closely to any literary creed. In prose three stand out: Thorgils Gjallandi (1851-1915), a farmer who wrote (in 1902) the first novel of high quality after Jón Thoroddsen; Gudmundur Fridjónsson (1869-1944), another farmer; and Jón Trausti (1873-1918), a printer who wrote magnificent novels dealing with life in Iceland during the eighteenth and nineteenth centuries, a direct precursor of Halldór Laxness.

In poetry the range was wider and the production much greater. Space only allows us to mention the three most important poets. Thorstein Erlingsson (1858-1914) at once a polished satirist and a lyrical nature poet; perhaps the first socialist in Icelandic poetry. Stephan G. Stephansson (1853-1927) went to Canada at the age of twenty and worked hard as a farmer all his life in very adverse circumstances, but he also became a prolific radical and idealistic poet of great range and depth, writing all his works in Icelandic. He is among Iceland's greatest poets. Einar Benediktsson (1864-1940) was the cosmopolitan *par excellence* in Icelandic literature, although he had deep roots in national culture and traditions. He was a great visionary and the herald of a new age. He was one of the most insistent advocates of the new technological age, flashing vivid visions of the great future awaiting Iceland once the power of the waterfalls had been harnessed. Einar Benediktsson was a great entrepreneur and adventurer, living like a king in foreign countries for many years, making titanic efforts to raise foreign capital to harness water power, exploit mines and further trade. He was already a legend in his lifetime—reputed, among other achievements, to have sold the *Aurora Borealis* to an American businessman. Appropriately, he is buried in the National Cemetery at Thingvellir along with Jónas Hallgrímsson, whose bones were brought home from Copenhagen after the Second World War.

Just after the turn of the century a number of promising young writers, finding it too difficult to make a living in Iceland, emigrated to Denmark and found a large public in Scandinavia. The first of these was Jóhann Sigurjónsson (1880-1919), a dramatist—author of *Eyvind of the Hills,* based on the story of an Icelandic outlaw of the eighteenth century and made into a film in Sweden by Victor Sjöström—and the first modernist in Icelandic poetry. Others were Jónas Gudlaugsson (1887-1916), Gudmundur Kamban (1888-1945), and Gunnar Gunnarsson (1889-1975), who wrote a large number of books, mainly novels, some of which placed him in the front rank of Scandinavian authors in this century. All the authors who emigrated to Denmark also wrote some of their works in Icelandic and translated others from one language to the other. One Icelandic author writing in German gained considerable renown for books about his boyhood experiences in the north of Iceland: he was Jón Svensson, or Nonni (1857-1944), a Jesuit scholar and teacher.

The First World War and the years after may be said to mark a turning-point in Icelandic literature, both poetry and prose. The attainment of sovereignty was not only of paramount importance in political, social and economic matters, but it also gave rise to a new cultural flowering, mainly in literature and the fine arts, a subject to which we return in Chapter 8.

Notes

1. Q uoted from Knut Gjerset, *History of Iceland,* New York 1925, pp. 326-7.
2. Op. cit., pp. 327-8.
3. Op. cit., p. 328.

PART THREE

THE REPUBLIC OF ICELAND

6. The Modern Nation-State: Politics and Society

The Coming of Statehood

It is convenient, although arbitrary, to talk of a 'new age' beginning with the establishment of the Republic of Iceland on 17 June 1944. Iceland had been a sovereign state since 1918 and largely autonomous since 1904, and it is arguable that the nation simply recuperated, with the renaissance of the nineteenth century. In a nation's history there are few meaningful landmarks dividing one age from another. There was a gradual loss of independence after 1262, and a gradual reconquest of it after about 1845.

However, 1944 must be considered as symbolically the most important year in Iceland's political history, even though it represents no very radical change in the political development of the nation, for it stands at the beginning of an entirely new age in terms of economic and cultural development. With the Second World War the country's isolation came to an abrupt and rather uncomfortable end. Iceland was thrown, largely unprepared, into the maelstrom of international affairs with all the attendant complications, problems and dangers. In a sense the Icelanders finally came of age in this period.

In the years 1918–44 there had been some notable events. A new constitution was adopted in 1920, and in the same year an Icelandic minister plenipotentiary was accredited to Copenhagen. Also in 1920 a Supreme Court was established with five judges. After 1919 the Icelanders gradually took over the surveillance of their territorial waters with their own coastguard.

The most spectacular single event of the period was the celebration of the Althing's millenium in 1930, which lasted three days and in which some 40,000 Icelanders participated. It was the largest gathering ever to congregate on Icelandic soil. King Christian X of Denmark and Iceland (he had also visited the country in 1921 and 1926) and Crown Prince Gustav Adolf of Sweden attended, and there were numerous government and parliamentary delegations from Nordic and other countries including Britain, France, Germany, the United States, Canada, the Netherlands and Czechoslovakia. The US Congress presented the statue of Leif Erikson sculpted by Sterling Calder (father of the pioneer of mobile sculpture, Alexander Calder), which now stands near the old centre of Reykjavík. In connection with the festivities the first modern hotel was opened in Reykjavík, the Hotel Borg.

In the half dozen years preceding the millennial festivities there had been a marked boost to the economic life of the country, but soon afterwards the Great Depression set in, and dominated the whole of the next decade up to 1940, when Iceland was occupied by British forces. With the German occupation of Denmark on 9 April 1940, all connection between Denmark and Iceland was instantly severed. The Icelanders therefore had to take immediate steps to meet the situation. On 10 April 1940 the Althing unanimously adopted the following resolution:

'Seeing that the situation which has been created makes it impossible for the king of Iceland to exercise the powers assigned to him by the constitution, the Althing announces that for the present it commits the exercise of these powers to the government of Iceland.' On the same day the Althing decided that '... Denmark is not in a position to execute the authority to take charge of the foreign affairs of Iceland ... nor can she carry out the fishery inspection within Icelandic waters ... therefore the Althing declares that Iceland will for the time being take entire charge of said affairs.' In the following year the Althing elected a regent for one year at a time to discharge the duties assigned to the king by the constitution. This new status of Iceland which was in force until the Republic was established was recognized by the governments with which Iceland was in contact during the war.

On 17 May 1941 the Althing unanimously adopted the following resolution:

The Althing resolves to declare that it considers Iceland to have acquired the right to a complete breaking off of the union with Denmark, since it has now had to take into its own hands the conduct of all its affairs, Denmark being no longer able to deal with those matters which it undertook to deal with on behalf of Iceland in accordance with the act of union with Denmark: that on the part of Iceland there is no question of renewing the Act of Union with Denmark, although it is not considered opportune at the present time, on account of the prevailing situation, to proceed to a formal dissolution of the union and the settling of a final constitution for the country, this however not to be delayed longer than the end of the war.

On the same day the Althing resolved 'to declare its will that a republic be established in Iceland as soon as the union with Denmark is formally terminated'. These resolutions were sent to the king and the Danish government. The matter was taken up again in 1944, when the three-year period prescribed by the Act of Union (see p. 136) came to a close. On 25 February 1944 the Althing unanimously adopted the following resolution: 'The Althing resolves to declare that the Danish-Icelandic Act of Union of 1918 is terminated.' This resolution was then to be submitted to a plebiscite and, if approved, would take effect as soon as the Althing had again voted on it. On 8 March the Althing adopted a constitution for the Republic of Iceland which was also to be submitted to a plebiscite. The voting on both these measures took place on 20-23 May 1944. Of the voters 98·61 per cent came to the polls, and 97·35 per cent of the votes cast were in favour of the proposal to terminate the union with Denmark, while 95·04 per cent approved of the constitution.

On 16 June the Althing confirmed the results of the plebiscite by two resolutions which were unanimously adopted. The formal establishment of the Republic of Iceland then took place at Thingvellir, on Lögberg (the Mount of Laws), on 17 June 1944, the birthday of Jón Sigurdsson. On the same day the president of the new republic was elected by the Althing to a four-year term. The choice fell on Sveinn Björnsson (1881-1952) who had been the Icelandic minister to Copenhagen from 1920 and the regent of Iceland from 1941. Greetings and good wishes to the Icelandic people were conveyed by special official representatives of the United States, Britain, Norway, Sweden and Free France. The ambassador of the Soviet Union, which had recognized the Republic, was also present. Later in the day, after the formal ceremony was over, a telegram arrived from King Christian X expressing his best wishes to the people of Iceland and the hope that the bonds of friendship between Iceland and the other Nordic countries might remain strong. It has to be said that for a long time many Danes were embittered by the way in which the dissolution of the union was handled, while they were themselves under Nazi occupation. Such feelings are now fortunately a thing of the past.

The proceedings at Thingvellir on 17 June 1944 took place in the open air, as in the old times. The day was cold and rainy, but nevertheless over 20,000 Icelanders assembled at this holiest of national shrines where so much of the nation's history had been enacted. When the foundation of the republic was formally declared by the president of the Althing, there were chimes from the old church at Thingvellir and a great hush fell on the crowd. Throughout the country the chimes echoed over the radio to which the rest of the population listened intently. It was an occasion never to be forgotten by those who experienced it.

Three decades later, on 27 July 1974, another great event took place at Thingvellir when the nation celebrated the 1100th anniversary of the settlement of Iceland. It was one of the brightest ⸜ and hottest days for many years, and the crowd exceeded 50,000, almost a quarter of the whole nation, even though the event was televised and broadcast by radio. The 'national poet' Tómas Gudmundsson read a long poem composed for the occasion, and the main speakers were the Nobel Prize laureate Halldór Laxness and the President of Iceland, Dr Kristján Eldjárn, a distinguished archeologist. On 27 July the Althing, assembled at Thingvellir, passed a resolution allotting a large sum of money to stopping the erosion of the island and on reclamation of what had been lost already. The anniversary year saw the 'ring road' around Iceland at last completed with the bridging of the many dangerous and fickle glacial rivers in the south-east. This last stretch of some twenty miles shortened by three-quarters the route from Reykjavík to the south-east.

The celebrations in 1974 were attended by many 'Western Icelanders' (Canadians of Icelandic descent), who have kept alive Icelandic culture and language through three generations, and still publish an Icelandic weekly in Manitoba. A year later they in turn were visited by groups of Icelanders when they celebrated the centenary of the first Icelandic settlement in Canada.

World War and Cold War—International Relations

On 10 May 1940, exactly one month after the Icelanders had taken full charge of their affairs, their country was occupied by British forces. Faced with the fact that one established method of Nazi strategy was the invasion of any potentially useful neutral state, the British government decided to anticipate the Germans in Iceland. There was no Icelandic army, navy or air force, and there were no means of preventing the use of Icelandic ports by German warships and seaplanes, and so the British forces moved in. They did not interfere with the administration of the country beyond what was deemed absolutely necessary from the military point of view.

The war had far-reaching effects on Iceland. The foreign forces were quite numerous and were stationed all over the island. Construction of roads, army camps and other installations required vast manpower, and suddenly there was full employment throughout the country with ample opportunities to earn easy money quickly. Wealth increased rapidly and an inflation set in. The standard of living rose steeply. But this new situation had obvious drawbacks, chief among them being a radical dislocation of traditional values and the demoralizing effect of easy money. The result was a kind of *nouveau riche* vulgarity which had been almost unknown before the war.

In late June 1941 the British minister announced to the Icelandic government that the British forces in Iceland were required elsewhere, but at the same time stressed the necessity of having Iceland well protected. The president of the United States had also stated that for the security of the Western Hemisphere he was prepared to send forces to Iceland to replace the British. An agreement to that effect was made between Iceland and the United States on 8 July 1941, after which American forces moved in and remained indefinitely, even though there was an interval between the autumn of 1946 and the spring of 1951.

The American government in 1946 asked for permission to keep three military bases in Iceland for a period of ninety-nine years, even though the agreement of 1941 had explicity stated that it would withdraw all its military forces as soon as the war was over. This request was unanimously rejected by the Althing. However, after violent debates in the Althing and at public meetings all over the country, the two governments entered into an agreement on the use of the Keflavík Airport which stipulated that the Americans should have the use of the airfield as a staging-post for its transport aircraft, necessitated by the occupation of Germany. To many Icelanders this merely meant that the armed forces had changed into civilian clothes.

When the North Altantic Treaty Organization (NATO) was formed in 1949, Iceland became one of its founder-members—again after a spell of violent debates and strong opposition from the Left. This happened partly through pressure from the Norwegian government which did not under any circumstances want foreign troops on its soil. In the treaty between Iceland and NATO it was unequivocally stated that no military forces would be stationed in the country in peacetime. However, two years later, on 5 May 1951, a new secret agreement was made concerning the 'defence of Iceland' which was only revealed to the Althing when it met the following autumn, after US forces had long since moved in and settled at the Keflavík Airport. In a preamble to this agreement it is stated that Iceland cannot defend herself alone, and that in an unstable world situation her lack of defences exposes her and her peace-loving neighbours to dangers—a reference to the Korean War on the other side of the globe. The agreement provides that Iceland shall allow the United States military facilities for the maintenance of the peace and safety of the country itself and the region covered by the North Atlantic Treaty. Since 1951 there has been a military contingent at the Keflavík base and at various strategic points around the country. Thus the neutrality so clearly stated in the constitution of 1920 was once and for all abolished. The question of the American military presence in Iceland has, more than any other issue, divided the nation into two opposing camps and has entirely destroyed the national unity which existed for the first few years after the founding of the Republic.

One of the expensive items on the budget of a modern state is foreign representation. At present Iceland has diplomatic relations with fifty-two countries and has nine embassies abroad: in Belgium, Denmark, West Germany, France, Norway, the Soviet Union, Sweden, the United Kingdom and the United States. The nine ambassadors accredited to these countries are concurrently accredited to the other countries with which Iceland has diplomatic relations. There are also permanent delegations at several international organizations of which Iceland is a full or partial member: the United Nations, NATO, the EEC, EFTA, UNESCO and the Council of Europe. In addition to the diplomatic missions Iceland has honorary consular representatives in about 125 places all over the world.

Beside the international bodies already mentioned, Iceland is a member of the Nordic Council, OECD and several organizations affiliated to the United Nations, such as the International Monetary Fund, the International Bank for Reconstruction and Development, the International Finance Corporation, the International Development Association, the World Health Organization, the Food and Agricultural Organization and the International Labour Organization. Iceland also joined the General Agreement on Tariffs and Trade (GATT).

Since 1944 Iceland has been involved in four international disputes, all of them concerning the extension of the country's fishery limits: to four miles in 1952, to twelve miles in 1958, to fifty miles in 1972, and to 200 miles in 1975. These disputes have generally gone by the name of 'Cod Wars'. The main opponent in all of them was the United Kingdom, but West Germany, Belgium and other countries have also been party to some of them. There have been clashes at sea, especially when the British government sent warships to protect British fishing vessels, but only one life has been lost, that of an Icelandic coastguard officer. The first three disputes were settled by temporary agreements, and the fourth one found the same solution in 1976.

Government and Public Finance

Political life in Iceland is traditionally rather turbulent and unstable, in contrast to the three Scandinavian countries. Few governments stay in power for the full four-year term allowed by the constitution between general elections (the only exceptions being 1934–42 and 1959–71). There were four political parties in the Althing until 1969, when a fifth was added by a splinter group from one of them. In order of their strength they are: the

Independence Party (conservative), founded in 1929 after a merger of the Conservative Party and the small Liberal Party; the Progressive Party (agrarian-centre), founded in 1916; the People's Alliance (socialist), founded in 1968; the Social Democratic Party, founded in 1916, and the Union of Liberals and Leftists, founded in 1969. A Communist Party was founded in 1930, but in 1938 it merged with the left wing of the Social Democrats to form the United People's Socialist Party, which in 1956 formed a loosely connected electoral alliance with a new left wing of the Social Democrats after yet another schism in their party, under the title People's Alliance which was turned into a full-fledged party in 1968, carrying the same name, while a splinter group formed the Union of Liberals and Leftists—all rather complicated.

According to the constitution the President of the Republic is elected for four years by a plebiscite and has functions similar to those of constitutional monarchs (the presidential election in 1944 was an exception to this rule). It has become a custom or an unwritten law that the President can remain in office as long as he chooses, that is until he resigns or dies; a President in office has never been opposed by a rival candidate, if he wished to stand for re-election after the prescribed four-year term. Thus there have only been three Presidents since 1944, the last one elected in 1968.

The cabinet is led by the Prime Minister who forms the government. Cabinet ministers have a seat in the Althing by virtue of their office, but non-elected cabinet ministers are very rare; they have the right to vote only if they are elected members. Most ministers hold more than one portfolio. There has never in the history of the Republic been a one-party majority government, but always coalitions or rarely minority governments.

Since the constitutional reform in 1959 the Althing consists of sixty members elected for four years. There are eight electoral districts, each represented by five or six members, except for Reykjavík which elects twelve members. Forty-nine members are returned by the electoral districts, while eleven seats are allocated to the parties which are, proportionally, not fully represented. Suffrage is universal for all Icelandic subjects over the age of twenty.

In all there are 224 local and municipal bodies. Each district has its own council in which every parish has one representative. In municipal councils the number of representatives varies from seven to fifteen, but parish councils have three to seven members.

Considering that the entire population of Iceland is roughly that of a medium-sized city in other countries, it will be realized what tremendous efforts are needed for the Icelanders to run a modern state with its institutions, foreign representation and all the other necessary trappings. Outside observers often wonder how this is possible, and it is indeed expensive for such a tiny group of people. But one important factor in all such considerations is the absence of military expenditure, a heavy burden on most states. There are various ways of financing the non-profitable institutions. A special entertainment tax (on dances, cinemas, etc.) goes to the maintenance of the Symphony Orchestra, the National Theatre, and local theatres around the country. Fines imposed for infringement of the liquor laws and from the sale of confiscated liquor as well as for unseemly conduct in public go to the Cultural Fund, founded in 1928, which grants certain kinds of stipends and runs a publishing enterprise. A national lottery, begun in 1933, provided the funds required to build the University of Iceland, completed in 1940, and still finances all the University's building expenses. Many other institutions, mostly humanitarian, have used lotteries for the same purpose. The State Broadcasting Service (radio and television) is largely self-supporting, securing much of its revenue through advertising. Various other institutions are also self-supporting, while others, like the National Library, the National Museum, the State Art Gallery, the People's Art Gallery, the Natural History Museum, etc., have to be subsidized.

Demographic Trends

In 1880 there were only three towns in Iceland, where 5 per cent of the population lived. In 1900, out of a total population of 79,000, the towns still only accounted for 11·4 per cent. By 1920 about 43 per cent of the population lived in towns and villages with more than 200 inhabitants. By 1973 there were nineteen towns and thirty-seven villages where 86·2 per cent of the population lived, leaving only 13·8 per cent in rural districts. In 1925 the population of Iceland passed the 100,000 mark, and in 1967 it reached 200,000. At that time the inhabitants of Reykjavík numbered a little over 80,000.

The population of Iceland has thus risen very rapidly during the last decades, because the birth rate is about 28 per thousand and the death rate only 7 per thousand—a rise of more than 2 per cent, which is twice that of the other Nordic countries. Infant mortality is also lower than in most countries, i.e. some fifteen per 1,000 births. Illegitimacy is higher in Iceland than in other European countries, or about 30 per cent, but a large number of such children are later legitimized by the marriage of their parents. In a large number of cases parents live together without formal marriage. The average life expectancy for men is seventy-one years and for women seventy-five. There are about 2,000 more males than females.

Administration of Justice

The judicial power in Iceland rests with local courts and the Supreme Court, established in 1920. The country is divided into seventeen districts and counties, each of which is administered by a district magistrate, and nineteen towns, each administered by a town magistrate. In Reykjavík there is a special judge for the lower criminal court and another for the civil court. There are also special courts consisting of an ordinary lower court judge and lay judges, for instance the Maritime and Commercial Court, the Labour Court, etc. Other special courts are organized on different lines, the most important being the High Court of State, which delivers judgment in first and last instance in cases brought against cabinet ministers in connection with the discharge of their official duties. There are fifteen members, partly chosen from district and town councils. This august court has never been convened since it was established seventy years ago, which is not to say that cabinet ministers in Iceland are paragons of virtue, but rather indicates the high degree of political corruption among the Icelanders and their total indifference to the behaviour of their political leaders. The Ecclesiastical Court is a special court of appeal consisting of three judges from the Supreme Court and two ecclesiastical members. It passes judgment in the last instance in cases under its jurisdiction. Juries are not employed in Iceland. The office of State Prosecutor was created in 1961. The judges of the Supreme Court and the regular district judges are appointed 'for life', that is to say they can hold office until the age of 65–70 and cannot be removed from office except by a court judgment.

Organised Religion

The Evangelical Lutheran Church has been the Established Church of Iceland since the middle of the sixteenth century, though there has been complete religious freedom during the past century. About 97 per cent of the population are members of the Lutheran Church. There are also free-church members (Lutheran), a small Roman Catholic congregation, and a number of non-conformists, especially in the towns. The Roman Catholics and some of the non-conformist congregations, like the Seventh Day Adventists and Pentecostalists, have been recognized by the government and have the right to solemnize marriages and perform other clerical offices which are valid according to Icelandic law.

A strange chapter was added to the religious life of Iceland when a handful of zealots for the resurrection of the old pagan cult of Ásatrú secured official recognition on 16 May 1973, and set about organizing their sect. Their 'chief priest', *allsherjargodi,* has been legally empowered to give names to children, consecrate adolescents, marry the living and bury the dead, but the adherents of our ancestral gods have met great obstacles when trying to secure a piece of ground on which to build their temple and a separate plot to make their own graveyard. The first official outdoor *blót* ('sacrifice') in Iceland since the year 1000 was celebrated in August 1973 in Borgarfjördur, in ancient times the district of Egil Skallagrímsson, some 150 km. north of Reykjavík. It was held in front of a large plaster effigy of Thór.

Iceland forms one bishopric with its see in Reykjavík, which is divided into fifteen District Assemblies, each supervised by a Dean. There are 287 congregations served by about 110 ministers. There are two honorary vice-bishops (both doing ordinary clerical work), one for each of the old dioceses, who ordain clergy in the absence of the Bishop and have the authority to consecrate a new Bishop, if the former one has died or cannot for some other reason consecrate his successor. Both the Bishop and the clergy are public officials and must retire at the prescribed age of 65-70. Clergy receive salaries from the government, but are also paid fees by parishioners for performing special offices. The supreme authority in the Church is the President of Iceland. He delegates powers to the minister of justice and ecclesiastical affairs who along with the Althing governs the Church in non-religious matters. In religious affairs the Bishop of Iceland is the supreme authority together with the Synodical Conference, the Church Assembly (of laymen and ministers), and the Executive Council of the Church Assembly.

Among the prescribed duties of Icelandic clergymen is the exact formal recording of all births, deaths, and marriages, since the church registers are the only official records of such events. Every year they also take the census in their parishes, except in the larger towns, where it is the responsibility of the municipal authorities.

Broadcasting

The State Broadcasting Service came into being in 1930 and has a monopoly of broadcasting. Every radio or television owner has to pay an annual tax to the Broadcasting Service, but is entitled to use more than one set of either radio or television. Television has been operating since 1966 under the auspices of the State Broadcasting Service, but it is an independent institution owned by the state. Since 1961 an American TV station, which was initiated in 1955, has reached the larger part of the Icelandic population, having been vastly enlarged, although it was licensed only as a service to the American base personnel. This created bitter controversy which lasted for many years: the country's intellectuals were in the forefront attacking this flagrant breach of existing laws and the opening up of the whole society to a very one-sided foreign influence. This had nothing to do with isolationism, as many of the propagandists for the army station maintained, but rather a demand for more variety in foreign influences and a protest against the outrageous fact that such an undeniably potent manipulator of public opinion as television should be run by a foreign military power within the country, but outside Icelandic laws and regulations. The effect of the American station was particularly apparent during the Vietnam war, when only the official US government views were presented. The controversy did not subside until the military authorities at Keflavík decided to make arrangements to limit the range of their TV station. Directly and indirectly this touchy issue was the reason why Icelandic television was established with a programme of two to four hours six days a week, while the army station had a programme of seven hours on weekdays and up to fourteen hours at weekends.

The State Broadcasting Service runs a 100 kW long-wave station in Reykjavík, but there are relay stations in various parts of the country, one long-wave station in East Iceland and twenty-seven smaller relay stations broadcasting on medium wave and FM. In addition there are short-wave and morse broadcasts for weather forecasting and general news for Icelandic ships. There is a single daily programme on the radio of about sixteen and a half hours, broadcasting in Icelandic; it can be heard by the entire population, even though people in East Iceland often complain of poor service.

The extension of the television network around the country is almost completed, with some 97 per cent of the population now able to receive the broadcasts. There are nine transmitters and fifty-nine smaller relay stations. The weekly television programme amounts to some twenty-four hours (Thursday is the day of relief), of which about 30 per cent is Icelandic material, while the rest comes from other countries, mainly (over 40 per cent) from the Anglo-Saxon world. The small proportion of Icelandic material is due to lack of funds and personnel. One only needs to compare Norwegian television with twelve times as many employees as its Icelandic counterpart but with a daily transmission that is only a little longer. The foreign programmes are either dubbed or subtitled. There are some 64,000 radio licence holders in the country and some 48,000 television licence holders.

Advertisements on radio and television are not sandwiched between items on the programme, but read at fixed hours, six times a day on the radio and twice each evening on television. Programme time for advertising is not for sale, and the radio

authorities exercise censorship over advertisements. Some things
may not be advertised either on the air or in newspapers, among
them medicines, cigarettes and alcoholic drinks. Advertisements
containing propaganda or biased comparisons between commodities or other articles for sale are forbidden. So are notices about the
contents of political papers and meetings.

Every morning Icelandic radio broadcasts résumés of the
editorials of all political papers in the country, and the
deliberations of the Althing are extensively reported while it is in
session. The Althing has the unequivocal right to radio time
whenever it pleases. This usually happens once or twice every
session, and the broadcast debates go on for two whole consecutive
evenings. At one time it was quite common for funeral services to
be broadcast over the radio, but this is less frequent nowadays and
reserved for well-known citizens. But every Sunday morning at
1100 there is a religious service on the radio.

Complete impartiality in politics, public debates and disputes,
opinions, faiths and sects, associations and individuals is the
working rule of the State Broadcasting Service, a rule which it
often proves difficult to observe and is in any case a tiresome brake
on open and serious discussion. In the spoken part of the
programme lectures of all kinds are most common (more so than in
the other Nordic countries), followed in frequency by readings
from fiction and poetry. Radio plays are presented once a week,
and there are usually one or two serial plays on other weekdays
throughout the winter.

The staff of the State Broadcasting Service, including
programme personnel and technicians, numbered 244 in 1973, 119
in radio and 125 in television. The executive board is composed of
a permanent director, appointed by the President of the Republic,
and three managers—of finance, radio and television—appointed
by the Minister of Education, whose ministry controls the Broadcasting Service. There is also a seven-man Council, elected after
every parliamentary election and divided proportionately between
the political parties. Its chairman is appointed by the Minister of
Education. The Council decides and supervises the programme
policies of both radio and television and monitors the impartiality
of both services.

Education

Educational standards have long been high in Iceland. Illiteracy
has been non-existent since the latter part of the eighteenth
century. From that time the duty of providing elementary
education rested with the household under the strict supervision of

the local clergyman. Literacy was one of the conditions for receiving confirmation at the age of fourteen.

Under the Public Elementary Education Act of 1907 school attendance was made compulsory for children between the ages of ten and fourteen, parents being required to provide preparatory instruction up to the age of ten. In 1926 local educational authorities were permitted to extend the compulsion to children between the ages of seven and ten, and in 1936 all children of between seven and fourteen inclusive were obliged to attend school. Only in some remote districts have there been modifications to this rule. Since 1946 compulsory attendance covers the ages between seven and fifteen. Children aged seven to thirteen attend primary school, after which they enter the lower stage of the secondary school. This lower stage, which is closely related to the primary level, provides general education to the age-groups from thirteen to sixteen or seventeen, and sometimes for an additional one or two years if the school has a continuation division. But only the first two years of this stage are compulsory. The upper stage of the secondary school comprises grammar schools (gymnasia), which provide advanced general education, and various special and vocational schools. Higher education is provided by the University of Iceland and the Teacher Training College. The Technical College and the College of Agriculture (at Hvanneyri in Borgarfjördur) may also be said to provide higher education.

There is a primary school in nearly every community in the country. In 1971–2 there were 199 such schools with 27,727 pupils. In rural districts, where bus transport is not feasible, boarding schools are the commonest solution, and of these fifty were operating in 1971–2. In some sparsely populated areas instruction is given by travelling teachers, who spend one to three weeks on different farms, teaching the children there along with those of the nearest neighbouring farms. This old scheme has gradually been replaced by boarding schools; in 1971–2 there were only eight school-districts with teaching of this type. For younger children (aged seven to nine) in rural districts there are in many cases 'alternate teaching schemes', often owing to lack of space, facilities or staff, in which the children spend alternately 1–2 weeks at school and at home. Normally the school year lasts nine months in towns and large villages, from early September to late May. In small villages it lasts eight months and in rural districts seven or eight months. Where the 'alternate teaching scheme' is applied, the children get about three-and-a-half to four months of formal schooling a year.

In 1971–2 there were 132 secondary schools at the lower compulsory stage. The Ministry of Education publishes a common syllabus for the compulsory stage. The following subjects must be taught: Icelandic (language, literature and history), Danish, English, mathematics, Christian religion, social studies, history, geography, biology, physics-chemistry, handicrafts, domestic science, writing, art, music and physical education. Except for English and domestic science, these subjects are roughly the same as those taught in the primary school, but the standard is higher.

In grades 9 and 10, following compulsory education, there are two main sections. First, the *general section* may be subdivided into (*a*) an advanced theoretical sub-section, only provided in grade 9, which is a specialized preparatory section for those aiming at higher education, (*b*) a general sub-section, mainly for those completing their lower secondary studies without a practical emphasis, (*c*) a commercial sub-section providing instruction in some practical subjects connected with clerical work. The *practical section* emphasizes some manual subjects such as sewing, fishing techniques, carpentry, etc. This section may be divided according to the relative emphasis on these subjects.

State-controlled examinations are held at the end of grades 9 and 10. The examination after grade 9 covers the whole of the advanced theoretical sub-section. Until 1969 entrance to the grammar school (gymnasium) was virtually controlled by this examination, with an average of 6 on a 10 scale as the pass-mark. About 35 per cent of each age group usually try this examination, approximately 70 per cent (or about 25 per cent of each age-group) passing it. Since 1969 there has also been a state-controlled examination of the end of grade 10, covering four theoretical subjects and granting admission to various secondary schools of the upper stage, including grammar schools if the average mark is high. There is also a channel into grammar schools through continuation divisions where they exist. In 1971-2 there were thirteen schools with continuation divisions, only three of which, however, had both grades 11 and 12.

Most of the general secondary schools of the lower stage do not have boarding facilities. There are, however, eight boarding schools in rural districts, which had 1,030 pupils in 1971-2. The ordinary school year for the general secondary school is eight to eight-and-a-half months.

The secondary schools of the upper stage can be grouped into six main categories: grammar schools, special vocational schools, technical schools, art and music schools, adult education courses and a folk high school.

In 1975 there were seven grammar schools in Iceland, three in Reykjavík, one in Kópavogur which adjoins Reykjavík, one at Laugarvatn in the south, one at Akureyri in the north, and one at Ísafjördur in the north-west. An eighth school is planned in the east. Two special schools, the Commercial College in Reykjavík and the Co-operative College in Borgarfjördur and Reykjavík, have divisions leading to the matriculation examination.

The special vocational schools include eleven domestic science schools, two schools of farming and agriculture, 16 vocational trade schools, a marine engineering school, two navigational schools, a school of catering, a fishing industry school, seven schools for hospital staff (including two training schools for nurses providing practical and theoretical courses lasting three years). There is a Technical College founded in 1964; four fine arts schools, of which the most important is the School of Arts and Crafts in Reykjavík; a Music Conservatory in Reykjavík and twenty-seven other schools providing music education in all parts of the country. Six municipalities offer evening courses in various subjects. A Correspondence School has been operated since 1940, first by the *Samband,* since 1965 also by the National Trade Union Federation, and since 1975 by four other country-wide organizations—the Farmers' Union, the Seamen's Union, the Union of State and Municipal Employees, and the Icelandic Women's Federation. Since 1972 a folk high school has been operated at Skálholt by the church. Finally, there are eleven special schools for the handicapped.

In 1971 the Teacher Training College achieved academic status, requiring the matriculation examination or a comparative education for entrance. The first students studying under this new scheme began their three-year course in 1971, while the last students under the old scheme graduated with a teacher's certificate in 1973. In 1971–2 there were 701 students in the Teacher Training College, the majority of them studying under the old scheme. There are other special schools for teacher training, for instance in physical education, domestic science, fine arts and handicrafts, music and pre-school teaching.

Academic education in the full sense did not begin in Iceland until 1847 with the formation of the Theological Seminary. This was augmented in 1876 by a Medical School and in 1908 by a School of Law. These three institutions were merged in 1911 when the University of Iceland was established on the centenary of the birth of Jón Sigurdsson, and a fourth faculty of Philosophy was added, primarily dealing with Icelandic studies, such as philology, literature and history. The University building was opened in 1940, since when there has been continuous expansion in building as well as educational departments. Departments of dental surgery and pharmacy were added in 1945 and 1957 respectively to the Faculty of Medicine. Economics, with the accent on business administration, was added to the Faculty of Law in 1941. In 1962 the Faculty of Business Administration became a separate department, as did the Faculty of Dentistry in 1972. The Faculty of Philosophy was extended in 1942 to cover a variety of new subjects, including modern languages, and again in 1971 to cover classical languages, geography, general history and literature, philosophy and psychology. In 1940 courses in engineering were begun at the University and a Faculty of Engineering was established in 1945. The courses covered only the first part of the full engineering curriculum at Scandinavian technical universities, compelling students to complete their studies abroad. In 1965 courses were initiated within the faculty in mathematics, physics, chemistry, biology, geology and geography, mainly for the training of secondary school teachers. In 1969 the department was renamed the Faculty of Engineering and Science, and in 1970 a new Bachelor of Science four-year course in engineering was initiated, as well as three-year courses in mathematics, physics, chemistry, biology, geology and geography. Finally, a Faculty of Social Sciences was set up in 1973. In the University's first academic year forty-five students were enrolled, in 1961 there were 799 students, and in 1971 the number was 1,928. In the latter year 626 students were pursuing their studies at foreign universities.

Various research and experimental institutions and stations work in close co-operation with the University. The University Library is the second largest in the country, after the National Library. A Manuscript Institute, officially named the Arnamagnæan Institute, was founded in 1967 after an agreement had been reached between Danish and Icelandic authorities, securing the return of the great bulk of the precious Icelandic manuscripts preserved in Copenhagen since the days of Árni Magnússon.

All education at the Icelandic state schools is free. A sizeable part of national expenditure, about 20 per cent, goes to the educational system. Nevertheless, the local municipalities and parishes defray much of the expenses of elementary and secondary education, though the salaries of teachers are mostly paid by the state. School boards organize local education and are a mixture of official and unofficial members. The chairman of each board is politically appointed by the Minister of Education, while other members are elected by town and parish councils. Of a population of little over 210,000, the total number of people under some kind of educational instruction is roughly 58,000—a high proportion.

Health and the Common Good

Social legislation in Iceland is on a par with that of the other Nordic countries. The first legislation for old-age insurance was enacted in 1890, partly replacing general poor relief which had been locally administered since the time of the Commonwealth.

With the growth of the fishing industry a law covering industrial insurance was passed in 1903, and one introducing sickness insurance followed in 1911. The first national plan for social insurance came into operation in 1936. It has frequently been revised and improved, and since 1947 it is compulsory for every citizen, covering old age, disability, industrial accidents, maternity benefits, sickness, children's annuities, family allowances and benefits to mothers and widows. Unemployment insurance was introduced in 1956. There is universal health insurance, including free hospitalization, but patients pay part of their doctor's bills and for most dental care, except for children from five to fifteen years of age who receive free treatment. In 1970 some 15·2 per cent of the national income went to the net social security expenditure in Iceland. Social insurance accounts for about 80 per cent of net social security expenditures and for an even higher percentage of the finance. The five branches of social insurance are: pensions, health, industrial injuries, family allowances and unemployment. These branches are administered and managed by the State Social Security Institute, which is supervised by a five-man Social Insurance Board elected by the Althing.

Old age pensions are paid to persons who have reached the age of sixty-seven. Disablement pension at the same rate as the old-age pension is paid to persons between the ages of sixteen and sixty-seven whose working capacity is reduced by at least 75 per cent. Every woman widowed before the age of sixty-seven is entitled to compensation payment for six months after the death of her husband and for a further twelve months if she has one child or more uner the age of seventeen to maintain. When the compensation period is over, the woman is entitled to a widow's pension, if she was aged fifty or over at her husband's death. A children's pension is paid until the child reaches the age of seventeen, if one of the parents is dead or receives a disablement pension. In addition, widows and single and divorced mothers receive a mother's allowance. Lastly, the pensions insurance pays a maternity grant for each confinement. Family allowances (general children's allowances) are paid to all children up to the age of sixteen who are resident in Iceland. Unemployment insurance covers members of trade unions in towns and villages with the exception of civil servants and the like.

Since 1972 the Government has borne 86 per cent of the pensions insurance, while employer's contributions cover 14 per cent. The cost of health insurance is divided between the state (90 per cent) and local authorities (10 per cent).

All matters of public health come under the Director of Health (surgeon-general), appointed by the Minister of Health. Certain parts of the central administration are delegated to chief medical officers, although still under the authority of the Director of Health. This applies to tuberculosis control, school hygiene and the supervision of sanitary control. District physicians supervise health work at the local level and act as experts to local authorities. At present (1975) the country is divided into fifty-seven medical districts, each served by a state-appointed district physician, except in Reykjavík where the city physician is appointed by the City Council. Fifteen of the medical districts have a population of over 2,000 (including four with 10,000–13,000 people, and one, Reykjavík, with some 85,000 inhabitants). The remaining forty-two districts have populations of less that 2,000, and about half of them less than 1,000. In 1970 the total number of registered doctors in Iceland was 308, that is a ratio of one to approximately 660 people. There were 101 dentists. In almost every district there is a trained midwife who is usually also entrusted with (compulsory) vaccinations against smallpox.

In 1970 there were twenty-five general hospitals in Iceland with a total of 1,400 beds. Included is these numbers are five small cottages or sick wards attached to district physicians' residences with four to nine beds each. Counting maternity homes, sick wards in old people's homes and rehabilitation institutions, the total number of hospital beds available was 2,575 or 12·6 beds per thousand inhabitants.

In former times infectious diseases like diphtheria, scarlet fever, measles and influenza often caused high mortality, and typhoid was quite prevalent in the first decades of this century. These diseases have now mostly been wiped out. No case of typhoid has been recorded since 1947, and the last death from it occurred in 1939. Diphtheria has been controlled through extensive immunization, no case having been notified since 1953. Poliomyelitis first recorded after 1900, used to rise to widespread epidemics approximately at ten-year intervals, with occasional small outbreaks in between. In 1956, after the last epidemic had subsided, large-scale vaccinations were initiated, and since then very few cases have been reported, the last two in 1966. In bygone ages the nosology of Iceland was characterized by the prevalence of two diseases, leprosy and hydatid disease. Now both are nearly extinct. As late as 1896 there were at least 237 lepers in Iceland, a frequency rate of 3·2 per thousand. A lepers' hospital was opened in 1898. To prevent the spread of hydatid disease public information on the mode of transmission was publicized, restrictions on keeping dogs were enforced, mainly with a view to keeping them from access to sheep offal, and annual anthelmintic treatment of all dogs initiated.

In the early decades of this century tuberculosis was one of the most common causes of death in Iceland, reaching a proportion of 200 per 100,000 in 1932. By 1940 the rate had declined to eighty-six and in 1950 was down to twenty. Since 1960, when it was down to three, the rate has been one to two deaths per 100,000, so that tuberculosis is now less common in Iceland than in any other European country. The main weapon against the disease was the wholesale X-raying of communities, so that it could be detected in its early stages. Iceland was in fact the first country in the world to X-ray its entire population as a move against tuberculosis. Other contributing factors were the improved general resistance of the population and the introduction of effective drugs.

On the other hand, cardio-vascular diseases and cancer have steadily increased during the last decades. In the period 1966–70 cardio-vascular diseases accounted for 46 per cent of all deaths, and cancer for 20 per cent. About two-thirds (66·3 per cent) of all deaths in 1966–70 occurred at ages of sixty-five years and over, 82·7 per cent at ages of fifty and over. Half a century earlier (1916–20) only 48·7 per cent of all deaths were those of people aged fifty and more. In 1966–70 accidents (poisoning and violence included) accounted for 9·2 per cent of deaths at all ages, but for 32·2 per cent of all deaths of people under fifty.

The Vegetarian Movement in Iceland has been quite active and runs a very fine and popular rest and convalescent centre at Hveragerdi, the natural hot-water town, making use of the hot springs to cultivate fresh vegetables and provide hot mud baths. The Red Cross of Iceland has been active in various fields, among other things providing town children with summer vacation homes in the countryside, but its most important work has been in helping to provide relief for children and other people in distress both in Iceland (in connection with natural catastrophes) and in many foreign countries.

The Temperance Movement started in Iceland in 1884 and has since become influential, with a membership of about 10,000. Prohibition was in force from 1909 to 1935, wines being exempted after 1922. Strong beer is still prohibited, although it is produced in the country for foreign embassies and the American military contingent at Keflavík.

The Suffragette Movement began in the late nineteenth century. Women were granted partial voting rights in local elections in 1882, and received full rights in 1908. Since 1915 they have enjoyed general suffrage. The Boy Scout Movement was founded in 1912, as an appendix to the YMCA which was founded in 1899, but it has since become an independent body with a membership of some 4,000. Youth Clubs began to be formed early in the century on Norwegian and Danish models, and played an important cultural and social role in rural districts in the first few decades, but more recently they have mostly been occupied with athletics. The National Life-Saving Association has branches all over Iceland and stations at various points around the coast. It has helped to save hundreds of foreign and Icelandic seamen, often under very hazardous circumstances.

The first trade union, a seamen's association, was founded in 1894, but the first union of skilled workers was the Icelandic Printers' Union, founded in 1897 (an earlier printers' union was founded in 1887, but only lasted a short time). During the First World War trade unions began to make themselves felt, and in 1916 the Icelandic Federation of Labour Unions was formed, simultaneously with the Social Democratic and the Progressive Parties. In the same year the Labour Movement got its first representative elected to the Althing. The Federation of Labour Unions now comprises some 140 unions with a combined membership of over 40,000. An Employers' Association was formed in 1934. Strikes have been frequent in recent decades. In 1960–72 some 14·3 per cent of the labour force was involved annually in strikes. The average duration of strikes per striking worker was 9·9 days. With the growing influence of the labour movement many laws have been passed to ensure the fair treatment of workers in every field, especially after 1930. Since 1964 every worker has a minimum vacation of twenty-one working days.

In this chapter[1] the aim has been to emphasize a few of the salient features of the political ans social organization of the Republic of Iceland. Much interesting material has had to be omitted for reasons of space, but we will return to the subject in other contexts in the following chapters. The Icelanders have undoubtedly come a long way since their fumbling efforts only a century ago to regain what had been lost six centuries earlier.

Note

1. Much of the factual material in this chapter is derived from *Iceland 874–1974,* a handbook published by the Central Bank of Iceland on the occasion of the eleventh centenary of the settlement of Iceland, Reykjavík.

7. The Icelanders

Fortunate island
Where all men are equal
But not vulgar—not yet

This *haiku* stanza from W. H. Auden's poem 'Iceland Revisited', written in 1964, expresses a significant fact in modern Icelandic society, the absence of class distinction. The conclusion of the last line may, however, be a matter of dispute, since many Icelanders feel and will concede that with the tremendous material progress after the Second World War and the consequent emergence of a sizeable *nouveau riche* class, a certain amount of vulgarity is to be detected in the larger industrial and commercial centres.

In general every Icelander feels as good as his neighbour and is conscious of his worth. The absence of class differences indicates a highly developed democracy, but more correctly it reflects an essentially aristocratic outlook, taking equality for granted without insisting on it, setting greater store by independence and individual excellence. Since most Icelanders are the children or grandchildren of ordinary farmers or seamen, there is constant movement between all walks of life and little feeling of inferiority among the so-called working classes. Indeed seamen and skilled labourers are on the whole better off economically than public officials and professionals. For instance, a skipper might make as much as $5,000 in a three-month herring season, when it was a good one, but such fabulous catches as in the herring boom of 1962-6 may not recur in the near future. Each Icelandic fisherman takes about 130 tons from the sea in a good year, which is six times more than in any other country.

Even though intellectuals are underpaid in Iceland, compared to other groups, this does not mean that they are less valued. On the contrary they are highly respected, since they are looked upon as the wardens of the cultural heritage. Every national culture has certain ideals by which it distinguishes itself from other cultures, ideals which give substance and significance to human aspirations and lend a certain pattern to the way of life and thinking of a people. The old ideals, embodied in the Sagas and in Eddic poetry, are still very much alive. The regard for renown after death is pronounced, coupled with a deep-felt reverence for what is most enduring in human endeavour: learning and artistic ability. To be sure, the man of action is highly esteemed, but the type closest to the heart of the Icelander is the creative individual, the poet, the painter, the composer and the scholar.

It is always a little facile and often misleading to make sweeping generalizations about national characteristics. Individuals of each nationality are so dissimilar that they rarely fit into neat categories. Still, there can be little doubt that nations have certain traits that distinguish them from one another. These traits have been developed and conditioned by heredity, history and natural environment.

It has been observed that a striking similarity exists between the Icelanders and the Greeks—an observation the present writer, who has a long-standing and intimate acquaintance with the Greeks, is inclined to support. Considering the history and physical environment of both these small nations, this is less strange than may seem at first glance. Both nations live in barren and mountainous countries, with scant vegetation and wide vistas, and both rely a great deal on the sea for their livelihood. Both boast of a 'Golden Age' early in their history, followed by long centuries of foreign domination, finally succeeded by independence with all its attendant problems. Both nations carry the burden of a glorious heritage, which makes their present endeavours seem inconsequential by comparison. These might be some of the reasons why Greeks and Icelanders strike the foreign observer as similar. The similarity is reflected in many ways. Both Greeks and Icelanders are fiercely individualistic, competitive and independent, intensely concerned about justice, extravagantly interested in politics, unruly citizens, restless and curious about other people, open to foreign influences but intent on preserving their own heritage, romantically attached to their barren lands, gay and carefree (sometimes to the extent of irresponsibility), generous and hospitable, but astute in matters of business. Admittedly, the Greeks are less reserved than the Icelanders when dealing with strangers, but once the ice has been broken Icelanders are quick to catch up with their Mediterranean counterparts. Another common feature is a strong clannish tendency wherever Greeks and Icelanders live abroad in any appreciable numbers.

In the literatures of many nations there are characters who, as it were, epitomize the salient characteristics of their people. Does not the character of Odysseus typify the prominent traits of the Greek psyche? Ever restless, shrewd and brilliant, capable of the deepest feeling, practical, consumed with curiosity, heroic, with the epithets of 'godlike' and 'much-enduring', who at moments of supreme peril will say to himself, 'My heart, you must endure. Worse things than this you have endured before now.' Similarly, the highly complex character of Egil Skallagrímsson (see pp. 85-6) may be said to embody some of the outstanding traits of the Icelandic spirit. Restless, fiercely independent and stubborn, a man of action and enterprise, proud and fearless, practical in money matters, quarrelsome and irreverent, with strong appetites for food and drink (especially the latter), a devout friend and loving father whose grief drives him to the verge of despair, but above all devoted to his art, the poetic craft which at once relieves him of his grief and ensures his 'immortality'. No other character in Icelandic literature brings out to such a degree those apparently contradictory traits which make up the 'national psyche' of the Icelanders.

Egil Skallagrímsson may be said to unite in one person the two kinds of 'culture heroes' revered by the Icelanders: on the one hand the individual of great artistic or intellectual accomplishment, poet, scholar or sage; on the other hand the man of action, the entrepreneur who has made his mark in business or some other mundane undertaking. There are other Icelanders who have also united these twin ideals in their person, for instance Snorri Sturluson (1178-1241) the poet, historian and politician; Hannes Hafstein (1861-1922) the poet and Iceland's first premier; and Einar Benediktsson (1864-1940) the poet and financial adventurer.

In both categories, the artistic as well as the mundane, an important ingredient is original behaviour, not to say eccentricity, which in some cases may even make up for failure in a particular field. The Icelanders have always shown a peculiar weakness for eccentrics. In former times, when artists of any kind were unable to make a living, the social misfits and potential artists and poets used to travel singly or in groups from farm to farm, telling stories, drawing pictures, acting, composing verses, and so on. Today, if one has the courage or is sufficiently carefree to live like a tramp or half-crazed eccentric, he can make a tolerable living, but admittedly this old tradition is rapidly waning in the modern welfare state.

Without undue exaggeration it may be maintained that the supreme ideal of Icelandic culture is not honesty, integrity, sense of duty, or diligence, but *excellence* which will bring the individual fame or fortune or both, and preserve his renown after death, which is by far the highest honour. This extreme concern with excellence may partly be rooted in a feeling of inadequacy on the part of a small, materially poor and isolated nation, but it is also fostered and reinforced by pride in what the nation has accomplished against heavy odds.

The yearning for excellence is closely related to an uncommonly keen sense of history in the Icelanders. They live in the past more than most other people and consequently feel a strong urge to 'make history' themselves, to achieve something worth remembering and recording for future generations.

Now, excellence frequently entails honour in the ethical sense, but in the Icelandic hierarchy of values fame and fortune will precede honour when the need arises. The end often justifies the means, so long as a man is not found out and put to shame officially. Hence many individuals of dubious ethical standards are dear to the Icelanders for having succeeded in their undertakings or done something out of the ordinary. There is a corresponding 'magnanimity' with regard to human frailty in men of great achievements. Several outstanding poets and intellectual leaders have been failures in their personal lives, judged by ordinary social standards, and this certainly enhances rather than detracts from their popularity. Also failure on a grand scale seems no less worthy of remembrance than great success, and so the ideal of excellence is not, as might have been supposed, nearly always synonymous with success. In fact the only absolute and unequivocal attribute of excellence is that it be noticed and remembered, be it positive or negative. This has created in Icelandic society highly elastic moral standards, political and financial corruption going hand in hand with tolerance, since almost any manifestation of the will to excel is accepted, provided it is expedient and elegant. In this sense Icelandic society has some resemblance to the American: in both a certain kind of frontier mentality prevails.

Added to the ideal of excellence, and related to it, is a strong craving for experience of all kinds; this finds its outlet in travel and adventure, scholarly and artistic pursuits and all manner of 'licentious' living. This insatiable curiosity is nothing new, but goes back to the dawn of Icelandic history, when the Icelanders travelled over half the globe from America to Constantinople. Few people in the world travel more than Icelanders of today. In 1973 more than 20 per cent of the entire population travelled abroad. In the first group tour to the Far East (India, Thailand, Japan and Hong Kong), organized in September 1970 and conducted by this writer, there were twenty-five participants, most of them ordinary wage-earners, for example a taxi-driver, two carpenters, a shop assistant, five office girls, a motor mechanic, a farmer's wife, and so on.

Most probably it is a universal rule that the people who live closest to the elements preserve what is most enduring in the national character, that is to say the farmer and the seaman. Among them you are liable to find the most striking individuals. This, at any rate, is true of the Icelanders and the Greeks. The Icelandic farmer, not yet contaminated by the amorphous urban civilization, is a man worth meeting. Deeply rooted in old traditions, well versed in the Sagas and poetry, he is abreast of current events in the modern world, both at home and abroad, and discusses them intelligently with the visitor. He is naturally hospitable and avidly curious about all things human. For centuries it was considered the blackest of crimes not to receive a traveller and house him free of charge, and this attitude is still widely prevalent in the countryside, even though modern communications and tourism have applied a natural brake to the old hospitality. I have frequently experienced, when travelling in remote districts, that a farmer's wife came running with a pitcher of milk, offering the travellers refreshments and sometimes even inviting them to stay overnight. Similar things are common in remote Greek mountain villages. Riding across the south-west part of Iceland with my father and a foreign girlfriend many years ago, we would stop at farms each evening, where the horses were taken care of and we were put up in rooms with clean bed linen, being offered breakfast in the morning, all without charge. The foreign visitor at first thought we were lying to her, when we told her that the farmers refused to accept payment. Having been convinced of the facts, she found them even stranger when being lodged, without any fuss, in a room with two men.

Though Icelandic seamen work under ultra-modern conditions with all the most recent fishing equipment, they stubbornly retain much of the rough independence of mind inherited from times when conditions were harder. They are voracious readers, often reciting whole collections of poetry by rote, and eager to discuss the newest trends in literature and the arts. It is not at all uncommon for farmers or seamen to take part in public discussions in the newspapers about the state of literature or the merits of the latest innovations in poetry. Thus the writer and the intellectual still maintain a living contact with an articulate part of their public, making cultural discussion mutually rewarding.

In one sense the Icelanders live like one large but not very harmonious family. This is most vividly reflected in their news-papers, which often read like extensive family diaries with all the minutiae of daily life diligently recorded. There are the news reports from all over the country, including everything from the daily catches of the fishing vessels and the weather conditions in each district down to all kinds of accidents, such as farm fires, car accidents or even minor fractures suffered by individuals. Every day there are the birthday articles about individuals reaching the ages of fifty, sixty, seventy, seventy-five or eighty years, not to mention those who are even older. There are also the obituaries, frequently five or six in the same paper in a single day. These intimate biographical articles, which take up a considerable amount of space in the newspapers, are widely read since they appeal to an insatiable interest in genealogy among the Icelanders, no doubt stemming from the fact that most of them can trace their ancestry far back and most families have a common ancestor somewhere along the line.[1] Added to all this are the interminable discussions in the papers about everything you can think of, from literature, religion and astrology to shop service, taxes, dogs, street paving and behaviour in public places. These discussions are liveliest and most intense during the darkest months of winter and are mostly conducted by the man in the street, since everybody feels free to express his opinions in public. However, these discussions have an unsavoury aspect in that a considerable number of them are anonymous.

All these ingredients make Icelandic newspapers quite intimate and in a sense provincial. Add to this the very pronounced interest in local politics, and you have a rather colourful press, but definitely not of the same intellectual quality as respectable newspapers in Europe or America.

There can be no doubt that the Icelanders are among the most avid newspaper readers in the world. In Reykjavík, a city of some 85,000 inhabitants, there are six dailies, four of them morning papers which are also distributed throughout the country, especially the two biggest ones, both of them conservative in content. The biggest has a distribution of well over 40,000, thus reaching a good three-quarters of all the families in the country. The other four newspapers range in circulation roughly between 4,000 and 20,000. In addition there is one large illustrated weekly in Reykjavík as well as three weekly papers, one attatched to a political movement, the two others mostly devoted to sensational journalism of the most primitive kind.

All the daily papers in Iceland are politically affiliated, three of them directly published by political parties, three of them supporting the largest party which has no official organ of its own. In addition to the Reykjavík papers there are weekly papers in more densely populated areas of the country, published by the political parties, which also deal with local matters of general interest in each district.

Newspapers in Iceland devote more space to party politics and are more politically coloured than their counterparts in other western democracies, and they are to that extent less reliable—also with regard to news, both domestic and international. There have been attempts to abandon strictly partisan journalism and open up the papers, but these have generally failed. One of the chief obstacles has been the attitudes of a large part of the reading public, especially the older generation, who have been accustomed to violent political debates and love nothing better—possibly a vestige of their Viking origins.

Even though the Icelanders are naïvely intolerant in political matters, they are exceedingly tolerant in most other respects, especially in moral and religious affairs. They have always been rather promiscuous, the rate of illegitimacy being around 30 per cent, but that figure is somewhat misleading, since a large number of children are legitimized later, when parents are old enough to work and can get married. There is no stigma whatever attached to illegitimacy, and unmarried mothers seem to have little difficulty in finding husbands. The father of an illegitimate child is obliged to pay a monthly allowance either directly to the mother or to the state, which then turns it over to the mother. When the father fails to pay, the state pays the allowance to the mother and then tries to extract the debt from the father; in some cases fathers flee the country to evade the tax collector. The rate of divorce is rather high, especially among people in their late twenties, and in general the Icelanders are somewhat lax about sexual matters.

In religious matters they are even more liberal. The Lutheran Church does not play any conspicuous role in national life beyond the traditional functions attached to baptism, confirmation, marriage and burial. Confirmation has become a purely social affair where lavish gifts and extravagant parties are the main ingredients. Even though the Icelanders care little about Christianity and organized religion, they are still an essentially religious people in a more general sense.

A survey in 1975, the first of its kind, conducted by the Department of Psychology at the University of Iceland, revealed that some 64 per cent of all Icelanders have had some experience involving the supernatural. Of those polled, 31 per cent stated that they have been aware of the nearness of a deceased person; 36 per cent claimed that they have dreamed about things that occurred later, and 27 per cent maintained that they had telepathic knowledge of distant events. The existence of elves and so-called 'hidden people' was considered possible, likely or certain by 55 per cent of those questioned, and the same percentage believed in the existence of ghosts.

The survey was quite extensive, the sampling being obtained from the National Registry through a random selection of 1,132 men and women aged between thirty and seventy, which represents one out of every seventy people in this age group. About 80 per cent of those polled were co-operative, and of these 53 per cent were women. The survey brought out some other interesting facts, such as that 92 per cent of the Icelanders never read the Bible, although 97 per cent consider themselves quite, somewhat or slightly religious. Some 52 per cent have visited a fortune-teller at some time during their lives; 41 per cent have sought the aid of a faith-healer, and of these 91 per cent feel that they benefited as a result. About 30 per cent have been present at public spiritualist seances, while 32 per cent have attended private seances. Of the last mentioned, 56 per cent report that they have communicated with the dead; and of those attending private seances, 83 per cent claim to have benefited from the experience.

Even though these figures may have startled some observers, they would hardly surprise those acquainted with old Icelandic literature, both the medieval Sagas and the eminently rich folklore of past centuries. Pagan traditions mingled with Christian ideas from the very start, and peopled the everyday world of the Icelanders with all kinds of strange and fanciful creatures. Their natural surroundings no doubt also contributed to the creation of this imaginary world. Through centuries of isolation and hardship they were plagued by volcanic eruptions, arctic ice and poverty. Being poetically inclined, in these circumstances they imagined their towering mountains and weird lava formations swarming with supernatural beings, with the result that nowhere else in Western Europe, with the sole exception of Ireland, has the field of folklore been so fertile.

Ancestor worship has been widespread from the days of the settlement 1,100 years ago, and so has belief in elves, sprites and other nature spirits. Ghosts have been as real to most Icelanders as their next-door neighbours. Dreams are also of tremendous importance and play a significant role in many people's lives. Added to this is a marked interest in all sorts of oriental occultism, animism and spiritualism, which has also gained a foothold within the Lutheran Church of Iceland itself. The Norwegian psychologist Harald Schjelderup maintains that spiritualism is most widespread in three countries: Puerto Rico, Brazil and Iceland. Mediums and individuals with 'psychic potentialities' abound in Iceland. Seances are frequently organized, both in private homes and in the largest auditoria, which are packed to capacity. During the winter 1969-70, by far the best attended gathering of the student body at the University of Iceland was a seance conducted by the country's leading medium, an unskilled labourer who has since visited universities in the United States and made an impression there. Many people make a living this way. Books about 'psychic experiences' and 'mysterious occurrences' are sure best-sellers every year. Curiously, men have made a greater mark than women in the field of 'psychic phenomena' in Iceland.

The belief in nature spirits finds many outlets: they are mainly looked upon as guardians, who visit people in their dreams to give them direction. There is a widespread popular belief in 'enchanted spots' which must on no account be touched or tampered with, so as not to inconvenience the good elves or 'hidden people' to whom they belong. A few years ago there were strong protests from a community in North Iceland on account of a plan to build a new road across one such 'enchanted spot'. The authorities gave in and diverted the road. In 1962 the newspapers reported a strange incident. To accommodate the 'hidden people', work on a new quarry was temporarily stopped. There are two versions of this incident. According to one version, the drills repeatedly broke; according to the other, they failed to work. The superintendent was at a loss until one of the workmen dreamed that a stranger came to him and announced that he was one of the 'hidden people' living in the rocks they were drilling. The stranger asked for time for him to find a new home and move to it. He threatened otherwise to keep on breaking the drills. A seer was consulted to act as intermediary in the dispute. Although somewhat shamefaced, the superintendent agreed to the terms of the 'hidden people', granting them time to move. When that had been accomplished, work on the quarry was resumed, and all went well. In 1964 a famous racehorse suddenly collapsed and died at a race in South Iceland, as a consequence of which there was speculation in the newspapers as to whether the accident might be due to supernatural causes since the owner of the horse had, many years earlier, mown an 'enchanted spot' near his farm and on that account lost his best milking cow. Such examples could be multiplied *ad infinitum* from all parts of Iceland.

The origin of the 'hidden people' (*huldufólk*) goes back, according to Icelandic folklore, to the Garden of Eden: one day Eve was bathing her many children in a stream when she suddenly heard the voice of the Lord calling. She hastily hid the unwashed children, and presented the ones she had washed to the Lord, pretending that they were all she had. This angered the Lord, who said, 'That which is hidden from me shall for ever be hidden from men.' The 'hidden people' are thus descendants of Eve's unwashed children, and they are invisible except to those with second sight or when they themselves wish to be seen. They frequently appear in dreams. Like their human neighbours, they live as cattle farmers and shepherds and are subject to human joys and sorrows. Some respected Icelandic scholars and writers have told about their childhood experiences playing with the 'hidden people'.

According to folklore, there are elves as well as 'hidden people' living in rocks and lava formations. The two terms seem at times to be interchangeable, but Jón Árnason, the great compiler of folk tales, quotes the 'hidden people' as denying that they are elves. However that may be, neither elves nor 'hidden people' are dainty fairies. On the other hand, the elves often appear to lead a more glamorous life than the 'hidden people'. Dressed in gorgeous raiment and living in splendid surroundings, they delight in enticing human beings to join them. They are most active at Christmas time. In the old days of rural Iceland the whole family

would go to church one Christmas Eve, usually leaving one person
to guard the farmstead. Throngs of elves would then swarm into
the house and dance all night. They would try to carry off with
them the person guarding the farmhouse or anyone caught
outdoors, tempting them with all kinds of blandishments and offers
of gold, silver and precious stones, as well as delicious food and
wines. If the person thus tempted succeeded in resisting the offers
until dawn, the elves would leave him or her, as well as all the
wealth they had offered. But woe to anyone who accepted any of
their offers, like Ólaf Liljurós, the Knight of the Lily and the Rose,
of ballad fame, who yielded to the charms of the elfin maidens and
was stabbed to death when he kissed one of them.

Wicked trolls or giants are also supposed to live among the vast
lava fields and awe-inspiring volcanoes of the wild and uninhabited
interior. Some of them are two- or three-headed, and they will
come down to the settlements—usually those along the coast—and
carry off beautiful maidens to their lairs.

There are few, if any, places in the world where belief in ghosts
is more prevalent or persistent than in Iceland. Ghosts have a long
history in Iceland and stories about them are legion. There are
many kinds of ghosts: revenants who come back from the grave to
torment the living, *sendings* sent by the living to torment or punish
an enemy, wraiths of those who haunt the spots where they died,
fylgjur or accompanying spirits who go ahead of living people to
announce their coming.

Stories of these phantoms go back to the early history of
Iceland. Most famous of the early ghosts was Glám in the *Saga of
Grettir the Strong*, written in the early fourteenth century. Glám
was a big, uncouth Swede who came to live in Iceland and was
hired as a shepherd by a farmer named Thórhall, who was having
trouble in finding a man to tend his sheep because his farm was
haunted. Glám scoffed at the idea of meeting a man-killing ghost:
he certainly was not afraid. But one day his body was found, blue
all over and swollen big as an ox: he had apparently been killed
after a fight with an evil spirit. He was buried on the spot. But
soon his ghost began to walk, seen by many who declared that he
was bigger and uglier than he had been in life, with a hideous
gleam in his eyes. Many went mad at the sight of him. He took to
riding upon the roofs of the houses at night, almost breaking them
down. He killed the cows in their stalls as well as the men who
took care of the cattle and herded the sheep. He created such
havoc that nobody could be induced to work on that farm until
finally Grettir Ásmundsson, the strongest man in all Iceland, came
to the haunted region and agreed to work as shepherd. Grettir met
the ghost and after a famous battle killed it, cut off its head and
burned its body. Glám was never seen again, but ever after Grettir

was afraid to walk in the dark, strong and powerful though he was, since he had seen the terrifying eyes of the ghost at the moment of death.

Another typical ghost story is related in the classical *Eyrbyggja Saga* from the thirteenth century, describing events shortly after the adoption of Christianity in the year 1000. A farmer in West Iceland, named Thórólf, was drowned with five of his men on an errand to fetch dried fish. The boat and the fish drifted ashore, but the bodies of the men were never found. At the funeral feast, the guests were flabbergasted when all the drowned men walked in dripping wet and took their places before the fire. Believing that the apparitions had been accepted by the sea queen *Rán,* the guests greeted them in an ordinary manner. But when the ghostly band reappeared night after night, along with the ghost of another farmer, Thórir, who had recently died, and those of Thórir's followers, covered with dirt from their graves, all the people fled.

This happened just before the celebration of Yule (Christmas), and it was thought that the visitations would stop as soon as the holidays began. But they continued throughout the holidays and were accompanied by much illness and many deaths in the region. Realizing that he needed help to rid his home of these unwelcome guests, the farmer finally secured the services of a priest who summoned the ghosts to a trial, cited them for haunting the house without permission and making people ill and killing them. Declared guilty, the ghosts accepted the verdict and left in peace.

A leading Icelandic prose writer Thórbergur Thórdarson (1889-1974), who was a devout Communist, wrote a book on recent occurrences similar to those of *Eyrbyggja Saga* and taking place in the same region, which is even more dramatic than the ancient masterpiece. He also wrote a hair-raising biography of the most noted male medium of this century.

Apart from widespread belief in *sendings,* ghosts called up from the grave and sent to avenge a wrong suffered, whether imaginary or real, and in *mórar* and *skottur,* the male and female forms of itinerant ghosts haunting the countryside and growing in number with every death in the region, perhaps the most distinctly Icelandic superstition of all is belief in the *fylgja* (plural *fylgjur*). The *fylgja* is 'a guardian spirit, really a second ego, originally a man's soul assuming the form of some animal or of a woman and accompanying him through life.'[2] According to Icelandic folklore, every man and woman has his or her *fylgja* which appears to the second-sighted before his or her arrival. The *fylgja* may have the form of some animal; it maay appear as a ball or as streaks of light; it may be the moon floating in the air, or it may be another person. Balls and streaks of light are good *fylgjur,* but the moon floating in the air is a very bad *fylgja,* foreboding evil. *Fylgjur* are classified as personal or of the family variety. The latter foretells the arrival of the members of a certain family from generation to generation. The most renowned family *fylgja* is Thorgeir's Bull, which announces the coming of the members of the Thorgeir family—a creature known all over Iceland. It is characterized by a loud bellow and often foretells a change in the weather.

Besides stories of 'hidden people'-, elves, giants and ghosts, Icelandic folktales have much to say about mermen and mermaids, sea and river monsters, psychic and other supernatural phenomena. There is in Iceland a peculiar concern for the physical remains of the dead, bones being removed from one grave to another at the direction of dead people who appear in dreams. This concern is also conspicuous in some of the Sagas, for example in connection with the bones of Egil Skallagrímsson, Snorri Godi, Grettir the Strong and his brother Illugi. It is a characteristic feature of the folktales. In modern times there have been some extraordinary incidents in this context, such as when the bones of Iceland's national poet, Jónas Hallgrímsson (1807-45), after being transferred from Copenhagen to Reykjavík, were stolen and taken to his birthplace in North Iceland, in accordance with his own wishes conveyed in a dream, before they were retrieved and buried at Thingvellir. This incident was satirized by Halldór Laxness in his novel *The Atom Station*.

There are many reasons, both obvious and hidden, for the prevalence of superstition in Iceland. Among the more obvious ones are the climate of the country and its eerie landscape. Shut off for centuries from the outside world except by sea, surrounded by towering cliffs and living in isolated farmsteads which, especially in the north and east, were often buried in snow during the long and dark winter months, the inhabitants naturally saw ghosts in the dark, heard them shriek in the storms raging on rooftops and shake the doors in their ramshackle houses. Huddling together in the dark of the *badstofa* (combined bedroom and sitting-room), listening to the pounding of the gales and the squeaking of planks which roused the dogs, setting them to howling in the dark passages, the family naturally thought that the dogs had seen something 'unclean'. As winter progressed and the food supplies became scanty, cheeks grew paler and eyes duller, and people saw wraiths everywhere. Then, with the coming of light and summer, the imagination was stirred and the ghostly stories grew and expanded.

The Icelander still entertains a strong belief in the supernatural and is strongly inclined to fatalism, which is also a salient trait of the ancient Eddic poetry and the Sagas. The notion of predestination is very much alive. One does what one is fated to do, and dies at a preordained moment. This is expressed with the word *feigur,* which is the exact equivalent of the English word 'fey' in its original sense, still used in Scotland. Its opposite is *ófeigur* (also a personal name) or 'unfey', and an Icelandic proverb is to the effect that 'the fey cannot be saved nor the unfey brought to death'. This notion is especially deep-rooted among seamen and those who work at dangerous occupations. It is also one of the central notions of Icelandic literature.

All these remnants of age-old beliefs and primitive superstitions exist side by side with a modern outlook towards science and technology and a thoroughly utilitarian mentality. For all their occult leanings, the Icelanders are exceedingly curious about modern discoveries in every field of technology. There is something almost childlike about their infatuation with novelties. They are 'gadget-happy' to the extent that no new article is left untested. This is especially true of kitchen equipment and cars. In a country where roads are notoriously bad for most of the year and cars are two to three times as expensive as in the nearest countries on both sides of the Atlantic, there is one car to every four inhabitants. This is no doubt due partly to native curiosity and the feeling that much catching up has to be done in a hurry, but it also reflects a determination to overcome the formidable obstacles created by the natural environment and by historical retardation. Within no more than two generations the Icelanders have leaped more or less from medieval living conditions to an ultra-modern welfare state. No one unfamiliar with Icelandic history will readily understand what these changes have meant to a people for so long harassed by misfortune. This may well be one reason why some foreign observers have detected a 'split personality' in the Icelandic nation.

That impression may also be caused, at least in part, by the difference between the Icelanders and most peoples in Western Europe where Christianity took root and created a distinct culture. Here it might be helpful to make use of a distinction which the American cultural anthropologist Ruth Benedict employed in her very interesting study of the Japanese, *The Chrysanthemum and the Sword.* She discusses two types of culture which she calls 'guilt culture' and 'shame culture'. The former prevails in Christian societies where the emphasis is on the duty of the individual to God and to his neighbour, leading to a sense of guilt when he falls short of fulfilling his duties. This culture is concerned with the profound problems of good and evil and fosters an awareness of man's tragic predicament. In shame cultures there is a kind of 'innocence' regarding the world, or rather an immature concern with appearance rather than essence.

In the former respect, she says, even though a man may belong to a guilt culture, he may also feel ashamed of his bad table manners or tactlessness—things which certainly could not be called sins. But in a shame culture people merely become ashamed of acts which ought to make them conscience-stricken. This kind of shame is, however, very strong, and cannot be relieved by confession-therapy as can a guilt-ridden man's sense of sin. A man of the shame culture is concerned only that his bad behaviour be kept secret, and therefore he would hardly pour out his shame in the confessional or participate in other such counselling services provided by various religious groups. Instead of making provisions for the admission of sins to priests or to gods, the shame cultures hold ceremonies for good luck.

In shame cultures, she says, society is the judge rather than a man's conscience, and since shame is a reaction to other people's criticism, man can be shamed by being publicly ridiculed and rejected, or by imagining that he has been.

Ruth Benedict's description of shame culture seems tailor-made for Icelandic culture as it is expressed in Edda and Saga and in the basic outlook of modern Icelanders. According to one Eddic lay, everything on this earth is perishable except a man's good reputation or renown. The central action in all the major Sagas is in one way or another tied to honour and affronts to it.

Essentially the Icelanders, despite all their cultural achievements, are children of nature, not much bothered by the complex and refined attributes of more sophisticated and orderly societies. They tend to give free rein to their desires, constructive as well as destructive, sustaining an innate belief in a universal order where good and bad must contend as freely as possible in order to bring out the best as well as the worst in each individual. They are averse to absolute standards in any sphere of life. Therefore they are more practical or realistic than idealistic. They approach every issue emotionally rather than rationally (this does not contradict their lack of idealism, since idealism is usually rational). Their way of thinking is poetic rather than philosophical. Their way of feeling is epic, not tragic, which ties in with their culture being one of shame, not guilt. The Icelanders are immature in the way youth is immature. This is an asset as well as a liability. It makes for abandon, immediacy, curiosity, thirst for experience and uncomplicated enjoyment of life, but it also creates social instability, irresponsibility, superficiality, and the danger of mistaking appearances for essences.

The Icelanders are a rather quarrelsome lot. They love heated arguments and verbal fencing, frequently just for the fun of it. In this respect they resemble their Irish cousins. They like to think of themselves as rational people, whereas in actual fact they are highly emotional. Their attempts to rationalize their views in quarrelsome discussions are often hilarious. It is noteworthy that they have never produced any original or profound thinker.

Philosophy is almost non-existent, whereas poetry flourishes. In literature their preference is for the epic style, the descriptive passage, the flowing narrative, to the exclusion of the analytical, the philosophical or the psychological approach.

There are of course many obvious contradictions in the Icelandic character. Icelanders, for all their savage past, are by nature a gentle people, affectionate to children and kind to most animals. They abhor any sort of overt cruelty. At the same time they can be fiercely aggressive in politics, which is one sphere where their Viking ancestry shows up when they are sober (in a drunken state they *are* Vikings). Icelandic politics are very personal and rather corrupt by Nordic standards. Nepotism is common and appointments to public offices are almost invariably political, although the system of state employment is the European one. In this respect, too, the Icelanders resemble the Greeks.

The original language of the Sagas is still alive in Iceland, the oldest living language in Europe. The present-day shopkeeper or farmer, children at play, or a boy and girl courting use the same terms as the old heroes. There is merely a slight change in orthography. New terms are invented from old roots for outlandish things such as telephone, radio and television, jet and helicopter, transistor and camera, astronaut and satellite, electricity and atomic energy, geology and geography, music and literature, philosophy and psychology, automobile and jeep, propaganda and production. There are almost no international words in the language, which makes it rather difficult for Icelanders to learn foreign languages, yet they seem on the whole to be natural linguists, many of them commanding one or two or even more foreign languages. A special committee is in session for coining Icelandic words for new concepts, and a law has been passed forbidding parents to give their children non-Icelandic names.

One Icelandic peculiarity is in the use of personal names. There are very few family names in Iceland and the adoption of new family names is illegal. The second name is derived from the father's first name, and the suffix denotes the sex of the child. Thus Jón Gunnarsson marries Anna Magnúsdóttir; they name their daughter Erna Jónsdóttir and their son Agnar Jónsson. Erna Jónsdóttir retains her maiden name when she marries, which sometimes causes embarrassment when Icelandic married couples register in foreign hotels. People normally address one another by their Christian names, and personal names in the telephone directory as well as in other similar catalogues are listed alphabetically under the Christian names, which also causes confusion to foreigners. Greetings to everyone from the President to the street sweeper are by tradition on a first-name basis.

Even though the population of Iceland is small and there are no local dialects, there is considerable local patriotism in the country, dating back to earlier times when the districts were more isolated than today. Traditionally the inhabitants of Northern Iceland have a reputation for being rather proud and sometimes even haughty. The people of Thingeyjarsýsla in North-east Iceland (around Lake Mývatn) are reputed to be especially culture-conscious. In the last century they were almost 'a nation within the nation' and had much the same standing as the New Englanders in the United States. Today their excellence is less obvious, and a large part of the population has moved away, mostly to Reykjavík and Akureyri. Moving west, the inhabitants of Eyjafjördur (around Akureyri) are reputed to be proud of their wives, the people in Skagafjördur of their horses, and the people of Húnaflói simply of themselves. The inhabitants of the Westman Islands off the south coast have exhibited a marked inclination for Texas-style independence and have even tried to put themselves outside Icelandic jurisdiction in certain matters. They celebrate their own 'National Festival' every August.

The Icelandic sense of humour is of the ironic kind, rough and robust. It lacks the casual subtlety and refinement of Danish humour and is more akin to the American brand. On the other hand, the Icelanders are highly sensitive to jokes about themselves and naïvely sensitive to criticism, especially from foreigners, a defect which is complemented by their childish delight in compliments. This is no doubt a remnant from the colonial period which created in the Icelanders a certain inferiority complex *vis-à-vis* foreigners that they have not yet been able to shake off. Consequently they tend to exaggerate both their own worth and the magnitude of affronts.

One of the compliments most often repeated by foreign visitors and relished by the natives is to the effect that Icelandic women are among the most beautiful in the world. Taken as a statement of fact, this is obviously quite correct, but as a compliment it somehow leaves one dissatisfied, since feminine beauty is a caprice of nature and does not belong to those achievements which merit special praise.

In general the Icelanders are honest in their financial dealings, although they have a peculiar inclination (probably also to be found in other countries) to cheat the state and other official institutions, both with regard to taxes and a good day's work. They have a reputation for being extremely unpunctual and fond of night-long parties in their homes. Nevertheless, they do work hard. It is not at all uncommon for an individual to hold two or more jobs. A man who is a taxi-driver at night may be a policeman or a teacher during the day. A teacher is likely to work in a fish cannery or on a trawler during the summer. This is partly due to a very high cost of living and a general Icelandic tendency to live beyond one's means.

Crime has been negligible in Iceland, but has greatly increased in more recent years. It is mostly limited to petty larceny, smuggling, embezzlement and suchlike. Murders are rare, but suicides are rather common and on the increase. The prison system is extremely lenient, and on special occasions all but the most serious criminals are let out. The saying goes that all Icelandic prisoners have their own keys, which is a slight overstatement, but on the whole they enjoy considerable freedom, and it has happened on several occasions that a prisoner left his cell and went out to commit burglary or have some fun at a dance, returning to his cell after the event. One serious burglary was actually traced to a prisoner who was supposed to be locked up and was found in his cell after the mystery had been solved. Drunkenness is a common nuisance, frequently accounting for petty crimes.

An indication that some of the old Saga spirit is still alive in the Icelanders is a true story which happened a few years ago at Mosfell, near Reykjavík, the farm where Egil Skallagrímsson spent his last years and hid his treasures before taking his leave. In 1887 the old church there was torn down against the bitter protests of some of the parishioners, the parish being amalgamated with a church some distance away, leaving the proud Mosfell valley without a church. When the building had been torn down it was discovered that the church bell, dating back to the fourteenth or fifteenth century, was missing. Nobody seemed to know what had happened to it. Some seventy-five years later a new and very modern church was erected at Mosfell. On the day of its consecration, 4 April 1965, the old bell was unexpectedly returned and placed in the choir of the new church, where it has rung for every ceremony that has taken place in the church ever since. The family living in the neighbouring farm had appropriated the bell, when protests against the demolition of the old church were in vain, and guarded it until a new church was built—hiding it, of all places, in the heap of manure which traditionally stands outside every farm in Iceland. Another instance of the almost Viking-like temperament of the modern Icelanders has been the so-called 'Cod Wars' with Britain in 1958, 1972 and 1975–6, where small Icelandic gunboats kept up a contest with British men-of-war inside the new fishery limits, frequently coming to serious and dangerous clashes. In 1958 the war was actually carried on for a while with a contest of wits between an Icelandic gunboat captain and the officer in charge of one of the British frigates, each trying to outwit the other with appropriate and pointed quotations from the Bible. It was generally agreed among journalists of many nationalities that the

Icelander carried the day in that contesst, as his countrymen eventually did in the 'Cod War' itself.

Notes

1. When the Duke of Edinburgh visited Iceland in 1964, a Reykjavík newspaper published a genealogy made in 1949 by a clergyman in Reykjavík, tracing the ancestry of Queen Elizabeth II back thirty-four generations to one of the original settlers of North Iceland, *Audun Bjarnarson,* the grandson of an English earl. His great-granddaughter was the mother of St Ólaf, King of Norway (*d.* 1030), whose daughter married Ordulf, a duke in Saxony, who died in 1074. From him there was an unbroken line of German dukes down to Ernst August, the first electoral prince of Hanover and the father of King George I of Great Britain (reigned 1714-27). W. H. Auden half-jokingly claimed to be descended from the same Audun, and indeed most living Icelanders could trace their ancestry to him, if they took the trouble, thus proving their distant connection with the British royal house.

2. Webster's New International Dictionary.

8. Artistic Endeavours since the Icelandic Renaissance

The History of the Book

Iceland has been uniquely a country of books since the twelfth century. Long before Gutenberg, people all over Iceland were busy copying manuscripts of the literary treasures of the nation as well as foreign masterpieces. In the sixteenth century the printing press came to Iceland: the first book to be published in Iceland, *Breviarium Holense,* was issued in 1534, and there is evidence of at least one other book, *Four Evangelists,* published by Bishop Jón Arason, before the Reformation (1550). During the remaining years of the sixteenth century forty to fifty books were published in the country, but the first book known to have been actually printed in Iceland was published in 1559, the third volume of *Korvínspostilla (Passio Corvini),* translated by Odd Gottskálksson (the two previous volumes were printed in Rostock in 1546).

In the seventeenth century a total of 225 books were published in Iceland, and of these 198 were printed in the country. The eighteenth and nineteenth centuries saw a slow but steady growth in book publishing, but no definite statistics are available until 1888 (see Table below), the year before the Booksellers' Union of Iceland was founded by three publishers. That union set up an effective distribution system which greatly increased book consumption in the country.

Considering that the population of Iceland during those eighty years rose from a mere 75,000 to about 200,000 (and is thus still one of the smallest in the world), the quantity of books published during the period is truly enormous. The *per capita* output of titles is three to four times that of the other Nordic countries and about twenty times that of the United States. On the other hand, far fewer copies are printed of each title than in many other countries, notably the big ones. The number of copies is in the range 300–600 for books on specialized subjects or by little-known authors, up to 15,000 for best sellers (a very small number have been published in editions of 25,000 copies). The average number of copies is somewhere between 1,200 and 1,500. About 500,000 copies of Icelandic books are sold each year in Iceland, or about 2·5 copies per inhabitant; whereas US publishers sell around 700 million

BOOK PUBLISHING STATISTICS SINCE 1888: I

	1888	1901–10	1911–20	1921–30	1931–40	1941–50	1951–60	1961–70
Total books published	59	?	1,130	1,561	2,451	4,790	5,022	5,734
Lowest annual total		56	100	112	170	302	428	500
		(1901)	*(1914)*	*(1921)*	*(1931)*	*(1942)*	*(1953)*	*(1963)*
Highest annual total		131	140	205	322	604	585	656
		(1906)	*(1916)*	*(1930)*	*(1939)*	*(1946)*	*(1960)*	*(1968)*
Fiction (Icelandic)*	4	54	69	108	147	263	272	455
Fiction (translated)	1	139	117	153	279	821	515	796
Poetry (Icelandic)	4	103	81	130	180	256	305	256
Poetry (translated anthologies)	1	7	8	6	9	13	22	18

* Sagas not included. Over 300 volumes of Sagas were published in the period 1888–1970.

BOOK PUBLISHING STATISTICS SINCE 1887: II

	No. of books*	% of total
Total published	19,909	100
Fiction (Icelandic)	1,128	5·66
Fiction (translated)	2,429	12·24
Poetry (Icelandic)	1,257	6·31
Poetry (translated anthologies)	83	0·42
Other selected categories		
Educational	1,109	5·57
Juvenile (translated)	986	4·95
Religious	958	4·81
Biography	950	4·77
Literary history	70	0·35

* Includes pamphlets.

Icelandic books published in Canada (approx.)	970
Icelandic books published in Copenhagen	940
Translations of Icelandic books published in:	
Germany	370
Norway	210
Sweden	160
Great Britain	140
USA	110
Other countries (approx.)	320

copies. Although the latter figure represents some 3·5 copies per inhabitant, Icelanders buy in addition a great number of books in foreign languages, especially English, German and the Nordic languages.

Out of approximately 600 books published in Iceland each year less than 100 are literary works, and of these less than one-third have any notable literary quality. Books worthy of serious consideration are thus fewer than thirty each year, and only half of these are of Icelandic origin.

During the last three decades the number of books published in Iceland has remained more or less at a standstill, but actually there has been a marked decline in the number of copies issued. In other words, there are fewer copies of each book being published at present than some years ago, despite the fast-growing population. This is due to many reasons, the chief being an immense growth in newspaper publishing, and a vastly greater variety of leisure activities available, such as those provided by amusement centres, cinemas, concerts, theatres, travel at home and abroad, and so on. Still, there are over fifty publishing houses, including three large book clubs.

Periodicals

The history of Icelandic periodicals is a complex maze where publications of all sizes and various runs are hard to trace. In the last century and a half there has been a vast number of periodicals, most of them extraordinarily short-lived and some barely surviving the throes of birth (see statistics below). The first Icelandic periodical was founded in 1780, an annual mostly concerned with agricultural matters and public enlightenment. It held out for fifteen years. Then came *Skírnir,* the oldest periodical still surviving in all Scandinavia, which was published under its present name in 1827, replacing a publication which had begun ten years earlier. *Skírnir* was printed in Copenhagen until 1890, when it

PERIODICAL PUBLISHING STATISTICS SINCE 1887

No. of different periodicals published	1,400
No. of periodical issues:	
Total	9,263
1888	17
1916	61
1932	101
1949	212
1962	286

moved to Iceland. It is now an annual of solid book size (usually 240 pages) and deals exclusively with literary and other cultural matters.

Obviously only a fragment of the periodicals in these statistics dealt with general literary or cultural affairs; the great majority were trade magazines and other specialized periodicals. At present there are only four substantial literary and cultural periodicals published in the country, two of them annuals (*Skírnir, Andvari*), and two quarterlies, *Eimreidin* and *Tímarit Máls og menningar,* the latter published by a book club. In 1967 the periodical of the Co-operative Movement of Iceland, *Samvinnan* (founded 1907), was turned into a socio-cultural bi-monthly magazine with a circulation of about 6,000, but this development was discontinued in 1974 and it reverted to its old format.

Poetry, Traditional

Until the turn of this century cultural life in Iceland, although vigorous, was highly uniform. It was confined to the literary arts, especially poetry, with a sprinkling of handicrafts and folk music. Painting, drama, and musical composition were almost non-existent. The novel was resurrected in the middle of the nineteenth century but did not flourish until after 1900.

Poetry was always produced in quantity. During the centuries following the collapse of the Commonwealth a particular metric form was evolved and adapted to the retelling in verse of long narrative sequences. Much of the old Saga material was turned into verse during those centuries. This peculiar verse form was called *rímur* and is still alive, especially in the so-called *stökur* or *lausavísur*—alliterative four-line stanzas whose rhyme-schemes have become so elaborate that over 2,000 varieties have been recorded. The most complex varieties are those called *hringhenda* and *sléttubönd*: the latter can be read backwards as well as forwards, and occasionally upwards and downwards and crossways as well, all the time making perfect sense and observing all the very strict rules of alliteration and rhyme. Sometimes these stanzas have the opposite meaning when read backwards. Indeed, there are stanzas which can be read in ninety-six different ways, making sense all the time. This popular art has been a favourite pastime among the public for centuries and is still widely practised, as may be seen in the newspapers almost every day. There are also occasional competitions in this kind of verse-making over the radio. These stanzas have much in common with skaldic verse, from which they are partly derived, their poetic value being minimal, but they indicate a lively interest in verbal virtuosity among the people at large.

After the nineteenth-century upsurge of romantic and nationalistic poetry, inspired largely by the *Edda* and the Sagas, which was followed by a brief spell of realist poetry at the turn of the century, modern Icelandic poetry may, by an arbitrary division, be said to have come into being with the publication of two first-volumes by the poets Stefán frá Hvítadal (1887-1933) and Davíd Stefánsson (1895-1964). These were entitled respectively *Songs of the Vagabond* (1918) and *Black Feathers* (1919). With their youthful enthusiasm and *joi de vivre*, simple and natural diction, and lack of earnestness, and the musical quality of their verse, these poets ushered in a new poetic epoch. Stefán frá Hvítadal published three more collections of poems which, however, could not compare with his first book, and he never attained the stature of Davíd Stefánsson who was a prolific writer and became a 'national poet'. In his later poetry Davíd Stefánsson drew richly on folklore and was able to recreate some of the nation's sad, mystical mood. He also wrote effective satirical poems, but his principal themes are sorrow, lost loves and faded dreams.

Both these poets were traditional in form and outlook, although they introduced fresh themes and diction. The same is true of Tómas Gudmundsson (*b.* 1901), the most accomplished formal master among modern poets and the most difficult to render into foreign languages. He is an aesthete with an exquisite lyrical note and an ethereal quality which sets him apart from his more robust and socially conscious contemporaries. He has only published four collections of poems, the latest in 1950. Many of his poems celebrate the sights, sounds, smells and good old times of Reykjavík. His poetry is pervaded by nostalgic memories of youth and playful fancies about everyday life, but in his most recent book, written during and after the Second World War, the oppressive reality of war, blood, tyranny, and madness has also entered his field of vision. Tómas Gudmundsson is the only living 'national poet'.

Three other traditional modern poets—Jóhannes úr Kötlum (1899-1972), Gudmundur Bödvarsson (1904-74) and Snorri Hjartarson (*b.* 1906)—are noteworthy, mainly for renewing old forms and employing fresh modes of expression within the old tradition. In general the traditional poets of this century have been preoccupied, in varying degree, with the same issues as their predecessors of the last century: nationalism, the beauties of the country, the purity of the language, the consciousness of a great historical and literary heritage.

'Atom Poetry'

The traditional poets, each in his own way, have dealt with many significant issues of their time and have largely tended to be descriptive and 'extrovert'. Much of the content of their poetry could easily be transcribed into prose (losing much of its lustre in the process). When we turn to the so-called modernistic poets or 'atom poets', as the Icelanders somewhat derisively call them, their work is on the whole more 'difficult' in the sense that they are more introspective and complex and less immediately comprehensible. They have moved away from the outward excellence of metre and high-sounding diction, making less frequent use of stock images and clichés, seeking their own idiom and symbols, often private ones, to capture the more evanescent qualities of intuition, sensibility and feeling, which are the main business of all real poetry. This has in many cases resulted in a loosening-up of strict metric forms and in freer modes of expression, but at the same time in greater precision in diction and imagery, which has become more daring, rich and variegated.

There are naturally all kinds of gradations among the younger Icelandic poets—some being more and some less lucid. The evolution has been slow and the new trends came much later to Iceland than to most other countries, due no doubt to the ingrained reverence of most Icelanders for the old tradition with its emphasis on lucidity and strict metric rules (alliteration being chief among them). Most significant poetry today has departed, to a greater or lesser extent, from the old traditions: in an anthology of new poetry published in 1954, in which twenty poets were represented, only seven used traditional metres, nine wrote free verse, and four used both. In the years since then the modernistic trend has become much more dominant.

Although there had already been fruitful innovations and experiments in the modernistic vein by poets like Jóhann Sigurjónsson (1880-1919), who was Iceland's leading playwright, writing in Danish and Icelandic, and Jóhann Jónsson (1896-1932), the first spokesman for a conscious modernistic revolution in Icelandic poetry was Steinn Steinarr (1908-58), a skilful versemaker in the traditional style, but above all a poet of sensibility and integrity. He established modernistic poetry in Iceland against heavy odds, especially with the last of his five collections of poems, *Time and the Water* (1948), a cycle of twenty-one poems, each reflecting the poet's own self, time, the present, and the timeless.

The modernistic poets are a curiously incoherent group with little in common except their determination to follow their own bent and write significant poetry in a fresh and stimulating way. With only one or two exceptions, they have not enjoyed popularity among the common run of readers, but they were the most expressive and articulate interpreters of reality in Icelandic literature during the first two decades after the Second World War.

The pioneers of 'atom poetry' include, along with Steinn Steinarr, Jón úr Vör (*b.* 1917) who, with his collection *The Fishing Village,* made one of the most original contributions to the new free-verse tradition; Stefán Hördur Grímsson (*b.* 1920) who has published three slim volumes, testifying to his lyrical talent, fertile imagination and sure sense of form and rhythm; and Hannes Sigfússon (*b.* 1922), a subtle and 'difficult' poet of the visionary type, whose verbal force and allusive qualities make him one of the most remarkable poets of his generation.

Slightly younger are two poets who have made lasting contributions to Icelandic poetry, even though they are very dissimilar in every respect. Sigfús Dadason (*b.* 1928), strongly influenced by French thinking and poetry, is a philosophical as well as a political poet of fine sensibility, whose two collections are landmarks in modern poetry for their perception and linguistic nuances. Hannes Pétursson (*b.* 1931), author of seven widely read and discussed volumes of poems, is sometimes referred to as the 'prodigy' of Icelandic post-war poetry. He is a vivid and comparatively 'easy' poet who mingles old and new motifs and metres to good effect and has a rare ability to give historical subjects fresh significance.

Still younger is Thorsteinn frá Hamri (*b.* 1938) who, with six volumes of poetry and two outstanding novels, is by far the most interesting and accomplished poet under forty. As to themes, his poetry is deeply rooted in old traditions, but he has gradually evolved a very personal poetic style, combining modern sensibility with a rather traditional diction and imagery. Many of his poems express an inner struggle, contrasting his original rural and new urban milieux.

As indicated earlier, collections of poetry were more numerous than works of fiction during the eighty-year period 1877-1966. The amount of books of poetry is still very high, reflecting the number of promising young poets as well as good older ones. At least a score of excellent post-war poets could be enumerated, but a mere listing of names has little practical meaning. Like their colleagues in fiction, most modern Icelandic poets express a deep-felt apprehension about the future of their tiny people in an encroaching world, with special emphasis upon the alarming American intrusion into national affairs through the military base af Keflavík.

Poetry is still a potent factor in the cultural life of the nation and its practice even seems to be on the increase, to judge from official poetry readings in 1974-6, the last of which filled the largest auditorium of Iceland to capacity, although most of the eight young poets presented were little known.

The Novel

The variety and vitality of Icelandic poetry were in no small measure due to the co-existence of more than one poetic tradition from the very beginning. In the realm of prose this was not the case. Here the epic-realistic style of the Sagas reigned supreme and was dominant in Icelandic prose writing until the mid-1960s, with surprisingly few deviations.

The modern epic-realist tradition reached its peak in two writers—in most respects dissimilar—who had a far-reaching influence on all later prose writing in Iceland. The older of the two, Thórbergur Thórdarson (1889–1974), created a sensation with his essays and eccentric memoirs from 1924 onwards. They were revolutionary, both in style and ideology. His radical socialist outlook was mixed with a curious interest in occultism and supernatural phenomena. His self-mockery gave sparkle as well as weight to his scathing social satires and frontal attacks against the ruling order.

Another revolutionary author of international stature is Halldór Laxness (*b.* 1902), who was awarded the Nobel Prize for Literature in 1955. With his narrative powers and vivid dramatic style he has done more than any modern novelist to renew Icelandic prose, and indeed he dominated the literary scene in Iceland from the mid-1920s to the mid-1960s. In his heyday he was an odd mixture of a universal creative genius and a partisan essayist propagating radical socialism; however, he made a point of separating his art and his social and political thinking, with the result that his novels are largely free from those tendencies which too often mar the works of socially conscious writers. He has a surprisingly wide range of styles and subjects, so that no two of his novels resemble each other in anything but their felicity of expression and power of character portrayal. Many of his fictional characters have become as much household figures in Iceland as the ancient Saga heroes.

Laxness's first significant novel was *The Great Weaver of Kashmir* (1927), a stylistic *tour de force,* mingling autobiography, philosophical speculation, mysticism, surrealism and Roman Catholicism. Its author was then converted to socialism in the United States, and from 1930 he concentrated his creative effort on the social scene and above all on character. From 1931 to 1946 he wrote four novels, *Salka Valka, Independent People, World Light,* and *The Bell of Iceland,* which capture the Icelandic scene more completely than any other works written in Iceland since the Saga Age. In 1948 he published a brilliantly executed and consciously tendentious satirical fantasy on contemporary Iceland, *The Atom Station,* which prompted some older patriots to demand that its translation into foreign languages should be forbidden. In 1952 came *The Happy Warriors* based on certain classical Sagas and written with unfaltering skill in the idiom of the thirteenth century. It is a thorough deflation of the ancient heroic spirit, and understandably upset some classical scholars in Scandinavia. In 1957 Laxness again surprised his countrymen with a finely wrought, almost lyrical novel describing life in Reykjavík at the turn of the century (translated into English as *The Fish Can Sing*). This was the least socially critical of his novels and inaugurated a new phase in his writing. The picaresque novel *Paradise Reclaimed* (1960) was a further departure from his earlier works; it is essentially a philosophical fable about man's quest for the infinite, partly set in the Icelandic Mormon settlement in Utah.

At that point Laxness suddenly turned to the theatre and wrote several plays with moderate success, but this detour was misguided, since his peculiar talent is above all epic, and not dramatic in the theatrical sense. The upshot was that he returned to the novel and published in 1969 *Christianity at the Glacier,* a quasi-fable on the theme of the self-effacing, saintly man of inner peace and natural charity pitted against the man of the world with all the trappings of power and financial success. This is also the theme of his best-known play, *The Pigeon Banquet,* and of most of his later work, including *A Country Chronicle* (1970), a description of the Mosfell Valley near Reykjavík where he was brought up at a farm called Laxnes (hence his pen-name). In 1975 he published his childhood memoirs. His earlier book of autobiographical sketches, *A Poet's Time* (1963), aroused great attention both in Iceland and abroad owing to the author's scathing revelation of his own gullibility while under the spell of Communism. After that he turned increasingly away from social affairs and towards a conservative attitude.

The dominant theme of Icelandic fiction after the First World War was the rapid emptying of the countryside and the resulting collision between the old rural way of life and the new urban society which was searching for its own identity, style and valid traditions. Icelandic novelists tended to exalt and romanticize the old values, stressing rural idylls and peasant virtues in the face of an amorphous urbanization. This was invariably done in the tested epic style of the Sagas. The overwhelming majority of Icelandic novels treated this subject in one way or another right up to the mid-1960s, a strange fact when one considers that already before the Second World War about 70 per cent of the entire population lived in towns and fishing villages—this percentage has, of course, greatly increased since then. The emphasis on pastoral novels tended to make Icelandic fiction rather uniform, since the same theme was exploited in one novel after another with only slight variations in style and approach. One explanation of this may be that the whole of society was in such a financial and social turmoil that all guiding principles of conduct and all traditional values were more or less blurred. The new urban society had not yet evolved the clear patterns necessary for significant novels in the traditional vein, nor had the novelists developed new techniques to deal with a totally new situation. Nor should it be overlooked that Laxness dominated Icelandic prose writing, both as an inimitable model and as an oracle, and his utterances seemed to have the impact of papal bulls. His younger and less experienced colleagues simply shrank from departing from the path he had laid out so masterfully, even if none of them could ever hope to rival him. Thus, paradoxically and perhaps unintentionally, Laxness in one sense halted the development of Icelandic fiction by tying it down to one definite mode of expressing reality. Admittedly, he was himself an undisputed master of the epic manner and might therefore be excused for sticking to it and insisting on it; but many a younger writer, who might more fruitfully have taken a different path, was mesmerized by Laxness's brilliance and force, and swallowed his superficial arguments in favour of epic fiction without demur. With the waning influence of the ageing and mellowing Laxness in the early 1960s, this state of affairs started to change.

Of the old school of novelists Gudmundur Hagalín (*b.* 1898) has been one of the most prolific, but his output is uneven. Of his many novels two stand out as permanent contributions to modern letters, both depicting memorable individuals of almost heroic stature. *Kristrún in Hamravík* (1933) is the story of a wretched widow of upright character who struggles for financial independence, and *Sturla in Vogar* (1938) deals with a hardheaded and formidable farmer who thinks only of himself and his own interests, until he learns the hard way that co-operation is the basis of civilized society. In both these novels the author used the salty language of the north-western peninsula. Hagalín was one of the most active cultural commentators in Iceland during and after the Second World War.

Of novelists who emerged in the 1930s, two stand out. Gudmundur Daníelsson (*b.* 1910) began by publishing realistic contemporary novels, but later turned to historical subject-matter. He is a romantic, with a strong preference for powerful primitive characters who sometimes take on almost mythic proportions. His most satisfying novel is *Blind Man's Buff* (1955), a modern allegory of two young people in search of 'real life'.

Olafur Jóhann Sigurdsson (*b.* 1918) is a highly sensitive and lyrical novelist, endowed both with acute psychological insight and a strong feeling for nature. His best novel is *Shades of the Soil* (1947) about a young man's first love and his subsequent departure from home. Two of his novels, *The Mountain and the Dream* (1944) and *Cold Spring Soil* (1951), treat of the irreconcilable antithesis of the rural population's dreams of a happy life and the harsh everyday reality. *The Machine* (1955) describes the consequences of a foreign military force on Icelandic soil as reflected in the consciousness and development of a young journalist. After a long interval he published in 1972 a much-discussed novel, *The Nest*, dealing with the endeavours of an elderly author to strengthen his ties with those life-forces and values of which he feels he cannot be deprived in a hostile world. Many individual passages in his writings are among the most beautifully written in modern Icelandic prose. In 1976 he became the first Icelander to receive the Nordic Council's annual Literary Prize for a selection from his last two collections of poetry, an unusual fate for a novelist.

Of post-war novelists a handful stand out for their originality and force. The first real *avant-garde* Icelandic fiction writer was Thor Vilhjálmsson (*b.* 1925), whose first publications were three collections of original and colourful short stories and sketches. These stories contain little movement or tension and less characterization; they resemble 'still lifes' more than stories. He finally turned to the novel with two large and intricate works, *Quick, Quick, Said the Bird* (1968) and *The Cry of the Beetle* (1970). Their subject is the individual searching for his identity in a crumbling world of lost values and faded ideals. Two later works of fiction are simpler in construction and more satirical regarding his fellow-countrymen. He has also published several collections of essays on contemporary arts, mainly the cinema and painting, both of which have influenced his writing. As one of the most important innovators in Icelandic prose writing and an indefatigable commentator on the contemporary scene, he has been important to younger writers.

Indridi G. Thorsteinsson (*b.* 1926) writes in the traditional manner, but with a difference. His principal works expound the inexorable principle which forces the rural population to abandon their farms and move to towns and fishing villages, and deal with their frequently sad fate in the new and unfamiliar environment. His two best novels are *Soil and Sons* (1963), which deals with the painful uprooting of a young farmer from his ancestral farm where his old father decides to carry on with his hopeless toil, and *A Thief in Paradise* (1967), an idyllic fable describing the pastoral serenity of an isolated parish which is suddenly disrupted by the intrusion of a new settler and his family. Some readers have seen in the latter a sly reference to the American military presence in Iceland.

Gudbergur Bergsson (*b.* 1934) produced, with his novel *Tómas Jónsson Bestseller* (1966), perhaps the most significant literary revolution since Laxness published *The Great Weaver of Kashmir* in 1927. It broke away from all the hallowed narrative and compositional norms, and opened up entirely new possibilities for Icelandic fiction. The novel has the form of a monologue conducted by a senile old man, Tómas Jónsson, who is in the process of writing his memoirs. The time element is wiped out: everything happens simultaneously, in the present, whether memories or the sensations of the moment's needs; there are no absolutes in human existence, everything is relative and illusory, all boundaries between inner and outer reality disappear, the personality is dissolved and objectified, or transformed into other personalities. There is a feeling of physical decay, darkness and death. In the copious and often coarse descriptions of contemporary Icelanders the author draws a terrible picture of social and political decay and sterility.

In his later books Gudbergur Bergsson has continued to explore the various manifestations of the 'anti-life', the wretched and pitiful existence we all accept. He is merciless in his cruel humour and his exposure of the clichés in everyday thinking habits and values, and like Laxness in *The Atom Station* he has searchingly and wittily demonstrated the demoralizing effects on the nation at large of the American military base at Keflavík.

In the mid-1960s for the first time women writers entered the front ranks of Icelandic fiction. There were two of them, both skilful and clever satirists, but very dissimilar in style and approach. In her second novel *The Snare* (1968), Jakobína Sigurdardóttir (*b.* 1918) gave a worker's view of the conditions created by the establishment of foreign industrial concerns in the country, leading to the gradual degeneration of all initiative on the part of the Icelanders. This reflected powerfully the anxieties felt by many Icelanders at the increasing range and power of foreign interests in their country. Her third novel *The Living Water* (1974) treats the same theme: it too tells the story of a labourer, brought up in the countryside, but who suddenly revolts against his inextricable involvement in a society he loathes, and finally loses his way entirely. These novels by a farmer's wife in the north-east of Iceland certainly testify to a living literary tradition among the ordinary people.

Svava Jakobsdóttir (*b.* 1930) is an ambivalent author who seldom makes direct statements. Her first novel *The Lodger* (1969) was superficially a realistic narrative of a young couple's marriage and housing problems, but this concealed a mordant political satire, one of the most remarkable in Icelandic literature. Svava Jakobsdóttir is also a sensitive short-story writer and an adroit playwright.

Many other writers have contributed to the development of Icelandic fiction since the Second World War, but their contributions have been less weighty than the ones listed above, even though individual works have been fresh and stimulating. In general two main tendencies may be said to have dominated the literary endeavours of the Icelanders in this century. First, a steady preoccupation with defining, crystallizing and deepening the peculiar features of the nation's history and character, with constant reference to the natural environment of the people. Second, a more recent but deeply felt need to synchronize Icelandic culture with contemporary reality, to validate it in a modern context and in the world at large.

Dramatic Literature and The Theatre

Dramatic literature is comparatively young and still rather under-developed in Iceland. The Reykjavík Theatre Company was founded in 1897 and has maintained regular performances almost without interruption ever since. In towns and villages round the country there have also been active amateur dramatic groups. The first trained stage actors came from Copenhagen in the 1920s, but were not in a position to make a profession of their art until the National Theatre was inaugurated in 1950. Nevertheless, the Reykjavík Theatre Company kept up a remarkably fine repertory under the guidance of a handful of skilled directors and actors.

The repertory consisted understandably mostly of translated plays, since native pieces were few. The two most notable Icelandic playwrights, Jóhann Sigurjónsson and Gudmundur Kamban, settled in Copenhagen and wrote their plays in Danish, although they were also performed in Iceland.

The first Icelandic dramatist was Sigurdur Pétursson (1759-1827) whose slight but humorous pieces were performed by students of the Latin School of Reykjavík (the present Gymnasium), a tradition that still lives on. Of other early dramatists mention should be made of the 'national poet' Matthías Jochumsson whose play *The Outlaws* (1861) has become a classic. Indridi Einarsson (1851-1939), an economist by profession, was the first Icelandic author to write exclusively for the stage. A number of his romantic plays, some based on folktales, are still sometimes performed. He was the originator of the idea of a National Theatre. Other 'early' playwrights were the prolific novelist Einar Kvaran (1859-1938), the politician Sigurdur Eggerz (1875-1945), the scholar Sigurdur Nordal (1886-1974), the diplomat Tryggvi Sveinbjörnsson

(1891-1961), the poet Davíd Stefánsson, and a number of other enthusiasts. Few of them had any noteworthy impact on the development of dramatic literature in Iceland, except perhaps Davíd Stefánsson who wrote four plays, of which *The Golden Gate* (1941), based on a folktale, became a great popular success and classic, and Sigurdur Nordal, whose single full-length play *Resurrection* (1945), written partly under the influence of Pirandello, was in its own way a milestone.

These two plays may be said to represent, broadly, the two main paths pursued by post-war dramatists in Iceland. *The Golden Gate* is a humorous and salty version of an Icelandic folktale about a devout peasant woman who saves her good-for-nothing husband from damnation by undertaking a gruelling pilgrimage to the Golden Gate, clutching his reluctant and unrepenting soul in a bag, and smuggling it into heaven when all entreaties prove in vain. When the play was first staged in 1941 it broke all previous box-office records and has been revived several times, not only in Iceland.

Resurrection is an ingenious and witty drawing-room drama about the individual's search for identity and his struggle against the rules imposed by bourgeois society, but in the middle the realistic framework is suddenly shattered and the play enters upon a journey into the realms of unbridled fantasy. This was the first major departure from traditional forms in Icelandic drama; however, the author was insufficiently experienced to succeed fully and too preoccupied by other tasks to pursue this new path. But some younger dramatists have followed in his footsteps and made all kinds of experiments, while others have stuck to old traditions and endeavoured to renovate them as Davíd Stefánsson did in *The Golden Gate*.

It was with the advent of the National Theatre and its subsequent competition with the Reykjavík Theatre Company that younger playwrights first began to appear. The first and most prolific of these was Agnar Thórdarson (*b.* 1917), who started out as a novelist, but then turned to radio and stage drama. His comedy *Atoms and Madams* (1955) was a great popular success, portraying the newly rich society of Iceland after the Second World War, and contrasting the prosperous superficiality and rootless modernity with the old moral values of rural Iceland, represented by an awkward but honest peasant.

Another playwright to emerge in the 1950s was Jónas Árnason (*b.* 1923), who first produced two musicals in collaboration with his brother, a composer. The first dealt with political and commercial corruption in the capital, where a cabinet minister and a businessman conspire to have Christmas postponed by a parliamentary decree, as the goods they have been expecting from abroad will not arrive in time for the lucrative Christmas shopping season. The second piece dealt with one of those typical big-time operators in a fishing village who own almost everything, directing the 'spiritual' life of their dependants as well as their mundane affairs. Both these musical farces were interlarded with romantic love stories to the accompaniment of attractive songs, making them popular at the time, but their themes were highly topical and their treatment is dated. In 1975 Jónas Árnason produced his best work, a comic description of the arrival of a small British military contingent at a remote spot in Iceland during the War, where they meet a highly original lighthouse-keeper. The play was successfully staged in Ireland in 1976.

The third playwright to emerge in the 1950s was Halldór Laxness who adapted his great novel *The Bell of Iceland* for the stage when the National Theatre was inaugurated, and later wrote four original plays with varying success. The first of these, *The Silver Moon* (1954), a dull and rather sentimental treatment of the effect of the American military presence in Iceland, was received with mixed feelings. Then came *The Chimney Play* in 1961, followed by *The Sun Knitting Works,* written a year later but not staged until 1966. Both were interesting attempts to create a personal dramatic style by mixing farce, satire, allegory, realism and a bit of Brecht, but neither one succeeded, although both plays contained interesting and powerful passages. The plays were rather difficult to follow, the author's warning about a symbolic interpretation only adding to the confusion. He characterized them as 'social comedies' which merely begged the question. Perhaps these strange plays can best be understood as a kind of dramatic exposé of the author's spiritual and political development at the time, his revaluation of life and his bitter political disappointments. In 1966 his best play, *The Pigeon Banquet,* was staged. Here he managed to dramatize a very static and undramatic individual, and to endow the whole play with a certain theatrical elegance, even if some of the episodes failed to come off. Three of his other novels were dramatized in the early 1970s and enjoyed great box-office success.

It may be claimed with some justification that in 1962 a new epoch began in theatrical writing and repertory, although such time categories are always misleading. In the early 1960s a number of young playwrights made their appearance and were presented by the two professional theatres and a new experimental group, *Gríma* ('Mask'). In the season 1962-3 two authors established themselves definitely as Iceland's leading young playwrights: Jökull Jakobsson (*b.* 1933) and Oddur Björnsson (*b.* 1932). In the following years both of them added valuable works to the repertory and were followed by a number of other young playwrights, chief among them being Gudmundur Steinsson (*b.* 1925),

Erlingur E. Halldórsson (*b.* 1930), Birgir Sigurdsson (*b.* 1937), and Nína Björk Árnadóttir (*b.* 1941).

This lively development in turn led to one of the most exciting theatrical events, a *Hair*-inspired musical satire, composed, directed and acted by a group of dedicated young actors. Owing to its familiar frame of reference and immediate appeal, this piece (*The Pop Play Óli* (1970), tracing the education and schooling, indoctrination and moulding of a boy, Óli) was more effective and successful theatrically in Iceland than *Hair,* even though the latter had a longer run. As another example of the same phenomenon, a group of actors from the National Theatre went to Greenland in 1974 in the company of an anthropologist to collect material for a short play, *Inuk,* which they composed and produced with such success that it has since been shown in both Western and Eastern Europe, all over Latin America and in the United States, taking laurels at several international theatre festivals. The technique of the production was such that a translation of the words was not absolutely necessary; foreign audiences were merely given short résumés of the action. This group enterprise has been the greatest success so far in Icelandic theatre history.

If we stick to the rough division indicated earlier, between a traditional and more experimental approach, we may say that Jökull Jakobsson pursues the former line, following more or less in the footsteps of Davíd Stefánsson and earlier Icelandic playwrights, while Oddur Björnsson and many of the young playwrights are more or less experimental and thus follow the example of Sigurdur Nordal.

Jökull Jakobsson has written many full-length plays, all in his peculiar manner of lyrical impressionism in a naturalistic setting. His themes have some resemblance to those of his great model, Chekhov: the devastating effect of time on the individual, the cruel gap between dream and reality, the inability to communicate by means of words even though they are used in profusion.

Birgir Sigurdsson, who is in some ways close to Jökull Jakobsson, made his début in 1972 with a prize-winning play describing the routine life of a young factory worker and his wife in very realistic terms, but with a strong poetic undercurrent. His theme is the antithesis between the workaday world of imposed duties and the youthful dreams of people who crave a more human existence.

Oddur Björnsson has pursued a quite different road from these playwrights, and has constantly experimented with form and content. His three one-act plays staged in 1963 were unprecedented in Icelandic drama, highly comic and at the same time intensely sad, almost tragic. A fourth, *Amalia* (labelled a tragedy), presented at the Icelandic Arts Festival in 1964 and later on television, showed the author fully in control of his medium: this play too is at once extremely funny and intensely tragic and moving. *The Horn Chorale,* his first full-length play, also staged by the National Theatre, was a musical which treated the same folktale motif as Jóhann Sigurjónsson's *The Wish* in a highly modernistic vein. A student of theology conjures up the Devil in the hope that his arrival will bring the Icelanders to their senses, but the Devil merely becomes one more good joke in the existence of a people whose chief preoccupations are novelties, sensations, tourism, festivals, fashion shows and aviation. The hero gives up the idea of improving the world and enters the service of the country's biggest company (an airline).

Two of the other experimental playwrights are, each in his own way, under the spell of Brecht and his epic theatre with a sprinkling of personal absurdism. Erlingur E. Halldórsson is perhaps the more consciously Brechtian. Three of his plays have been staged—all clearly allegories of the social and national condition of Iceland under American 'military protection'. Gudmundur Steinsson has written a number of plays, four of which have been staged, two by Gríma and two by the National Theatre. *The Presidential Candidate* (1964) described the ascent of a politician and the means he employs to reach his goals, and *Native Soil* dealt with the American base at Keflavík and the humiliating position into which the Icelandic employees are forced *vis-à-vis* their 'protectors'.

This brief résumé of Iceland's post-war drama, from which several authors have been omitted, shows that much searching and experimenting is going on, and a number of Icelandic authors are writing interesting plays, but by and large the theatre depends on imported material, because native dramatic literature is only just coming of age. To reach full maturity it will need much more time, better accommodation, and above all more experienced and inventive directors.

The beginnings of the National Theatre go back to 1923 when the Althing levied a special amusement tax to be put into a 'National Theatre Fund'. A committee was formed to organize the fund, invest it and make preparations for erecting a theatre building. The Depression and the War delayed the final inauguration till April 1950. The National Theatre operates from September till the end of June, with occasional summer tours of local theatres around the country. The theatre director and the five-man theatre council, composed of representatives from the four largest political parties and one from the actors of the Theatre, all have life tenure, and a new law to change this state of affairs has long been pending in the Althing. From the beginning the National Theatre has also presented one or two operas or musicals each season. Since 1973 there has also been a small experimental stage in the basement of the Theatre, where experimental or *avant-garde* plays are staged.

The Reykjavík Theatre Company is run by a private enterprise although it has considerable financial support from the municipality. The core of the company is a group of salaried professional actors who each season stage eight to ten plays. The company is still housed in the same little theatre, seating 210 people (the National Theatre seats 661), near the lake in the old centre of Reykjavík, where it started in 1897. Here the theatre director is appointed for five years at a time, and the theatre council is also elected for fixed terms. The company occasionally tours the country with one of its productions. There is good co-operation between the two theatres as well as stiff artistic competition.

Painting I

Painting and sculpture had a tenuous existence in Iceland until the present century. This was mainly owing to natural circumstances—the country's population being small and scattered in more or less isolated farms, while there was no moneyed, leisured class to subsidize artistic activity. However, there is evidence that talent was not lacking. Wood-carving was widely practised from the earliest times, mainly to decorate homes and places of worship. Many fine examples of such work are to be found in the National Museum. Tapestry-weaving was also popular, and illuminations in surviving manuscripts indicate high artistic skill. Embroidered clothes were much in vogue, richly ornamented with gold and silver. All this can be verified in the National Museum. Portraits have also been painted in considerable numbers for the last three centuries, mostly by clergymen.

In the seventeenth and eighteenth centuries some ten artists, who worked mainly in the Baroque tradition, stand out. One of them was Gudmundur Gudmundsson (1618-90), a wood-carver and sculptor, and another Hjalti Thorsteinsson (1665-1754), a portraitist. However, the most gifted portraitist was Saemundur Magnússon Hólm (1749-1821), the first Icelander to study at the Academy of Fine Arts in Copenhagen, where he was awarded numerous prizes. Contemporary with him at the Academy was Bertel Thorvaldsen (1770-1844), the son of an Icelander living in Copenhagen, who became in his lifetime one of the most celebrated sculptors in Europe, living mainly in Rome. Saemundur Magnússon Hólm became a clergyman in Iceland after spending fifteen years in Copenhagen, and his great talents went to waste in the terribly adverse conditions of his native land. His career is a telling illustration of the hopeless situation of artists in the poor and primitive society of Iceland. Two of his contemporaries, who also studied fine arts, settled in Denmark and Norway, while a third, Thorsteinn Illugason Hjaltalín (1770-1817), the first Icelander to devote his life entirely to fine arts, settled in Germany and never returned to Iceland. The first Icelander to study abroad with the avowed intention of becoming an artist in Iceland was Thorsteinn Gudmundsson (1817-64), a painter in the primitive manner whose lack of determination coupled with inadequate artistic ability resulted in a meagre and mediocre production.

Two men may be said to have given Icelandic painting an impetus around the middle of the nineteenth century. The older of these was Helgi Sigurdsson (1815-88), a versatile writer and artist who was also the first Icelander to study photography. He made some fine drawings and oil portaits of leading Icelandic intellectuals while he was studying medicine in Copenhagen, but after his return to Iceland, where he took holy orders, he devoted his varied talents to other tasks, such as collecting antiquities. Part of his collection was the embryo of the National Museum, founded in 1863. He also wrote the first systematic essay on the principles of art known to have been written in Icelandic.

Sigurdur Gudmundsson (1833-74), who conceived the idea of a National Museum and was its first director, was a man of many parts, dividing his energies between painting, antiquities, the theatre and many other tasks. He was responsible in 1862 for the first production of *The Outlaws,* a play he had inspired and partly written, and his stage designs for that performance, which still survive, were the first Icelandic paintings of natural scenery. Sigurdur Gudmundsson, who worked in the neo-classical tradition, was a gifted artist, but he was first and foremost a man with a mission, a pioneer who has left an indelible mark in the cultural history of his country, even though his artistic output was limited. Ironically, he died of starvation in 1874, the year when his compatriots were celebrating the millennium of the settlement.

Two famous Icelandic vagabonds of the last century were potential artists who went to seed. Gudmundur Pálsson (1830-84) was a fine wood-carver who studied abroad, but took to drink and vagrancy after his return to Iceland. Sölvi Helgason (1820-95) was self-taught, an excellent and productive draughtsman and calligrapher. He was imprisoned in Copenhagen for common lawbreaking in 1854-7, but otherwise spent his life wandering from one farm to another, drawing quaint, primitive pictures and writing on order. The most important self-taught man of the late nineteenth century was Arngrímur Gíslason (1829-87), a versatile artisan who also wandered from farm to farm at certain times and was an alcoholic. His portraits of peasants and their families have a strong personal character. He was the first Icelander to depict a historical incident, the burning of a famous church in North Iceland in 1865.

As the nineteenth century came to an end and the dawn of independence was felt to be near at hand, there was a general awakening in all spheres of national life, not least in the fine arts. About the turn of the century a number of gifted artists entered the scene and established painting and sculpture as potent factors in Iceland's cultural endeavours. Fortunately, they found ready eager acceptance among their countrymen. These were individuals who gave themselves wholeheartedly to their art, for better or worse, and reaped rich rewards for their devotion.

The first three artists of the new generation to go abroad for thorough studies were the sculptor Einar Jónsson and the painters Thórarinn B. Thorláksson and Ásgrímur Jónsson. Einar Jónsson (1874–1954) was a dreamer and romantic, who came to Copenhagen when Realism was gaining ground in the arts. Some of his early works, sculptures like *The Outlaws* and *Proletarians*, reflect his struggle between Romanticism and Realism, but he soon withdrew into his own world of fantasy and religious mysticism, and created works that became progressively more allegorical. After the First World War the Icelandic state built him a workshop and museum in Reykjavík where he worked for the rest of his life in almost total seclusion, and where most of his works are to be seen. There are a number of his sculptures in public places in Reykjavík.

Thórarinn B. Thorláksson (1867–1924) came to painting comparatively late while still pursuing his trade as a bookbinder in Reykjavík. He was the first Icelander to receive a public grant for studies abroad, and spent almost nine years in Copenhagen. There his interest in landscape was aroused, and in 1900 he was the first Icelandic artist to go out into nature to paint, the result of which was the very first Icelandic exhibition of paintings, held the same year. All his life Thorláksson was an 'amateur' in the sense that he painted only in such time as he had to spare from breadwinning, but his best works, especially in his last years, nevertheless constitute an important and permanent contribution to Icelandic art.

Ágrímur Jónsson (1876–1958) is the great pioneer, the first of the three 'giants' (the others being Jón Stefánsson and Jóhannes Kjarval) who established painting as a basic strand in modern Icelandic culture. Ásgrímur Jónsson went at the age of twenty-one to Copenhagen, where he worked as a furniture painter while studying at the Academy of Fine Arts and in museums. In 1902 and 1903 he spent summers in Iceland painting mostly landscapes, and held his first exhibition in 1903. A long journey to Italy a few years later brought him into contact with Impressionsim, which opened up new avenues in his art. In 1910 the first exhibition of Icelandic art outside Iceland was held in Oslo with works by Ásgrímur Jónsson and Thórarinn B. Thorláksson.

For a long time Ásgrímur Jónsson was the grand old man of Icelandic painting, setting an example of integrity and devotion to art. His simplicity and strength of character became legendary. As a painter his strength lies in his fresh rendering of Icelandic landscapes and his suggestive interpretations of Icelandic folktales. He bequeathed his private collection of his own paintings to the Icelandic state, thus making about half his entire life's work public property. These works are on exhibition at his home in Reykjavík.

Jón Stefánsson (1881-1963) went to the University of Copenhagen in 1900 to study engineering, but soon gave this up for art studies, first in Copenhagen and later with Matisse in Paris. A man of strong temperament, he had to wage a hard and bitter struggle to master his medium, but the result was impressive. Perhaps no other Icelandic figurative painter has ever achieved such forceful composition.

The third great pioneer and the best-loved in Iceland was Jóhannes Kjarval (1885-1972), the most protean of them all, an uneven genius of extraordinary range and fecundity who seemed to embody the nature of Iceland, both visible and invisible, in his prolific production. He was the first Icelandic artist to go so close to nature as to select as his subjects a patch of grey lava or green moss, a narrow crevice, a small rock formation, or a few blades of grass. While Jón Stefánsson was a formal expressionist, Jóhannes Kjarval was a romantic one with strong surrealist tendencies.

After many years as a seaman on Icelandic fishing smacks where he used every spare minute to paint, Jóhannes Kjarval sailed for London on a trawler in 1911, supported by a group of young enthusiasts who had organized a lottery to raise the funds necessary for his stay abroad. In London he was refused admission to the Royal Academy School, but the museums were a revelation to him, and he quickly fell in love with Turner and his seascapes. In 1912 he was admitted to the Academy of Fine Arts in Copenhagen from which he graduated in 1918. His art, like that of Picasso, falls into many distinct 'periods', each characterized by a fresh insight, new technique and wider application of his talents. He was a masterly draughtsman, but above all he was an untiring innovator. In a very real sense he taught his countrymen to see Iceland with fresh eyes, as did the other pioneers, each in his own way, thus joining hands with the writers in defining, crystallizing and deepening the peculiar features of the nation's character with constant reference to its natural environment.

Painting II

In the wake of the three 'giants' came a number of very competent painters, most of whom received their training in Copenhagen. They more or less followed in the footsteps of the pioneers, repeating rather than adding to the original contributions. One of them, however, stands out for his unusual versatility. Gudmundur Thorsteinsson (1891-1924), best known by his nickname Muggur, studied at the Academy in Copenhagen in 1912-15. He followed many muses, being simultaneously painter, actor, musician and a great humorist, as manifested by his brilliant illustrations of folk and fairy tales. Even though his output is small and far from unified in style, Muggur has a notable place in the history of Icelandic art.

In the 1930s there were important developments and changes. Revolutionary ideas and techniques were introduced, and Iceland moved closer to international modes of expression. Gunnlaugur Scheving (1904-72), who studied in Copenhagen and Oslo, painted fishermen and peasants in their daily tasks in strong and simple forms. He was later increasingly drawn to historical subjects and especially to folk motifs.

Thorvaldur Skúlason (*b.* 1906) started his career under the strong influence of Ásgrímur Jónsson, his teacher, and Jón Stefánsson. His exhibitions in 1938 and 1943 in Reykjavík aroused lively interest and controversy, since he introduced a new and peculiar style which he developed for many years with much success, until he switched to pure abstractions at the end of the War. The main strength of his later work lies in strong and almost mathematical composition.

Another pioneer of abstract painting in Iceland, and the first to hold a purely abstract exhibition, was Svavar Gudnason (*b.* 1909) who stayed in Copenhagen many years before and after the Second World War and is generally considered one of the great originators of abstract art in Scandinavia. He is radically different from Skúlason, freer, more elastic and explosive, frequently playing with violent colours and contrasts. Perhaps, despite his long sojourns abroad, he is the most 'Icelandic' of the abstract painters, conveying the inner tensions of the Icelandic temperament and the contrasts of its environment. He too is widely known in Europe.

A close friend of Thorvaldur Skúlason was Snorri Arinbjarnar (1901-58) who also studied in Oslo. He was a delicate and atmospheric painter of houses and harbour scenes with a strong sense of form, moving from realist expressionism to near-abstract composition. Jóhann Briem (*b.* 1907), who studied mainly in Germany, is one of the most distinctive Icelandic painters of his generation, an exquisite colourist with a dreamlike quality and a preference for folk motifs. He stands midway between figurative and abstract painting, uniting the best of both. Jón Engilberts (1908-72), who studied in Oslo and Copenhagen, was a colourful, almost juvenile painter of primitive passions. The best of his uneven output is characterized by inspired virtuosity.

When we come to the post-war generation of painters, the diversity is even more baffling than in the preceding generations. This is no doubt a natural consequence of the opening-up of new horizons during and after the War. The young generation no longer went to Scandinavia for their education, but to the great centres of art in Paris and America. Abstract painting continued to develop and flourish until well into the 1960s, but it seemed gradually to have reached a dead end, and there was a slow return to the figure, mainly under the influence of English and American Pop Art. Man and his environment again became a respectable subject, having been practically outlawed by a whole generation of geometric and lyrical abstractionists.

There were many highly competent painters in the post-war group, but only a handful will be briefly mentioned here. Of these Kristján Davídsson (b. 1917), who studied in America and Paris, is the most protean. With a very flexible technique he has experimented with a great variety of styles, constantly seeking new outlets for his searching originality. He has had many different 'periods', each marked by his inspired mastery of style and intense feeling for his medium. Jóhannes Jóhannesson (b. 1921), who also studied in America, is a peculiar colour expressionist working in stark, compressed forms of great vigour. Karl Kvaran (b. 1924) is a constructivist of rare force and originality, concentrating on stark, simple forms and 'pure' colours. Eiríkur Smith (b. 1925) was in a sense an abstract extension of Kjarval, his art being 'landscape painting' in purely non-figurative terms, suggesting rather than imitating or reproducing natural phenomena, but around 1970 he turned to figurative painting under the influence of the English painter Francis Bacon, as did many of his younger colleagues, notably Einar Hákonarson (b. 1945). Sverrir Haraldsson (b. 1930), who may be the greatest original talent among his generation, started out as a geometric abstractionist, then moved through several interesting phases to a strange, mystifying type of landscape painting, where his facility sometimes seems to lead him astray. Hördur Agústsson (b. 1922) was one of the pioneers of abstract art in Iceland, and has made murals and worked on book-design with admirable results; he is also the principal authority on the history of Icelandic architecture, having studied its development through the ages for many years. Bragi Asgeirsson (b. 1931), who studied in Copenhagen, Oslo and Munich, has been a leading exponent of graphic art, besides being a good and highly experimental painter and an outstanding art critic. A large number of fine young figurative painters have come to the fore since the mid-1960s, some of them engaging in social realist or socialist painting, intent on making their art serve practical, political purposes.

Whatever the reason, many Icelandic women artists have made their reputation mainly abroad. Júlíana Sveinsdóttir (1889-1960) was the first Icelandic woman to become a professional painter, a highly sensitive, quiet and personal artist who never followed the beaten track and in time won a reputation throughout Scandinavia. Nína Tryggvadóttir (1913-68) lived most of her adult life in New York, Paris and London. She moved from realist expressionism to lyrical abstraction and enjoyed high esteem abroad for her colour compositions. She also achieved international renown as a stained glass artist with the first-ever one-man exhibition of glass windows at the Galerie La Roue in Paris in 1958. In the same year she executed a series of fourteen glass windows for the restored Romanesque church at Langweiler in Germany. She also made the huge mosaic altarpiece on the wall of the new Skálholt Cathedral as well as the outdoor mural on the Hotel Loftleidir in Reykjavík. Louisa Matthíasdóttir (*b.* 1917), living in New York since the early 1940s, also began her studies in Copenhagen and later studied in Paris. She has gained a high reputation in America for her strong suggestive studies of the human body and for her plaster heads. A younger painter, Gudmundur Gudmundsson (*b.* 1932), working under the name of Ferro and later Erro, is probably the best known internationally of all Icelandic artists, having had one-man shows in most major cities of Europe, America and Asia. He is a versatile and obsessed artist, cruelly witty and importune, whose monstrously surrealistic paintings of the machine age and human anatomy often take the form of distorted insects in an environment of huge steel construction. He has also had fun with Pop Art and his very personal brand of socialist realism.

This too short survey should make it clear that modern Icelandic painting is extraordinarily fertile and vigorous. In no other art-form has there been so much growth, invention and diversity of fine talent.

Sculpture

Strangely, sculpture in Iceland has not shown any vigour comparable to that in painting. After Einar Jónsson, a solitary figure outside the mainstream of modern art, there have been only a handful of noteworthy sculptors, some of them working abroad. The grand old man of Icelandic sculpture is Asmundur

Sveinsson (*b*. 1893), a veritable Proteus who has gone through all the phases from strictly classical to purely abstract forms. He studied for many years in Stockholm and Paris, visited Greece, and returned to Iceland filled with ideas which he gradually materialized in magnificent forms. He is at home in the Sagas as well as in Icelandic folklore, and has treated both subjects in his sculpture, sometimes in figurative, sometimes in abstract form. But he is above all a child of his own century, fascinated by modern progress and technology, as two of his well-known sculptures show: *Electricity* at the Sog power station near Thingvellir, and *Through the Sound Barrier* in front of the Hotel Loftleidir in Reykjavík. He works with equal ease in stone, cement, metal and wood. Many of his sculptures stand in public places in Reykjavík, while the best selection of his varied work is to be seen in and around the workshop which he built in Reykjavík with his own hands and has partly turned into a museum.

His younger contemporary, Sigurjón Ólafsson (*b*. 1908), is less versatile and much less productive, but he is a sensitive and powerful sculptor, and a master-portraitist. He spent many years in Denmark where a number of his works are to be seen, but since the War he has worked in Iceland, his poor health permitting, and produced some masterpieces, both realistic and abstract. Some of his sculptures may be seen at the National Gallery of Art in Reykjavík, while others are in various places around the capital. He has also made a colossal abstract relief on one of the outer walls of the Hydro-electric Power Station at Búrfell.

The most exciting and productive *avant-gardist* in Icelandic sculpture is Jón Gunnar Árnason (*b*. 1931) who works mostly in metal and plaster. His blood-curdling mechanical contraptions have created sensations at shows in Iceland and abroad. A number of younger sculptors have exhibited originality and seem destined to make significant contributions to Icelandic art in due time.

Just as in painting three women sculptors have mainly made their reputation abroad. Nína Saemundsson (1892-1966) studied in Copenhagen and worked in Paris and Rome until she moved to America in 1926. She spent four years in New York before settling permanently in Hollywood. In America she became well known with such works as *Spirit of Achievement* on the front façade of the Waldorf-Astoria in New York and busts of celebrities like Hedy Lamarr and Peter Freuchen, but in Iceland her renown is based on a few pieces in the National Gallery and one public statue, *Maternal Love,* in the old centre of Reykjavík. Gerdur Helgadóttir (1928-1975) lived in Paris from the 1950s and won fame and many international awards for her intricate metal pieces. She also worked in stained glass in Germany, France and elsewhere. Among her most ambitious work in that field are the windows of the new Skálholt Cathedral. A large mural of hers decorates the outer wall of the Customs Building near Reykjavík harbour. Ólöf Pálsdóttir (*b.* 1920), a traditionalist of severe and simple forms, is well known in Scandinavia. Some of her pieces are exhibited at the National Gallery of Art in Reykjavík.

Apart from the National Gallery of Art, which has permanent exhibitions of paintings and sculpture, and various individual museums run either by the state or by artists themselves, there are a number of exhibition halls in Reykjavík, most of which are booked throughout the winter by artists* whose exhibitions normally last two weeks. The best exhibition halls are in the Nordic House and in the new municipal gallery of Kjarvalsstadir, named after the great master, where there is a permanent Kjarval exhibition in one wing. Genuine interest in painting and sculpture is widespread, exhibitions are well attended, and works of art sell well—so well, in fact, that most homes in Reykjavík and the larger towns have originals hanging on the walls—not all of the very best quality, needless to say. There are a few art schools, one of which is run by the state under the name The Icelandic School of Arts and Crafts. It gives three- to four-year courses, but most serious artists complete their studies abroad. Exhibitions of Icelandic art abroad are frequent, but there is dire shortage of foreign exhibitions in Iceland—for very natural reasons. All in all, the growth and vitality of art in Iceland is one of the happier and more telling results of the general national awakening in the earlier part of the twentieth century.

Music

Nobody knows with any certainty what musical traditions the settlers of Iceland brought with them. The *skalds,* when reciting their poems, are said to have sometimes sung them, and in the ninth century attempts are known to have been made at polyphonic song. The melody was sung in consecutive or parallel fifths and octaves. This system has been preserved in the so-called duet or quint song.

Christianity brought new musical trends. When the first bishop of Hólar, Jón Ögmundsson (1106-21), established a school at his see, he hired a French priest to teach singing and rhyming, the French at that time being prominent in music; also, the bishop himself had been in Paris and Rome and was a highly educated man and a good singer. Candidates for priestly orders had to be trained in Gregorian chant. After the Reformation, the great bishop Gudbrand Thorláksson had some hymn-books set to music and printed in 1589 and 1619. In 1594 he also published the so-called *Grallari (Graduale),* a book that was printed with few alterations nineteen times, the last time in 1779. It was the principal song-book until the late nineteenth century.

Popular secular songs were sung from earliest times, but they were not written down until the end of the nineteenth century—a work still in progress. The oldest form was the duet song, but the more common one was the so-called *rímur*-song, sung to the long *rímur*-cycles already mentioned. The folk music of Iceland has an ancient and unusual ring which sets it distinctly apart from that of other Western European countries. A great quantity of these songs have been collected since the turn of the century. Some have been issued on gramophone records, and there are societies round the country still cultivating this form of music.

Of native Icelandic instruments only two are known. They were rather primitive: one was a form of fiddle with two to four strings, and the other was the *langspil* with three strings. Both were placed on a table and played with a bow. The melody was played on one string, while the others were scraped with the bow to produce harmonic sounds.

About the middle of the nineteenth century European influences on Icelandic music began to be felt on a small scale, mostly in church music. Pioneers in this field were organists at the Cathedral of Reykjavík. In the late 1850s three-part and four-part singing began to be practised, and about 1860 the first choir was formed. Church choirs are now to be found in every parish, and every church has an organ.

At the millennial festivities in 1874 commemorating the settlement, the present national anthem was sung for the first time. The composer was Sveinbjörn Sveinbjörnsson (1847-1927), the first Icelander to devote himself full-time to music. For most of his adult life he lived abroad, mainly in Edinburgh, where most of his works were published.

The turn of the century saw the beginning of a period of increased choral activity; brass bands made their appearance; music was played in the home, and gradually singers and musicians began to appear in public. A number of minor composers wrote songs which became quite popular. Following the First World War new impetus came with young composers who had studied abroad. Páll Ísólfsson (1893-1974) came home in 1920, after long and successful studies in Germany, and was the leading figure in the musical life of his country for over four decades. He was organist at Reykjavík Cathedral and conducted symphony orchestras, choirs and brass bands. He was also the first director of the Conservatory of Music, founded in 1930. His very active life understandably thwarted his creativity, but he nevertheless found time to compose some significant vocal and instrumental music.

The year 1930 was in a sense a turning-point. A symphony orchestra, which for some years had existed in embryo, now received a permanent conductor and teacher, and the State Radio began its operations. In 1932 the Music Society was founded and became one of the most important factors in the musical life of the capital, taking charge of both the Symphony Orchestra and the Conservatory. It also ran an excellent choir. It arranged performances of the first major choral works and the first opera to be staged in Iceland. It gives ten subscriber concerts every season and has had many world-famous performers besides all the principal Icelandic musicians and singers.

The Conservatory of Music, still partly supported by the Music Society, is simultaneously a popular school for people not intending to make music a career, a college and a professional school for future musicians. In its first thirty years nearly 100 students graduated from it, many of whom are now active in Icelandic music. The Conservatory has done much to promote music throughout the country, and in recent years similar colleges have been established in all the larger towns outside Reykjavík.

Another important milestone came in 1950, when the National Symphony Orchestra became a semi-official body, and the National Theatre was opened. For the past few years the Symphony Orchestra has been under the auspices of the State Radio, and has functioned simultaneously as a radio orchestra and a theatre orchestra (in the National Theatre) as well as giving up to twenty independent concerts every season, and special youth concerts. These concerts are all well attended and form an important feature in the cultural life of Reykjavík. All the public concerts of the orchestra are broadcast, as are many special concerts. As already mentioned, the National Theatre functions partly as an opera company, producing operas and musicals, either with Icelandic singers or with individual foreign artists. Although Icelandic musicians have on the whole not suffered from unemployment, the same cannot be said about the singers, who only get intermittent assignments. Therefore most of them have settled abroad. In the late 1950s and early 1960s the three principal tenors of the Copenhagen Royal Opera were Icelanders.

Besides Páll Ísólfsson there were a number of Icelandic composers active before and after the Second World War. Jón Leifs (1899-1968) and Hallgrímur Helgason (*b.* 1914) collected folk melodies and used them as basis for their compositions. The former was an ambitious composer and the pioneer of modern music in Iceland. Björgin Gudmundsson (1891-1961), Karl O. Runólfsson (1900-70), Jón Thórarinsson (*b.* 1917) and Jórunn Vidar (*b.* 1918) also wrote ambitious vocal and instrumental music, but it was first with the post-war generation of composers that

Icelandic music made significant strides and aroused attention and interest abroad.

Among the more prominent of the younger composers, Jón Nordal (*b.* 1926) has composed fine orchestral pieces developing from the older national style to more advanced techniques. Jón Ásgeirsson (*b.* 1928)represents the national style initiated by Jón Leifs, but develops it further; among his many interesting works is the first Icelandic opera *The Lay of Thrym,* which had its première at the International Arts Festival in Reykjavík in 1974. Its libretto is based on various Eddic poems. Leifur Thórarinsson (*b.* 1935) has composed mainly orchestral and chamber music. Thorkell Sigurbjörnsson (*b.* 1938) is one of the most prolific *avant-gardistes* with a highly personal style. Atli Heimir Sveinsson (*b.* 1938) is a highly gifted composer with an extremely varied output, who may be said to have explored all the *avant-garde* techniques. He was the first Icelander to be awarded the Nordic Council's biennial Music Prize, for his *Flute Concerto* (1975). Magnús Blöndal Jóhannsson (*b.* 1925) has been a pioneer in Iceland of electronic music and is still active in that field.

In 1970 a biennial International Arts Festival was inaugurated in Reykjavík, sponsored jointly by the Municipality, the Ministry of Education, Nordic House, the professional theatres and all the artists' associations. One of its principal instigators was the Russian-born pianist Vladimir Ashkenazy, who is married to an Icelandic pianist and is himself a naturalized Icelandic citizen. Needless to say, music is the main ingredient in the Festival, which has secured the co-operation of numerous world-renowned musicians in every field.

9. The Infrastructure

Communications

The roads of Iceland are much poorer than those in most other countries with a comparable standard of living. Until the turn of this century there were no roads to speak of, and the horse was practically the only means of communication and transportation besides boats. Organized road building began around 1900, and the first roads were only intended for horse-drawn traffic. There have never been any railways or trams, but in 1913 the motor-car was introduced, and after that road-making progressed rapidly. By 1930 all the most important districts had been linked by roads, but winter road communication remains difficult in many places, notably in the north and east. In 1939 there were a little over 2,000 vehicles in the country, but by 1974 the number had shot up to 63,000, of which 6,000 were trucks and lorries and 800 passenger coaches. Private companies run regular coach services throughout the country, and in Reykjavík and Akureyri there are bus services run by the municipalities.

Every year has seen expansion of the road system. In 1927 there were 1,300 km., in 1947 about 5,200 km., and in 1974 about 11,000 km., including local country roads (about 2,000 km.). Most of the existing roads are only of earth and gravel, but in recent years about 150 km. have been laid with a hard surface in three directions out of Reykjavík. The maintenance of the vast road system is a heavy burden on the Icelandic taxpayer. All the large rivers and many of the smaller ones have now been bridged.

There are many good natural harbours in Iceland, except on the south coast, and at present there are regular coastal services between all the main ports. Until the First World War most of the cargo traffic, both coastal and trans-oceanic, was handled by foreigners, mainly Danes and Norwegians, but with the establishment of the Iceland Steamship Company in 1914 most of the coastal services, in addition to trans-oceanic transport, came into Icelandic hands. In 1929 the State Shipping Department was established to take over the coastal services, while the Steamship Company concentrated on foreign transport of goods and passengers. During the Second World War Icelandic shipping suffered heavy losses, but since the war older ships have been disposed of and new ones bought. By 1974 the Iceland Steamship Company had nineteen cargo vessels, having disposed of its only passenger ship, which for decades carried tourists between Reykjavík, Leith and Copenhagen. This fleet, with a gross tonnage of about 35,000, sails to many ports in Europe and America. In 1946 the Federation of Iceland Co-operative Societies (Samband) put its first ship into operation and in 1975 had eight vessels, including two tankers, with a gross tonnage of 11,000. Altogether there are nine shipping lines, making a merchant fleet of fifty ships with a gross tonnage of approximately 56,000, but if all vessels of 100 tons and over are included, the number becomes 340 and the gross tonnage 136,000. The rapidly increasing size of the fishing fleet mainly accounts for the large number of vessels. Despite the size of the Icelandic merchant fleet, it only transports about half the country's imports and exports, while Icelandic ships play some part in international traffic elsewhere.

The first lighthouse in Iceland was only built in 1878, on Reykjanes, the south-western peninsula. There are now 110 lighthouses, ten radio-beacons (with twenty-five more specifically for aircraft) and two stations for radio direction-finding on Faxaflói.

Air traffic was first introduced in Iceland in 1919 when a small aircraft was bought and used for two years on flights to many parts of the country. An airline company was founded in 1928 and operated a few years. Regular air services started in 1938 with the formation of Icelandair, which has maintained domestic scheduled flights ever since. Another company, Loftleidir Icelandic Airlines, was established in 1944 by a few young pilots returning from their training in Canada. Until 1952, both these companies handled the domestic services, but after that Icelandair has been mostly responsible for them along with a number of smaller private companies.

Air services in Iceland are especially important, because of the limitations of the road system, and the inaccessibility to ordinary vehicles of large areas of the country in the winter. Icelandair's planes have often been called upon to perform extraordinary tasks, such as transporting whole flocks of live sheep from remote districts or dropping supplies to scientific expeditions on the Greenland Ice Cap. In 1973 Icelandair carried more than 183,000 passengers on internal routes, while also keeping up scheduled flights to several European countries. Loftleidir Icelandic Airlines concentrated on international flights between America and Europe via Iceland after 1952 and made remarkable progress by offering lower fares than other air carriers on the Europe–America route.

In 1973 Icelandair and Loftleidir Icelandic Airlines pooled their interests and have jointly offered scheduled flights to Copenhagen,

Oslo, Stockholm, the Faroe Islands, Glasgow, London, Luxemburg, New York and Chicago since 1974. During the summer they also fly to Frankfurt-on-Main and Greenland. An indication of the expansion of the two airlines is that in 1950 they carried 5,700 passengers on scheduled flights, while in 1973 they carried 592,843.

In 1906 a submarine telegraph cable was laid from Scotland to Iceland, and in the same year telephone lines were established in Iceland itself. Radio-telephone submarine cable linking Scotland and Iceland (Scottice) came into use in 1962, and a year later a similar link with Canada (Icecan) was opened.

Agriculture

Iceland was until this century basically an agricultural country, but since the turn of the century fishing has become progressively more important to the economy. As late as 1870 agriculture employed about 75 per cent of the labour force, but only half the working population at the turn of the century, and in 1974 it only accounted for 11 per cent. Of necessity, agriculture has always been limited in scope and variety. The cultivated areas only amount to about 1 per cent of the country, but it is estimated that 5 to 10 per cent of Iceland could be cultivated. The active growing season is no more than four months, from May to September, and farming is based almost exclusively on cultivation of grass and animal husbandry. The quality of the grass is good; it is usually harvested twice every summer and is stored either dry as hay in barns or in silos for winter feed. The cattle have to be fed for eight months and sheep for five or six months. Generally nine-tenths of the farmer's income is derived from livestock and more than half of that from the sale of milk, from which various dairy products are made. Grain was once grown in the country, but due to bad climatic conditions in the sixteenth century it was no longer profitable. In recent decades barley and oats have been grown experimentally with some success.

Despite the great decrease in agricultural manpower, the number of farms remained fairly stable down to the last few decades. For some 250 years the number of farmlands fluctuated between 6,150 and 5,350, but between 1955 and 1970 the number fell from 5,210 to 4,660. The average size of a farm is about 300 hectares, but the sizes actually vary from 150 to 1,200 hectares. The average stock per farm is 180 sheep and thirteen cattle, including eight dairy cows. The number of cattle in 1972 was 65,280 (36,580 dairy cows), representing nearly a threefold increase over the previous fifty years. Sheep account for about two-thirds of the total agricultural production in the north-west, north-east and east. In 1933 there were 728,000 sheep in the country, but through the introduction of Karakula sheep in that year with the idea of improving the breed, about two-thirds of the native stock were infected in the following years, so that by 1949 the number of sheep had fallen to 402,000. In 1960 the stock had increased again to 834,000. During the summer season the sheep population rises to as many as approximately 2 million head, at least half of which is slaughtered in the autumn. Conservation specialists maintain that there are far too many sheep in Iceland and point to the fact that erosion and overgrazing have lately reached catastrophic proportions. It is estimated that about half the soil and vegetation of Iceland has been lost since the country's settlement, while much of the rest has greatly deteriorated. At present land reclamation and afforestation do not make up for what is lost every year, mainly due to overgrazing.

But the Icelanders love their sheep—of their total meat consumption, mutton accounts for some 80 per cent. In the 1930s a winter-fed sheep gave 10 kg. of meat, but by the 1970s this had risen to 16·5 kg., with an annual average increase of 1 per cent. The annual production of milk per cow has increased about 1·5 per cent, from 1,780 kilos in 1920 to 3,520 kilos in 1972.

The impressive increase in agricultural productivity is directly related to extensive land reclamation carried out since early in this century and to the total mechanization of agriculture after the Second World War. The total area of cultivated hayfields amounted to about 1,000 hectares in 1885, about 17,000 hectares at the turn of the century, and over 82,000 hectares in 1970. In the 1920s hay from meadows amounted to 48·5 per cent, but in 1970 the figure was less than 2 per cent. The acceleration in land reclamation was made possible by the use of track-laying tractors with bullgraders and bulldozers, introduced in 1942 and gradually replacing the wheeled tractors and small track-laying tractors previously used. Excavators were introduced in the same year, making possible large-scale drainage of pastureland. Between 1942 and 1972 some 19,000 km. of ditches were dug, almost half of this for draining pastureland. Tunnel drains were introduced in 1962 and by 1971 some 39,400 km. had been laid. The greater part of all cattle pasture is on cultivated land, and sheep are as a rule grazed on improved fields in spring and autumn, while they are moved on to common grazing lands in the uplands in midsummer.

Horses are still a prominent feature of the Icelandic environment, though their practical use belongs to the past. They are now mostly used for sport, but are also exported. In 1943, a peak year, there were 61,876 horses in the country; thirty years later their number had declined to 39,209. The export of live horses started around 1850; the most significant period was 1870–1930, when 2–3,000 horses were exported annually.

According to price-levels and output-volume in 1972 agricultural produce could be divided as follows: cattle 50 per cent, sheep 33 per cent, horses 2 per cent, hothouse and garden produce 5 per cent, pigs and poultry 7 per cent, subsidiary income 3 per cent. Sheepskins are about 20 per cent of the volume of mutton production. About two-thirds of the wool is used industrially, as raw material for cloth and knitted fabrics.

In 1973 there were nineteen dairies in Iceland, eight more than in 1963, with a total quantity of milk weighed in amounting to 109,751 tons in 1972, which was equal to 87 per cent of the whole marketed quantity. There are some fifty legally authorized slaughter-houses, mostly owned by farmers' co-operatives, handling 11,827 tons of mutton in 1972 or 95 per cent of the total production.

In 1971 egg production was estimated at about 10 kilos per head of population (2,100 tons). The crops of potatoes, turnips and other vegetables are very much affected by weather conditions from one year to another. Farmers grow potatoes for their own use and, in a few areas, commercially. The total yield has been as high as 16,000 tons and as low as 5,000. In the best years potato production satisfies domestic demand, but about 40 per cent of the national requirements usually have to be imported. Hothouse cultivation began half a century ago and has developed rapidly, as is best seen by the total area under glass (in square metres): in 1929 1,200, in 1949 67,600, in 1972 113,000.

In the period 1935–70 agricultural productivity value increased nearly fourfold, showing an intensive growth rate of 4 per cent *per capita* each year.

The importing of agricultural machinery began in earnest in 1945 with 201 wheeled tractors. There were great fluctuations in the following years, reaching a peak of 810 wheeled tractors in 1966. At present every farm has one tractor, some three or more. Haymaking machines in common use are cyclomowers, singer wheel rakes, roter-speed, self-loading forage boxes or bailers, and harvesters and self-loading trailers for silage. Almost every farm has been equipped with a drying system, and most of the *ca.* 2,500 farms with dairying as their main activity have milking machines. At the end of 1967 Icelandic farmers had altogether 3,037 motor vehicles, mostly jeeps and lorries. Almost three of every four farmers are freeholders, their proportion having increased considerably over the past few decades. About half the leaseholds are government or institution owned, their tenants enjoying extensive legal protection and low rents. A burning problem on many farms is the lack of women.

Fishing

If agriculture is by far the most heavily subsidized industry in
Iceland, fishing comes next, even though it has been the very basis
of the national economy since the beginning of this century. It was
not until 1890 that decked vessels began to be used to any extent
by Icelanders for cod fishing, and shortly afterwards herring
fishing was developed. These have been the two most important
species caught in Icelandic waters. Herring fishing has been an
extremely unstable business; in good years it was lucrative and
earned great sums, but there could be many successive years when
the herring disappeared altogether. The last great herring boom
was in 1965-6, when the catches rose from 50,000 tons in 1955 to
750,000 and almost 800,000 tons in 1965 and 1966 respectively.
Cod fishing is much more stable and has until recently represented
about 30 per cent of the total quantity of fish taken by Icelandic
vessels. Various other valuable marine species are caught around
Iceland, the most important from the point of view of quantity
being capelin (its catch exceeded that of cod in 1972), saithe,
redfish, haddock, catfish, molluscs, ling, shrimps, plaice, Greenland
halibut, lobster, lumpfish, tusk and halibut. The Icelandic catch in
1972 totalled 725,327 tons, compared to 1,199,100 tons in 1965.
Herring represented a considerable part of the catch in 1965,
whereas the herring catch in 1972 was the only species not caught
in Icelandic waters, since a total ban on the exploitation of
Icelandic herring stocks is now in force for conservation. In 1972
the herring was caught mainly in the North Sea. The Icelandic
grounds are fished not only by Icelandic fishermen but by by many
other nations, such as the British, West Germans, Russians,
Belgians, Faroese, Norwegians, Polish, French, Dutch, and so
forth. The total catch of demersal fish taken in 1972 by the
Icelanders was 377,200,000 tons, while foreign vessels took
299,000,000 tons.

Whaling has been lucrative during the summer months since
1948, the species caught being fin whale, sperm whale and sei
whale. The catch in 1972 was 446, but it has fluctuated from year
to year between 280 and 450. The entire carcass of the whale is
utilized, the meat is either processed for human consumption,
pet-food and meat extracts, or together with the bones reduced
into meal. The blubber is processed into oil.

The average number of fishermen is 4,500-5,000, rising to some
5,500-6,000 during the height of the fishing season in March-Aoril
and July-August. The *per capita* productivity of the fishermen is
still among the highest in the world. Of the total labour force only
6 per cent are directly engaged in the fisheries, while 8·1 per cent
are engaged in fish processing.

From about 1930 fish on ice was exported to Great Britain and Germany, but after the Second World War the quick-freezing industry expanded greatly, and quick-frozen fish is now a major export. Formerly the greater part of the catches of cod and related species was salted and exported either wet or dried as klipfish. Now more than half of these species are filleted or frozen, while reduction into meal and oil is also extensive. A considerable part of the catch is normally sold fresh (on ice) for direct human consumption. The canning industry has not given the results hoped for, in spite of both private and official efforts. In 1966 the export value of herring products was just under 50 per cent of the total value of marine products, and in the period 1962-7 herring was the dominant export item, but in 1972 it only amounted to 6 per cent of the export value of marine products, while frozen fish represented 52·3 per cent, salted fish 18·8 per cent, marketed fish 11·2 per cent, dried unsalted fish 2·4 per cent, and meal and oil 13·9 per cent. The largest buyers were the United States (41·4 per cent), EFTA countries (25·6 per cent), Comecon countries (13·4 per cent) and EEC countries (10·9 per cent).

The fishing industry has accounted for between 15 and 20 per cent of Gross National Product, and the export value of fish and other marine products constituted 90 per cent of all export goods in the mid-1960s, but had declined to about 75 per cent by the mid-1970s, owing to the introduction of large-scale industrial production and the expansion of light industries and tourism. Even though these industries and other invisible earnings are taken into account, the contribution of the fishing industry is still dominant and amounts to about half of the total export value of goods and services.

The Icelandic fishing fleet has twice been entirely renewed and modernized since the Second World War and now ranks among the best equipped and efficient of the world. There are about ninety freezing plants all around the country with a total capacity of roughly 1,500 tons of fillet a day.

It should be clear from the foregoing that the Icelanders are more dependent on fisheries than any other independent nation in the world. This is also the reason why Iceland has so unswervingly and strenuously held to her right to protect and preserve the coastal fishing by extending her fisheries jurisdiction. The two overriding reasons for the Icelandic Government's decision to extend the fishing limits to 200 miles in 1975 (having extended them from three to four miles in 1952, to twelve miles in 1958, and to fifty miles in 1972) were on the one hand the urgent need to conserve the fish stocks in Icelandic waters that supply the Atlantic Ocean, and on the other hand the country's vital economic needs.

The need for conservation had gradually become ever more

evident. Without the Icelandic initiative to protect the important spawning areas on the continental shelf, Iceland and the other nations fishing in Icelandic waters would in the long run be the losers, as had already been indicated by the harm done to the haddock and herring stocks in these waters by over-exploitation. The drop in the herring stock has already been mentioned, but the drop in Iceland's haddock catch was from 53,506 tons in 1965 to 35,036 tons in 1969. The figures for the total haddock catch in Icelandic waters by all nations were 110,086 tons in 1946—and 46,613 tons in 1969.

Cod being the most important species in Icelandic fisheries, it was only natural that the Icelanders should be alarmed at the evidence that cod was being overfished. Scientists demonstrated beyond all doubt that the total mortality in the spawning population of cod was over 70 per cent in 1970-1, and that fishing was responsible for four-fifths of this amount. The average age of the spawning stock had been drastically reduced. Fish over ten years of age were extremely rare, whereas in 1950-5 fish up to fifteen years old were not unusual. Thus the increased fishing effort, with ever improving equipment, had sharply reduced the spawning potential of the cod stock. The cod is in a way similar to the salmon or capelin, the greatest part of the stock now having the possibility to spawn only once in its lifetime; the biological implications of this are bound to be extremely prejudicial to the survival of the stock. The North Sea was a chilling reminder of the consequences of overfishing. There were clear signs that trawling had led to overfishing in Icelandic waters even before the First World War. The decline was halted then by the chance that most foreign vessels were kept away from Icelandic fishing grounds during the war years. Before the Second World War the situation had again become so grave that attempts were made to reach an international agreement on conservation measures, which were to be applied in certain limited areas of the utmost importance as breeding and nursery grounds for the fish-stocks. These attempts were continued after the war, even though the situation had considerably improved during the war years, but they proved vain. The greatly increased catching capacity of the foreign vessels operating around Iceland in the post-war period made the problem more acute than ever. Therefore in 1948 the Althing passed a 'Law on the Scientific Conservation of the Fisheries of the Continental Shelf', authorizing the Government to issue the necessary regulations to establish areas and zones within the limits of the continental shelf, where all fishing should be subject to Icelandic jurisdiction. The United Nations' Law of the Sea Conference, initiated by Iceland and other interested nations, which convened in Venezuela in the summer of 1974, was favourable to the

Icelandic case, even if an international agreement was not reached at that stage, and the same is true of the Geneva Conferences of 1958 and 1960. There can be no doubt that the Icelandic principle will be accepted by the majority of nations attending the Law of the Sea Conference, and that the much-contested extension of Icelandic fishery limits will greatly contribute to safeguarding the fish-stocks of the North Atlantic.

Industry

Mechanized industry is a relatively recent development in Iceland, but its pace is rapidly accelerating, in spite of a dire lack of raw materials and capital. Some 26 per cent of the labour force are occupied in manufacturing industry (including 8 per cent in fish processing), of whom about one-third are women.

During the first half of the century the development of light industries was very slow, but with the mechanization of agriculture and fishing maintenance and repair firms inevitably came into existence. Industrial endeavours were at first mainly directed at the domestic market owing to the remoteness of the country from world markets. Tariff and locational protection of much of manufacturing industry did not further exporting. It was only in 1960 that a major reorganization of the import structure and the currency system was made by abolishing multiple exchange rates, making import licences more liberal, and lowering maximum tariff rates. Two devaluations of the *króna* in 1967 and 1968 resulted in increased manufacturing exports from 1969 onwards. These exports were also encouraged by entry into EFTA in 1970 and by various supplementary measures then put into effect. The annual production in manufacturing industry increased by 3-4 per cent in 1960-8, but in 1969-72 the increase was over 10 per cent. Manpower increased much less, so labour productivity must have taken a big step forward.

Since agriculture with its overproduction and fishing with ever diminishing catches cannot absorb the annual increase in the labour force, which is estimated at 2-3 per cent or an annual average of 1,760 people, further industrialization of the country is a necessity, whether one likes the idea or not. This was one reason why Iceland joined EFTA, others being to take part in the economic development of Western Europe, to increase competition in the domestic market and get rid of tariffs, thus strengthening the competitiveness of manufacturing industry, and finally to further exports of industrial products. In entering EFTA, Iceland was granted duty-free access to markets in the EFTA countries, but domestic tariffs were to be gradually removed over a period of ten years. Iceland was also given permission to maintain her substantial trade with the Soviet Union. In addition to these concessions, the Nordic Industrial Development Fund decided to provide Iceland with an interest-free long-term loan of $14 million to help her make necessary adjustments to the economy in consequence of joining EFTA. A trade agreement with the EEC became effective in 1973, except for fish products where decisions have been pending on whether the Community will let part of the agreement take effect before there has been an agreement in the fishery dispute, first with West Germany and then with the United Kingdom (since November 1975). This has done great harm to the Icelandic fishing industry.

During the period 1968-72 export of light industries (including fish canning) increased fivefold, the greatest increases being in wool products and knitted goods, furs and skins, canned fish products and diatomite.

The abolition of trade barriers, both quotas and tariffs, have undoubtedly made a large part of the Icelandic economy more competitive than before. In 1969 the total number of enterprises in manufacturing was 2,157. Of these about 750 were one-man firms and only about 150 firms employed more than twenty people.

The dairy industry has no foreign competition and its increase is on the whole determined by the amount of milk produced and the growth of the domestic market. In recent years efforts have been made to diversify this branch of industry by introducing new types of product, such as cheeses and yogurt. The chocolate industry, which at one time was quite prosperous, has had a difficult time since the abolition of import controls at the end of 1974. In the textile industry, production and labour productivity have increased considerably, more than the average for manufacturing industry as a whole. Yarns (*'lopi'*) have been exported mainly to the United States, Canada, Denmark and Yugoslavia. Blankets have been exported to the Soviet Union in large quantities, and so have standardized items, like sweaters, while fashion goods of special Icelandic design have had a great vogue in the United States and various Western European countries. Production and exports of knitted wool products increased by over 10 per cent annually in 1969-72. Carpet making is largely based on Icelandic wool and mainly directed at the domestic market. Icelandic wool carpets have to compete with imports, mostly of synthetic materials. The share of Icelandic producers has varied between 60 and 85 per cent. The hide, fur and skin industry is chiefly centred on export, which increased by almost 100 per cent in 1965-9. In 1972 exports amounted to twelve times the value of 1968. The shoe industry had difficult times after the freeing of imports in 1960, both production and employment drastically diminishing, but in 1970 this downward trend was broken. Employment in the garments industry decreased in 1964-7 owing to foreign competition, even though the quantity remained approximately constant, but production increased considerably in 1969-72, by over 20 per cent annually on the average. There have been great fluctuations in the fishing gear and paper carton industries, since they are closely linked to the fisheries, but even so production has increased appreciably. Both production and productivity in the furniture and fixtures industries have increased since 1960. Imports have been subject to a global quota, and the domestic market share is over 90 per cent. There has been no control of imports since the end of 1974, but exports have been on the increase. The production of paints has increased at an annual rate of 3-5 per cent. The domestic market was over 80 per cent in 1963-70, and exports have been increasing. Production of detergents and washing fluids had an annual increase of 4-5 per cent in 1960-8, of more than 20 per cent in 1969, and of more than 10 per cent in 1971 and 1972. The metal industry is mostly a service industry and depends heavily on the fisheries. Shipbuilding is carried on in many places around Iceland. Until 1965 shipyards were mainly occupied with repairs, but they have since increasingly directed their activities towards building fishing-boats, even sometimes for foreign markets. Plastics production has had an annual growth rate of 25 per cent since 1960, its products varying from insulating materials, fishing gear, wrapping material to cooking utensils. The production of ceramics from Icelandic lava has enjoyed growing popularity and is steadily increasing. Mink farming was reintroduced in the early 1970s after a lapse of many years, but it is subject to great fluctuations on the world market.

Next to her fishing grounds Iceland's greatest natural resource is undoubtedly energy which can be exploited on a large scale. This energy has two different sources, the hydro potential of the rivers and the geothermal potential of the vast natural steam areas of the country. Some major steps are now being taken to tap this precious source for power-intensive industry. The first step in this direction was taken in 1951 by building the State Fertilizer Plant at Gufunes, some 10 km. north-east of Reykjavík. The plant started production in 1954 and is based on electrolysis of water. About 11,000 kWh are needed to produce one ton of ammonia which is then processed into ammonium nitrate used for NPK fertilizers. In 1970-2 the capacity of the plant was increased to about 60,000 tons of NPK fertilizers a year, the production of which requires about 140 GWh per year (1 GWh = 1 million kWh).

Another large factory, though needing much less energy, is the Cement Plant at Akranes, across the bay from Reykjavík, whose production of over 100,000 tons of Portland cement a year makes the country self-sufficient in this material. The process is based on liparite calcareous sand which is dredged from the bottom of the nearby Faxa Bay.

A diatomite filter-aid plant at Lake Mývatn in the north-east started production in late 1968 with a capacity of 12,000 tons per year, and in 1973 its capacity had reached 22,000 tons a year. The main shareholders in the company, Kísilidjan, are the Icelandic Government and the Johns-Manville Corporation of New York, according to an agreement made in 1966. The plant gets its raw material from the bottom of the lake and uses geothermal steam as a source of heat to remove the water. This represents the first large-scale application of natural steam for industrial purposes in Iceland. All the production of the plant is exported.

By far the largest power-intensive enterprise in Iceland is the aluminium smelter at Straumsvík, some 14 km. south of Reykjavík, on the Keflavík road, a wholly owned subsidiary of Alusuisse of Zürich. The smelter was built under a contract signed by the Icelandic Government and ratified by the Althing in 1966, which stipulated that the smelter should have an ultimate capacity of 60,000 tons of aluminium a year, requiring some 120 MW of continuous power and consuming about 1,000 million kWh of electric energy per year. Production was to start in 1969 at a rate of 30,000 tons annually, reaching ultimate capacity not later than 1975. In connection with this vast scheme the National Power Company of Iceland (*Landsvirkjun*) was established in 1965, whose first task was to build a new hydro power plant on the river Thjórsá in the south with an ultimate capacity of 210 MW. The first stage of the Búrfell power plant with a capacity of 105 MW was completed in 1969 and full capacity was reached in 1974. Since all raw material for the aluminium smelter, including alumina and carbon electrodes, have to be imported, mostly from West Africa, a new harbour to accommodate cargo carriers of up to 60,000 d.w. was constructed at Straumsvík by the town of Hafnarfjördur and leased to the smelter company. Production of the smelter started in 1969 according to plan and amounted to 12,400 tons. Energy consumption in that year was 171 GWh. Since then production has increased year by year, and in October 1969 a new agreement was made calling for the ultimate capacity to be reached in 1972 and extending that capacity to 77,000 tons of aluminium a year. In 1973 the smelter produced 71,300 tons of aluminium and consumed 1,231 GWh of energy—or about 54 per cent of the total energy production of Iceland in that year.

The combined project of smelter and power station represented a total investment of $151 million, and is by far the largest industrial venture ever undertaken in Iceland. Aluminium amounted to about 17 per cent of total exports in 1973. The 550 employees of the smelter are among the highest paid workers in

Iceland and their contribution to the national product is correspondingly high.

The aluminium smelter has, however, been a hotly debated issue in Icelandic politics, mainly because it is wholly owned by a foreign company, which is run according to a special law enacted by the Althing and which pays a price for its electricity consumption that is said to be far below production costs. The contract between the Government and the Swiss company is valid for twenty-five years, which is considered very unrealistic in view of the constant inflation in Iceland, reaching the record proportion of 50 per cent a year in 1974 and 1975. In this context it is also pointed out that the state budget of Iceland is so small that a mere handful of medium-sized foreign companies could easily control the whole national economy.

Since 1971 systematic studies on the feasibility of power-intensive industries have been carried out by a committee under the authority of the Ministry of Industry. Its main task has been to find prospective industrial buyers of the electrical power from the new 150 MW Sigalda hydro-electric project, due to start production by mid-1976. Numerous foreign companies have shown interest in establishing power-intensive industries in Iceland. The Sigalda project is some 40 km upstream from Búrfell on the river Tungnaá, a tributary of the Thjórsá river. In 1973 a large reservoir of 1,000 GL capacity at Thórisvatn was completed, which will serve both the Búrfell and the Sigalda hydro plants, as well as other hydro plants anticipated in the future on the rivers Thjórsá and Tungnaá.

It has been estimated that technically harnessable hydro energy in Iceland amounts to some 35,000 GWh or 3·5 million kW a year, and that the geothermal potential is of similar magnitude. It is considered that some 60–80 per cent of the hydro potential could be harnessed when economical and ecological factors have been taken into account. Up to now only 7–10 per cent of this vast potential has been utilized. In 1974 about 47 per cent of the energy used in Iceland was imported (oil), 38 per cent was hydro-electric, and 15 per cent geothermal. The last figure may well be higher, since it is difficult to estimate the proportion of geothermal energy that has already been utilized.

A new plant using steam fields on a small scale is under construction at Karlsey on the northern shore of Breidafjördur in the north-west. In the initial stage it will produce 6,600 tons of seaweed meal annually, but the ultimate planned capacity is 25,000 tons. For drying the seaweed the plant will use 50 litres per second of 90° C hot water from the nearby low-temperature geothermal area of Reykhólar. All the products of the plant will be exported, and the Scottish corporation, Alginate Industries, by far the biggest alginate salts producer in the world, will be the main buyer. The chief shareholder will be the Icelandic Government, and there will be no foreign shareholders.

Other projects under consideration include the so-called Sea Chemicals Project on the Reykjanes peninsula in the south-west, which would use geothermal heat for recovering minerals from seawater and geothermal brine. The main efforts have been directed at producing salt and some by-products from the Reykjanes brine on the one hand, and producing magnesium chloride and soda ash, or ultimately magnesium metal and chlorine, on the other. A feasibility study on an annual production of 250,000 tons of salt and by-products was under consideration in 1975. This plant would be the first step in an industrial complex that could be of tremendous economic importance for the diversification of Icelandic exports.

Electricity was first introduced to Iceland in 1904 when a small stream in Hafnarfjördur, 10 km south of Reykjavík, was harnessed and a plant of 9 kW built. In the following thirty years electric supply utilities were established in most of the larger towns and villages. The largest plant during this period was the Ellidaár power plant on the outskirts of Reykjavík, which in 1922 had an initial installed capacity of 1,032 kW. Then came the large power plant on the river Sog, at Ljósafoss, with 8,800 kW installed capacity, which started operating in 1937 and was a significant step towards the complete electrification of Iceland, for it was the first time that more power was harnessed than was needed for one supply utility. Generation of electricity in 1973 totalled about 2,285 GWh, of which approximately 61 per cent went to power-intensive industries, while in 1968 the percentage was only 15 per cent for the fertilizer plant.

Foreign Trade

Iceland is more dependent on foreign trade than any other country in Europe. Its foreign trade (export and import) *per capita* is six times that of the United States, and almost three times that of Great Britain, and more than one-and-a-half times that of Denmark, Norway and Sweden. Imports have at times amounted to as much as 50 per cent of the Gross National Product. Commerce and services occupied 37·3 per cent of the labour force in 1971. In 1855 there were fifty-eight business firms in Iceland, but in 1973 the figure had reached 2,753, out of which 1,692 (61 per cent) were in Reykjavík and its neighbourhood. 49 per cent of the total number of businesses were owned by individuals, 51 per cent by partnerships, limited companies or co-operative societies, or by public bodies. The biggest exporters are a handful of sales organizations, such as the Icelandic Freezing Plants Corporation, founded in 1942, and The Federation of Iceland Co-operative Societies (*Samband*) founded in 1902, which handle almost all frozen fish exports and have subsidiaries in the United States for the final processing and distribution of frozen fish products. The Union of Icelandic Fish Producers, founded in 1932, handles all salted-fish exports. The Union of Stockfish Producers, founded in 1951, handles about 50 per cent of the stockfish exports. The Iceland Herring Board is the official agency handling all salted herring exports. The Canning Industry's Institute, established in 1972, is almost the only exporter of canned marine products. Almost all the exports of agricultural products are handled by the *Samband.*

A considerable part of the imports and the domestic trade is in the hands of the co-operative societies, which began to develop in the late nineteenth century and are most active in the rural areas and the towns outside Reykjavík. Since the Second World War the *Samband* has greatly expanded its activities and branched into manufacturing, shipping, insurance, banking and other fields. In 1972 it embraced fifty co-operative societies with a membership of 36,541, operating 195 stores. Since 1922 there has been a state monopoly on the import of alcohol and tobacco, with a revenue amounting to 9 per cent of the total revenue on current account in 1972. From 1936 to 1956 there was a state monopoly on the imports of potatoes and fresh vegetables, since when the Vegetable Trading Centre, operated by the producers' organizations, has functioned as a general sales agency.

Banking is of course an important factor in the Icelandic economy. There are three relatively large state-owned commercial banks, four private banks, and a Central Bank which formulates the monetary policy of the Government, acting as its adviser and as administrator of its economic policy. The Central Bank has the power, previously entrusted to the Althing, to fix the par value of the Icelandic currency (*króna*), and has the overall control of foreign exchange dealings. It also supervises all banking institutions. The two largest commercial banks now deal in foreign currency, apart from the Central Bank. The commercial banks have a network of branches all round the country. In addition there are about 100 savings banks, mostly in rural districts and half of them savings departments of local co-operative societies, which do not grant credit to the public, and are therefore not savings banks in the normal sense, but rather a means to finance the operation of the co-operatives in question.

Since the Second World War inflation has been the most constant and characteristic feature of the Icelandic economy, reaching a peak of over 50 per cent a year in 1974-5. This has been due mainly to Iceland's heavy dependence on foreign trade and the great fluctuations in both fish catches and world market prices. For all that, Iceland has achieved in this period a remarkable growth in real income and has maintained a high level of employment and social security. For reasons of geography, climate, and perhaps in response to favourable taxation legislation and the opportunities given by continuous inflation, the building industry employs an unusually large share of the labour force—11·3 per cent. It is estimated that over 80 per cent of all Icelanders own their apartments or houses. The quality of housing is probably exceptionally high, in contrast to the roads.[1]

Note

1. See Ch. 6, fn. 1, above.

10. The Country and its Seasons

Introduction: the Landscape

The natural beauties of Iceland have long been celebrated by natives and foreigners. Even if the landscape appears at first sight barren and naked (there are almost no trees in the country), you find all over the country beautiful green valleys and pastures, glittering rivers, calm, reflecting lakes and multicoloured mountains. Actually, the clear and extremely variegated colours are among the most distinctive characteristics of Iceland and can only be compared with the Mediterranean countries.

Lake Mývatn in the north-east, at the northern edge of the vast Ódádahraun lava desert, the fifth largest lake in the country, is by far the richest in natural life of all kinds. The water collects and seeps into the lake from underneath the lava, and no real river flows into it, even though a rather big one, the Laxá river, flows out of it. Bird-watchers flock to Lake Mývatn every year, for it is the home in summer of between 100,000 and 150,000 ducks of fifteen different species. The lake itself abounds in a special kind of very tasty trout, which live on the numerous midges from which Mývatn derives its name.

Around Lake Mývatn are interesting places like the Námafjall hot-spring area; the Hverfjall mountain considered the largest and most remarkable explosive crater in the world; the Dimmuborgir lava formations, with their unreal, mysterious appearance; the deep clefts in the lava where you can swim all the year round in underground lakes at a temperature of 27° C. under rocky vaults. In the lake itself peculiar lava formations protrude out of the water as well as many beautiful islands, most famous among them the Slútnes, where almost all the Icelandic flora are represented and grow with luxuriance.

The interior of Iceland is rich in magnificent scenery which is, however, rather chilly and overwhelming in its grandeur. The coastal regions are more attractive and congenial, especially the many fiords on the north-west and east coasts, while the north coast is full of fertile valleys flanked by splendid mountains. Aside from the spacious Borgarfjördur district, one of the most peculiar regions in the west is the Snaefellsnes peninsula with the arresting cone-shaped and ice-capped volcano at its tip, which is clearly visible from Reykjavík, some 200 km away, in good weather. In the south, apart from the national shrine of Thingvellir, there are many places of great beauty, such as the Thórsmörk close to Mýrdalsjökull, a remote paradise enclosed by high mountains, and the Thjórsárdalur valley along the Thjórsá river with its spectacular waterfalls, green brush growth and striking contrasts between vegetation and wasteland. This valley was laid waste in the first historical eruption of Hekla in 1104. Previously there had been nearly thirty flourishing farms there, one of which, Stöng, has been excavated, giving a clear idea of housing and living conditions in Iceland's early centuries.

An area of exceptional variety and grandeur lies south of the vast expanse of the Vatnajökull glacier, in the south-east corner of the country, a coastal stretch of some 100 miles from the Almannaskard mountain pass to the National Park of Skaftafell. Close to Almannaskard at the eastern end lies the prosperous and rapidly expanding fishing port of Höfn in Hornafjördur with one of the most modern and comfortable hotels in Iceland. The view of the towering glaciers and the mountain formations beneath them is a source of constant wonder to the traveller. The highway from Höfn to Skaftafell skirts several glaciers, some of them descending almost down to sea level, and traverses many glacial rivers. Among them is the only glacial river in Iceland to enter the sea by an adjoining lagoon, which by the way is filled with majestic icebergs and frequently also with thousands of seals.

The Skaftafell National Park, the first of its kind in Iceland, is in the most remote district of Iceland, which until recently could only be reached by horse or aircraft. The National Council for the Protection of Nature, founded in 1956, resolved unanimously in 1961 to work for the preservation of Skaftafell as a national park, having a year earlier received a proposal from one of its members, the geologist Dr Sigurdur Thórarinsson, to the same effect. In the explanation accompanying his proposal, he said among other things:

There can scarcely be any doubt that the natural beauty of the area surrounding Skaftafell in Öræfi is unsurpassed by any other inhabited part of Iceland. There are few other places, if any, where the grandeur of the landscape can be matched. There is a unique view not only of Iceland's highest mountain, but also of the country's biggest outlet glacier and its widest expanse of a glacial outwash plain. The area contains mangnificent mountains of varying shapes and many types of rock. There is found one of the interesting valley glaciers in Iceland, the Morsárjökull. Waterfalls and ravines renowned for their beauty are to be found there. The vegetation is more luxuriant and varied than in most other places, and the climate is probably more favourable than anywhere else in Iceland except in the neighbouring farm Svínafell. Apart from the glacial outwash plain,

Skeidarársandur, the Skaftafell area is endowed with such natural boundaries of glaciers and rivers that it could easily be protected and preserved without a great deal of costly fencing.

A generous grant from the World Wildlife Fund and a grant voted by the Althing secured the purchase of the estate of Skaftafell in 1967, since when it has been a National Park. It is the first of its kind in Iceland to be protected from a strictly nature conservation point of view, while the only other so-called national park in Iceland before that time, Thingvellir, was declared a sanctuary for historical reasons and has moreover been invaded by a large number of privately owned summer houses—an unheard-of arrangement in any national park.

The settlement around Skaftafell has a remarkable history. From the earliest days it was known as the Country Between the Sands and flourished until the middle of the fourteenth century. There were at least thirty farms, four parish churches, two annex churches and eleven chapels. Then in the spring of 1362 Oræfajökull erupted with the biggest cataclysm in Europe since the destruction of Pompeii, accompanied by a gigantic glacier burst from the western valley glaciers. The district was laid utterly waste, and when it was finally resettled it acquired a new name—a strange one for a place of human habitation—Oræfi, or Waste Land, which it still has to this day. Oræfajökull erupted again in 1727 and did much damage, but nothing to compare with the destruction of 1362. Another threat to the community was the volcanic activity of the Grímsvötn in the very heart of the Vatnajökull glacier. From this crater at intervals of about ten years an enormous volume of water emerged, often accompanied by volcanic eruptions, and forced its way up from below the Skeidarárjökull. This glacier burst generally began in the river Skeidará, but covered most of the sands, with a maximum discharge of about 40,000 cu. m. of water per second, or about seventeen times the volume discharged by the Rhine at the Dutch border. It broke up the margins of the glacier and gradually encroached on the grasslands of Oræfi from the west, driving the farms from the plain into a close group under the mountain slopes. Since 1938 the flooding has diminished, but has occurred at shorter intervals of 4-6 years. The three farms of Skaftafell formerly stood in the plain, where traces of their sites are still to be seen, but in 1820 they were moved about 600 metres up the slope where they now stand.

In the Skaftafell National Park 210 species of vascular plants have been found to grow, and the southern element in the Icelandic flora is more prominent there than in most other parts of the country. One species of fern, *Asplenium trichomanes,* is found in Iceland only in this area. Ecologists know that within the National Park they can study plant societies typical for elevations from the sea shore to the uppermost limits of vegetation in the mountains. The Skaftafell area is also interesting for ornithologists, and even more so for entomologists. A Swedish entomologist, Carl H. Lindroth, in a study of the flora and fauna of this area, has pointed out that it affords a unique example of the maintenance of organisms in close proximity to perennial ice.

Volcanoes

In the summer of 1965 eleven American astronauts came to Iceland as part of their preparation for landing on the moon. This was the first time their rehearsal programme had taken them abroad; they had previously made similar visits within the United States, to Oregon, Arizona, New Mexico and Hawaii. They were training themselves to walk the surface of the moon, but more especially testing their capacity to define types of rock and taking rock specimens. The area they visited is located around the volcano Askja, which last erupted in 1961-2, in the interior of North-east Iceland. The expedition included a group of scientists, one of whom declared at the end of the short visit: 'We could stay here a whole week if only we had time. A new thing comes up every minute. The landscape here is the closest we have ever been to what we imagine the moon to be like. The boys are thrilled.' Two years later another group of astronauts, visiting the same area, included Neil Armstrong, the first man to step on the moon in July 1969.

Many foreign travellers have been intrigued by the moon-like features of the Icelandic landscape. This is perhaps natural considering that an estimated one-third of the total output of lava on the earth since A.D. 1500 has come from Iceland's volcanoes. The new volcanic areas of Iceland cover approximately 13,500 square miles. In them some 150-200 volcanoes have been active since the Ice Age, and at least thirty of them have erupted since Iceland was settled, some of them more than twenty times. There have been over 150 recorded eruptions, which have occurred, on average, during the last few centuries every fifth to sixth year. Post-glacial lavas cover about 10 per cent of the total area of Iceland, which is 103,000 square km., including islands and skerries. Most of the older lavas have been covered with the peculiar particoloured moss so characteristic of the country. One unique feature of the new volcanic areas of Iceland is their variety of volcanic phenomena. They exhibit nearly every type of activity found in the world, making the country a volcanologist's and geologist's paradise.

The most common types of lava-producing volcanoes are crater-rows and shield volcanoes. A crater-row is the result of a single eruption from a fissure, producing both lava and tephra. The Laki crater-row, which erupted in 1783, extends about 30 km. and contains about 100 separate craters. In a period of about six months it poured out the greatest lava flow known in historical times, covering 565 square km.

The shield volcanoes are of the Hawaiian type, cupolas composed entirely of layers of lava with a crater on top. A typical example is the Skjaldbreidur near Thingvellir. These volcanoes are numerous in Iceland, but the only one that has been active in historical times is the new Surtsey volcano.

The highest volcanoes in Iceland are cone-shaped, the Fuji type, often with an ice-cap on top. They are not common, but among them are the biggest volcanoes such as Öraefajökull, Iceland's highest mountain (2,118 m.), Eyjafjallajökull (1,665 m.), and Snaefellsjökull (1,442 m.). Two of the most active volcanoes of Iceland are also ice-capped, Katla under the ice of Mýrdalsjökull, and Grímsvötn in the centre of Vatnajökull. Katla has erupted at least thirteen times since the settlement of Iceland, the last time in 1918. The eruptions of subglacial volcanoes cause tremendous floods—so-called glacier bursts—which for instance in the case of Katla may exceed the Amazon river in volume of water.

The most famous Icelandic volcano, Hekla, was known throughout the Catholic world in the Middle Ages as the abode of the damned. Since its first recorded eruption in 1104, which destroyed a vast area, including the Thjórsárdalur settlement, Hekla proper has erupted some fifteen times, causing great damage in the surrounding countryside. At the beginning of its 1947 eruption, starting 27 March, the eruption column rose to 100,000 feet and the lava covered 25 square miles. It lasted thirteen months. In May 1970 there were eruptions in a number of craters in Hekla, lasting for about two months.

Askja in the north-eastern highlands last erupted in 1961, but its eruption in 1875 was the last to cause great damage in the country.

Submarine eruptions are frequent off the coasts of Iceland, especially on the ridge south-west of Reykjanes. The last submarine eruption, near the Westman Islands, started visibly on 14 November 1963, building up three islands; one of them endured and was named Surtsey, with an area of nearly 1·5 square miles. The eruption continued for more than two years, building up a lava mass over 560 feet high. The name was given to the island by the State Topographical Committee and is derived from the mythological giant Surt who was believed in heathen times to be the God of Fire. From the point of view of geomorphology the new island is one of the world's most interesting natural phenomena, for scientists are enabled to give close study there to geological processes which ordinarily take thousands or even millions of years. From the same submarine fissure there were a number of other eruptions, two of them forming new islands which later returned to the ocean depths. The last one, in the summer of 1966, was just as powerful in its initial stages as the Surtsey eruption. The eruptions from this fissure are the second longest in this century, the longest being the Paricutin eruption in Mexico 1943-1950. The total amount of volcanic materials discharged in the Surtsey area amounted in July 1966 to 2·5 billion tons.

This was not the first volcanic activity in the area. In 1783 an island was formed not far from Surtsey, and the Danish government immediately decided to hoist the Danish flag on this new and unexpected acquisition. But when the expedition for this purpose arrived on the spot, the island had vanished—to the great enjoyment of the local people.

The most dramatic of recent volcanic eruptions started during the night of 23 January 1973 in Heimaey, the largest and only inhabited island of the Westman group, where more than 5,000 people lived in the most prosperous and enterprising fishing community in the whole of Iceland. On the island there was an old volcano, Helgafell, which had not been active for the past 5,000-6,000 years, but the 1973 eruption came from a mile-long fissure east of Helgafell, consisting of dozens of small craters forming a continuous row of fire east of the town, reaching all the way down to the sea. There had been stormy weather the day before, and all the local fishing boats and a number of others were therefore in port. At midnight the wind subsided and turned towards the east, thus saving the town from the burning cinders and ashes emitted from the craters. Within a few hours almost the entire population of Heimaey had been evacuated across the sound to the mainland town of Thorlákshöfn, four hours away, where buses awaited them and carried them to the various schools of Reykjavík where preparations had already been made for their arrival in the early morning. About 5,000 people had been moved without a single accident in the middle of a winter night. The eruption continued until 28 June, building up a new volcano, later named Eldfell, and causing terrible damage. About one-third of the town, including over 400 houses, was either buried or burnt by lava and tephra. The island was considerably enlarged by the new lava and the harbour vastly improved, even though for some time it looked as if it would be totally destroyed. There is no doubt that the direction of wind on that fateful night and during the following days saved the inhabitants from disaster, for when the wind changed showers of ashes and pumice rained over the town, burning many houses and making it dangerous to move out of doors. The present writer went to Heimaey during the first week of the eruption, escorting a photographer from *Esquire* magazine: it was one of the most nightmarish experiences of his life. Rescue work had already started. Large groups of volunteers were shovelling ashes from roofs and roads, covering windows facing the eruption site with sheet iron as a protection against the flying embers. Protective embankments were made, but these were of little avail. It was finally decided to try cooling the lava by pumping seawater onto its advancing edge. This proved effective and saved a part of the town, including the very important fish processing plants, the largest in Iceland. Luckily, the airfield on the island, which was on the north-western slopes of Helgafell, was only slightly damaged and could be used from the beginning in the rescue work, planes continuously coming and going carrying the disabled, some of the animals, valuable machinery, and so on. Both by sea and by air, cargo after cargo of furniture, household appliances, fishing gear, equipment and other useful articles was taken to the mainland, leaving behind a veritable ghost-town. The whole nation took part in the rescue work, the inhabitants of Heimaey finding temporary, and in some cases permanent, shelter in towns and villages all around the coast, but mostly in the south-west. Valuable help came from all the Nordic countries, and a large number of prefabricated wooden houses were brought in from Scandinavia and assembled in various places on the mainland. After the surviving part of the town of Heimaey had been cleared of ashes and the houses restored, part of the population started to move back, and gradually life returned to the Westman Islands. The surroundings were entirely new, as one of the greenest parts of Iceland had become one of the darkest.

The most recent eruption at the time of writing started on 20 December 1975, near Krafla in the north-east, where the first major power station utilizing natural heat was under construction. The station itself was not damaged, but the construction work halted for some time.

Except for one well-known reference (see p. 20), the *Sagas of Icelanders* are rather reticent about volcanic activity in Iceland, although there were a number of eruptions in the first centuries after the settlement. A folktale connecting the first historical eruption of Hekla (in 1104) with the renowned historian Saemund Sigfússon (see p. 30) tells how he deceived a woman in Saxony who, despairing of his return, sent him a golden box which he took to the top of Hekla and threw into the cleft. That caused the eruption. No doubt the volcanic activity in Iceland has coloured the sombre visions of the Sybil in *Völuspá*, the greatest of the Eddic poems. During the Middle Ages, Hekla was believed to be the Gate of Hell. When wars were waged in Europe, the souls of the damned were seen hovering over the volcano, in the guise of ravens, and plunging into the crater with screams of agony. Icelandic volcanoes later fired the imagination of the great fantasist, Jules Verne.

Earthquakes are frequent in Iceland, but rarely harmful. The most disastrous ones occurred in the southern lowlands in 1784 and 1896, leaving many farms ruined. The village of Dalvík in Eyjafjördur in the north was partly destroyed by an earthquake in 1934. Following the volcanic eruption near Krafla in December 1975, there were severe earthquakes for some weeks, destroying part of the fishing village of Kópasker in the north-east in January 1976.

Avalanches are common in the north-west, north and east, where the steep mountain slopes, covered with deep snow, threaten the inhabited areas. In many of these areas farms have been destroyed and people killed by avalanches, but the most gruesome disaster of this kind occurred in the town of Neskaupstadur in the north-east on 20 December 1974, when an avalanche destroyed a large fish-processing plant and some houses, killing thirteen people.

Thermal Activity

Connected with volcanism in Iceland is the vast thermal activity briefly discussed above. High-temperature activity is limited to the new volcanic median zone where there are fourteen solfatara (high-temperature) fields. They are characterized by steam holes, mud pools, and precipitation of sulphur. The main high-temperature areas are the Torfajökull glacier east of Hekla, and Grímsvötn in the Vatnajökull glacier. Next in order of size are Hengill east of Reykjavík, Kerlingarfjöll in the central highlands between the glaciers Hofsjökull and Langjökull, Námafjall at Lake Mývatn in the north-east, Kverkfjöll on the northern edge of the Vatnajökull glacier, and Krýsuvík south of Reykjavík. The total power-output of the Torfajökull area, which is the largest, is estimated to be equivalent to 1,500 megawatts. Some of the high-temperature areas have workable sulphur deposits.

Low-temperature areas number about 250 with more than 800 individual springs and are found all over Iceland, but they are rare in the eastern basalt area. The average temperature of the water is 75° C. (167° F.). The biggest hot spring in Iceland, Deildartunguhver in the Borgarfjördur district in West Iceland, has a flow of 150 litres per second. Some of the hot springs are spouting springs or geysers, the most famous of which is the Great Geysir in Haukadalur in South Iceland, from which the international word geyser is derived. It is located about 40 km inland from Reykjavík.

Up to 1810 it erupted precisely every third hour, then slowed down and only erupted every thirty hours, until it suddenly died out altogether in 1916. It awoke from its long sleep just as suddenly one hot summer day in 1935, since when it has been spouting intermittently. In recent years its whims have been pampered by doses of soft soap, which usually bring it to life, but lately it has again shown a certain reluctance to placate the avid tourists. At its best it ejects a column of steaming water to a height of 60-70 metres.

The Great Geysir is surrounded by a large number of smaller springs, the biggest and best known being the Strokkur which is active all the time. There are smaller spouting springs in other areas round the country, one which is very popular with tourists being on the outskirts of the small town of Hveragerdi, erupting every two hours and even more frequently when fed with soft soap.

A strange feature of the thermal areas of Iceland is the white vapour exuding from valleys, hillsides and mountains, giving the impression that the surface of the earth is merely a thin lid on top of a boiling cauldron. The smell in these areas is not pleasant and at times too strong for the delicate nostrils of highly civilized visitors. This is especially true of the seething blue-black sulphur pools in the hot-spring area of Námafjall near Lake Mývatn in North-east Iceland. The visitor is advised to move about with caution, for the reddish-yellow lava crust is thin, and more than one foolhardy tourist has been swallowed by the depths below, while others have been rescued at the last moment, terribly scalded. This is truly prehistoric landscape where the earth is not yet quite cold and we are in the middle of the cooling-off process.

Ice and Water

There is no lack of fire in Iceland, but there is also ice to substantiate the fact that the old Vikings were not altogether in the wrong when they named the island.

Glaciers cover 11,800 square km. or 11·5 per cent of the area of Iceland. But during the past few decades they have markedly thinned and retreated owing to a milder climate, and some of the smaller ones have all but vanished. The glaciation limit is lowest in the north-west (about 750 m.) and highest in the interior north of the Vatnajökull glacier (about 1,500 m.). Almost all types of glaciers are found in Iceland, ranging from the small cirque glaciers to extensive glacier caps reminiscent of the inland ice of Greenland. The latter are drained by broad lobe-shaped outlets or by valley glaciers of the alpine type.

By far the largest of the glacier caps is Vatnajökull in South-east Iceland with an area of 8,400 square km. It reaches a thickness of

1,000 m. One of its southern outlets, Breidamerkurjökull, descends to sea level. Other major glaciers are Langjökull (1,025 sq. km.) and Hofsjökull (990 sq. km.), both in the central highlands, Mýrdalsjökull (700 sq. km.) in the south, and Drangajökull (200 sq. km.) in the north-west.

On the tip of the Snaefellsnes peninsula, across the bay from Reykjavík, one of the smaller glaciers, Snaefellsjökull, may be seen in clear weather and affords a fascinating sight at sundown. The Icelandic glaciers are tempting for hardy adventurers, but many of them are dangerous to cross owing to rifts and crevices in the ice.

Due partly to the glaciers but also to heavy rainfall, there are many large rivers in Iceland as well as many smaller ones. Most of them stem from the glaciers and are consequently heavily laden with debris, turbid and often yellowish brown in colour. The longest is the Thjórsá river (230 km.) in the south with an average discharge of 385 cubic metres per second. The second largest is Jökulsá á Fjöllum (206 km.) in the north-east.

Icelandic rivers are chiefly of two types, glacier rivers and clear-water rivers. The former usually divide into numerous more or less interlinked tributaries that change their courses all the time and swing over the outwash plains lying below the glaciers. This is especially true of the rivers running south from Vatnajökull; in that area a permanent road with many long bridges was finally completed in 1974, making it possible to circle the island by car. The maximum discharge of the glacier rivers usually takes place in July and August.

Clear-water rivers are of two kinds. One drains the old basalt areas and has a variable discharge with maximum flow in late spring. The other kind drains regions covered with post-glacial lava and usually has small variations in discharge, so that these rivers are best suited for hydro-electric power production.

One of the most arresting aspects of the Icelandic scenery are the numerous and extremely variegated waterfalls all over the country. The most frequented by tourists is the Gullfoss ('Golden Waterfall', 32 m. high) near the Great Geysir. Others are the Dettifoss (44 m.) in the north, and the Skógafoss (61 m.) in the south.

Lakes in Iceland are abundant, but most of them are rather small. Some are formed by subsidence (Thingvallavatn, Kleifarvatn), others fill glacier-eroded basins (Lögurinn, Skorradalsvatn), still others are lava dammed (Thórisvatn, Mývatn), while a few are ice dammed (Grænalón). The five biggest lakes in Iceland are Thingvallavatn (83 sq. km.), which is 109 metres deep, Thórisvatn (68 sq. km.), Lögurinn (52 sq. km.), the lagoon Hóp (45 sq. km.), and Mývatn (38 sq. km.). The rivers in Iceland abound in salmon; and char and trout are plentiful in lakes and streams.

Vegetation

Geologically Iceland is still a young country, and its formation is still going on. It is in large part a table-land broken up by tectonic forces. Its interior consists entirely of mountains and high plateaux, devoid of human habitation. Its average height is 500 metres above sea level, the highest point being Hvannadalshnúkur in the Öræfajökull glacier in South-east Iceland, reaching a height of 2,119 metres. Only one-fifth of the country is lowland, the biggest plain being along the south coast which is the most fertile agricultural area. The country is, with the exception of its southern coast, richly indented with fiords and bays, from most of which great and small valleys run deep into the highlands. In the north-west, north and east the mountains extend to the coasts, often reaching greater heights there than in the hinterland plateau. The numerous gaping fissures running in a north-south direction in the north and in a north-east/south-west direction in the south are a striking feature of the landscape.

Only about one-quarter of the total area of Iceland has a continuous plant cover. This is due mainly to the unfavourable climate, volcanic activity, glacier movements and overgrazing. The vegetation has greatly deteriorated during the eleven centuries of human habitation, accompanied by extensive soil erosion. The once widespread birch-woods were destroyed by ruthless cutting and grazing, so that only stray remnants of them still survive. Since the Second World War steps have been taken to halt the erosion. Extensive areas have been protected from grazing, and reafforestation experiments with conifers have been made on a considerable scale. The largest trees are now found in the birch-woods Hallormsstadarskógur in the east and Vaglaskógur in the north. The rowan and aspen grow in some parts.

In general the vegetation in Iceland is subarctic in character and distinguished by an abundance of grasses, sedges, and related species. Grasslands, bogs and marshes are extensive, and there is much moorland and heathland. But all over the country, also in the inhabited lowlands, there are large areas of bare rock, stony deserts, sandy wastelands, and lava fields. The largest unbroken lava field is Ódádahraun, about 1,800 square miles.

There are about 500 species of seed-producing and non-seed-producing plants. The most common vegetation consists of various low-growing shrubs, especially heather, crowberry, bog whortleberry, bearberry, willow, and dwarf birch. The lava fields are first colonized by lichens and mosses, which are a striking feature in the landscape, especially in the south-west. At higher levels the mosses are less prevalent on the lava fields, while the lichens increase in quantity. These pioneer moss-lichen communities are in time succeeded by communities of higher plants.

Fauna

When Iceland was settled, the arctic fox was the only land mammal in the country. Foxes are still common all over Iceland and have frequently ravaged the sheep. The brown rat, the black rat, the domestic mouse, and the field mouse were later accidentally introduced by man. Reindeer were imported from Norway in the late eighteenth century, and there are many of them in the highlands of the east. In about 1930 mink was introduced for fur farming, but soon escaped in great numbers and reverted to the wild state, causing great damage to bird life and freshwater fish. Polar bears have occasionally visited Iceland on drift ice, but have always been killed shortly after their arrival. There are seventeen species of whale and two indigenous species of seal (the common seal and the grey seal); four other species of seal visit Iceland in winter. Whales are caught in considerable numbers during summer, and seals are also caught for their fur at certain restricted periods in some parts of the country.

The most common domestic animals are cattle, sheep and horses. Other domestic animals include pigs, dogs, cats, goats, hens, geese, ducks, turkeys and pigeons.

All told, 241 kinds of birds are known to have visited Iceland at one time or another. Of these seventy-two nest regularly, six are common passage migrants, about thirty are regular drift migrants or winter visitors, the rest being accidentals. Seabirds, waterfowl and waders are the most common indigenous birds. The most celebrated is the Icelandic gyrfalcon which in former times was highly prized and exported all over Europe and even to the East. It is now fully protected throughout the year. The huge white-tailed eagle, now rare, is also fully protected. The third indigenous bird of prey is the merlin. The rock ptarmigan (the most important game bird) and the eider duck are quite common, the latter being the object of the ancient eider duck farming. It is now rigorously protected by law.

There are two species of owl, one having come to Iceland since the turn of the century owing to the milder climate. Eight other newcomers in this century are the shoveller, the tufted duck, the pochard, the lesser black-backed gull, the herring gull, the common gull, the black-headed gull, and the starling.

Nesting passerines are represented by only nine species, no doubt mainly due to the scarcity of trees and insect life. The raven, the snow bunting, the redpoll, and the wren are resident species, while the meadow pipit, the white wagtail, the redwing, and the wheatear are common summer visitors. The starling has established itself in Iceland since 1940, but its breeding range is restricted. The swallow, the fieldfare, and the house sparrow have tried to breed in Iceland, but have not yet become permanent settlers.

The most common waders in Iceland are the golden plover and the whimbrel. Other common waders include the snipe, the redshank, the dunlin, the purple sandpiper, the ringed plover, the oystercatcher, the red-necked phalarope, and, less common, the black-tailed hawk and the grey phalarope.

Iceland is one of the major breeding grounds of waterfowl in Europe. There are no fewer than sixteen species of duck; geese are represented by two nesting species and three passage migrants. Iceland is one of the few places where the whooper swan is still a common breeding bird. It is most numerous on lakes lying on the borders of the central highlands.

On the towering bird cliffs along the coasts of Iceland the most important colonial sea birds are the common guillemot, Brünnich's guillemot, the razorbill, the puffin, the kittiwake, the fulmar and the gannet. All these birds have been caught for human consumption, and the eggs of some of them have been taken for the same purpose.

About 800 species of insects have been recorded in Iceland. As in other arctic and subarctic countries, the *Diptera* (flies, gnats, and midges) form the largest and most important group. *Coleoptera* (beetles) and *Hymenoptera* (bees and allies) are also fairly numerous, but ants are non-existent. Moths are the only fully indigenous representatives of the *Lepidoptera*. A few species of migratory butterflies, such as the red admiral and the painted lady, sometimes come to Iceland in goodly numbers, but never survive the winter. There are no reptiles or amphibians in the country.

Apart from salmon, trout and char, two other freshwater species of fish are also found, the eel and the three-spined stickleback. None of these five species is really freshwater fish, but they represent species that are establishing themselves in freshwater.

Plankton in Icelandic waters provides optimum conditions for a rich marine fauna. Salt-water fish number about 150 species, including cod, haddock, herring, Norway haddock, halibut, whiting, saithe, ling, plaice and lemon sole, which together form the basis of large-scale coastal fisheries. Only sixty-six of the 150 species are known with certainty to propagate in Icelandic waters, the others being migratory visitors or stragglers from oceanic waters. Shrimp and lobster fishing has lately become a lucrative occupation in some parts of the country, especially in the north-west and south-east.

The Weather

Sayings like 'If you don't like our weather, just wait a minute' indicate the variability of the Icelandic climate. It is cool, temperate and oceanic, influenced by the country's location in the boundary zone between two different air currents—the one polar, the other of tropical origin—separated by the polar front, and by the confluence of two different ocean currents, the Gulf Stream flowing clockwise around the south and west coasts and the East Greenland polar current curving south-eastwards round the north and east coasts, the two currents meeting off the south-east coast. A third element affecting the climate is the arctic drift ice brought by the polar current, which occasionally blocks the north and east coasts in late winter and early spring. The advance of drift ice causes a considerable fall in temperature and usually some decrease in precipitation.

Considering the northerly location of Iceland, its climate is much milder than might be expected, especially in winter. Summers are cool and winters comparatively mild. The mean annual temperature for Reykjavík is 5° C., the average January temperature being −0·4° and July 11·2°. Corresponding figures for Akureyri in the north are 3·9°, −1·5° and 10·9°C.[1] The wettest regions are in the south and south-east. The annual precipitation at Kvísker in the Öræfi district is more than 3,000 mm. and is the highest recorded along the coast, but on the southern slopes of Vatnajökull it may be appreciably higher, whereas in the highlands north of Vatnajökull it drops to 400 mm. or less.

The weather in Iceland depends mainly on the tracks of the atmospheric depressions crossing the North Atlantic. The passage of a depression some distance south of Iceland causes relatively cold and dry weather, especially in northern districts, while one passing north-eastward between Iceland and Greenland brings mild weather, moderately dry in the north. South-westerly winds, which are common, bring with them warm air, but also moisture which cannot cross the mountains on the south coast without being deposited in the form of rain and snow, thus maintaining the immense glaciers. Coastal areas tend to be windy, gales are common, especially in winter, but thunderstorms are extremely rare. The weather shows greater variation from one year to another than in most countries farther south. When the mean temperature in England, for instance, deviates 1° from normal, in Iceland the variation can be expected to be 3°.

Fogs are rather uncommon in Iceland except in the coastal districts of the east and north-east, and on the whole the air is marvellously clear. The *Aurora Borealis* is often visible, especially in autumn and early winter. For two to three months in summer there is continuous daylight, and in early spring and late autumn there are long twilights. The really dark period (3-4 hours of daylight in clear weather) lasts from about mid-November until the end of January.

There are, virtually, two seasons only in Iceland, and even they are not very clearly defined, except by the amount of daylight available. You may have warm summery weather in February and wintry weather in July or August, even with hailstorms. Night frost often occurs in early June and late August, making agriculture hazardous.

There are two distinct days marking the beginning of summer and winter. The Fist Day of Summer falls on the third Thursday of April and is a public holiday mainly devoted to the youngest generation. There are colourful children's processions through the streets of Reykjavík and other towns if the weather is reasonably good, which is not always. The First Day of Winter falls on the third Saturday in October, but it is not an occasion for celebration. The official celebration of the First Day of Summer, unique in the world, bears eloquent witness to the great esteem in which summer is held by the Icelanders.

In reality, summer does not usually arrive until late May or early June, lasting until mid-September if nature is benevolent. There is a saying that the Icelanders are constantly waiting for a summer which never arrives, and dreading a winter which never turns up either. It is possible to think of Iceland as a country of no seasons at all, and it would perhaps be appropriate to maintain that by European or American standards there are only spring and autumn.

There is, however, one feature that clearly distinguishes summer from winter in Iceland: the absence of darkness for some three months. This short and ethereal epoch has been a favourite subject for innumerable poets and versifiers. It casts a spell over the whole country and its inhabitants, quickening the pace of life, summoning the populace of towns and villages out into the countryside alive with multi-coloured flowers, gren pastures, colourful mountains, twittering birds, grazing sheep, cows and horses, chattering brooks and roaring rivers and waterfalls. Every weekend families flock to the countryside with their tents, climbing mountains, basking in the sun, or gathering berries in late August. One very popular pastime is exploring the uninhabited interior, either in sturdy mountain trucks that can make their way across roadless sands, lava and unbridged rivers, or on the small Icelandic horses which for centuries were called the Icelander's 'most useful servants'. Though extensive areas are without vegetation, there are scattered cases of lush green grass and brightly coloured flowers in the lee of the white ice-caps. Salmon-fishing is also very popular, but has recently become an expensive sport. Swimming, an obligatory item in the curriculum of all primary and secondary schools, is also widely practised in the many swimming pools with natural hot water all over the country.

The Icelandic Horse

All over the country large herds of grazing sheep and horses are to be found—in the mountains, near the highways and around the farms. The horse is almost as common a feature of the landscape as the sheep, even though it has lost most of its utilitarian or economic value. For more than a thousand years, from the ninth to the early twentieth century when wheeled vehicles first made their appearance, it was the only means of transport and thus had many vital tasks to perform carrying people from one corner of the country to another, transporting goods between the remote inland farms and the trading points on the coast, bringing home the hay from distant fields, rounding up sheep from the mountains in autumn, conveying new-born babies home from the midwife, sick people to the doctor and the dead to the grave. In addition, horsemeat has been a staple food in many parts of Iceland. Today the horse has only one practical function in the countryside—carrying the farmers in the autumn sheep round-up. Even this is now dwindling, and aircraft have in some cases taken over.

However, while the horse has been eclipsed in the countryside by jeep, tractor and mechanized haymaking, it has enjoyed a steadily growing interest and importance as a source of recreation. In Reykjavík there are hundreds of regular horseback-riders, and similar interest is being shown in other towns and in the countryside, where the rearing and taming of horses has become a lucrative occupation. This growing interest is not limited to Iceland. There are clubs encouraging and cultivating the use of the Iceland horse all over Western and Northern Europe. Why all this interest? One reason is that the Iceland horse has some peculiarities not found in horses elsewhere in Europe. It has five different gaits, of which the *tölt*, or running walk, in which the horse is so steady that the rider hardly moves in his saddle, is not found in any other horse in Europe (although it is common in Mongolian and some South and North American horses). The word *tölt* is of Germanic origin, and it has its counterpart in the Latin *thieldos*, the name for a gently moving mare in Imperial Rome.

The various riding clubs of the country organize long trips on horseback through the wild interior of the country, and arrange annual horse races and shows in their districts, while once every four years they join under the auspices of the National Association

of Riding Clubs and hold a country-wide meeting. The last and by
far the biggest meeting of this sort was held in July 1974, in
Skagafjördur in North Iceland, where no fewer than 3,000 horses
were gathered from all parts of the country, out of which some 400
took part in the shows and races. After this meeting the present
writer, with four companions, took some twenty-five horses across
Iceland down to the south coast, riding 10-12 hours a day through
the wilderness of the interior, stopping mid-way at Hveravellir
between the two large glaciers Langjökull and Hofsjökull to have a
much needed bath in a natural swimming pool hundreds of miles
from any inhabited area. This five-day trip was one of his most
memorable experiences, strenuous and exhausting though it was.

The size of the Icelandic horse is on the average about 133 cm.
(13·1 hands), and its weight 380-400 kg. The horse matures slowly
and should preferably not be tamed until it is 4-5 years old. On the
other hand, it has a long life-span, often 23-25 years. The hair
changes according to season, being shaggy in winter and short in
summer. There are about 40,000 horses in Iceland, of which more
than half are semi-wild and remain out of doors all the year, often
without needing any fodder at all during a normal winter.

One of the best *Sagas of Icelanders,* the *Hrafnkel's Saga,* has a
horse as the central motif, indicating that the horse had religious
significance in heathen Iceland. The prohibition against eating
horsemeat after the adoption of Christianity stemmed from the
practice of eating it in heathen religious ceremonies. The horsefight
was a popular amusement at public gatherings during the
Commonwealth period. Many great poems celebrate the vigour,
fidelity and wisdom of the Iceland horse, which also figures
prominently in folklore and fiction. The oldest written account of
the nature and manners of the Germanic peoples is in Tacitus'
Germania, in Chapter X of which a feature of the coexistence of
our ancestors and their horses is described in a way that is
recognisable to anyone conversant with Norse mythology and the
Eddic poems:

But what is unique about this nation is that it tries to obtain omens and
predictions from horses. The animals are reared at public expense in the
aforementioned sacred woods. The horses are snow-white and have never
been used for any non-sacred work, and when they have been harnessed
to the divine chariot they are accompanied by the priest, the king or the
head of state, who study their neigh and snort. No oracle is more sacred
than these horses, not only among the populace, but also among the
chieftains, for although the Germans regard the priests as the servants of
the Lord they regard the horses as his confidants.

Conclusion: the Seasons

Disregarding individual tastes, perhaps the most thrilling experience in Iceland is to spend a summer night out in the wild country amid mountains, lava fields or meadows, with not a person in sight and not a tree to disturb the sweeping panorama. The sun may be resting on a mountain top, hiding behind a range or lingering on the horizon. The silence is so vast that it hurts the eardrums; only the sound of the body throbs in them. Perhaps a stray bird crying in the distance now and then breaks the stillness. The eyes travel far, take in the magnificent landscape and the splendid sky—coloured like a painting by Turner. The solitude of the body is at once frightening and exhilarating in this silence: the individual, engulfed by nature, discovers his true proportion within the universe, and is both depressed and strangely elevated by a powerful feeling of unity with the elements.

For the rural population of Iceland the brief summer season is of paramount importance, since all the hay for the domestic animals has to be made and stored in barns and lofts before winter. At the end of April the farmer turns the sheep out on the pastures. Lambing is in late May and early June and usually coincides with the first growth of grass. The sheep are shorn of their shaggy coats of winter wool at the end of June, after which they are driven to the common grazing land in the interior where they forage for themselves for some ten weeks. In late June the cows are also turned out on to the pastures, but driven home for milking every evening and usually housed overnight. In July comes the haymaking, and not a blade of grass is wasted, since the flocks depend upon the hay for fodder throughout the long winter.

About mid-September the farmers from each district co-operate in gathering the sheep from the common grazing land and drive them to a common fold in each district, where they are then sorted and taken away by the individual owners. Every farmer has a registered ear-mark for his sheep, so that there is never any doubt about the ownership, all lambs having been ear-marked in the spring. The sheep round-up may take a week or more, and the farmers have provisional huts in the mountains where they stay at night while searching the highlands. The sorting of the fold is an occasion for great festivities and merry-making where the whole countryside turns up. The round-up did not always bring in all the sheep, so that a second search was made later, usually by a man with special qualifications. Such a search is the theme of Gunnar Gunnarsson's masterly story *The Good Shepherd (Advent)*, which has been translated into many languages.

From the dawn of their history winter has been one of the dominant factors in the mental as well as the physical world of the

Icelanders. In every respect it has shaped their destinies, coloured their outlook and conditioned their daily existence. In their folktales and poetry, and even in the theatre, it has been personified by a white-haired, long-bearded, dignified old man, named King Winter, who was a kind of father figure, representing both the benevolent and the harsh aspects of a strict master of the house.

Extending as it does over some seven months of the year, winter cannot be treated lightly in Iceland, even though in later years it has become much milder than it used to be, so that it now resembles autumn more than anything else. In its cruel guise it has wrecked innumerable ships on the coasts of Iceland, causing numerous deaths and untold misery over the centuries. It has ravaged farmsteads, often submerging them under snow for weeks or even months on end. It has kept the individual farms and their inhabitants more or less isolated for long periods. It has tormented and killed the livestock, especially the sheep. And it has made Iceland one of the world's most difficult lands for farming and agriculture.

But winter also has its more pleasant aspects which, strangely enough, seem to make a more lasting impression, at least on the average Icelander. Among these are the very long winter nights with their occasional moonlight and the Northern Lights dancing across the sky like gracefully draped ballerinas whenever the weather is clear during the early part of winter. There are the tantalizingly short but wonderfully brilliant days of midwinter when the sky is clear, and the curiously twilit days when it is cloudy. There is the feverishly gay and colourful Christmas season, with multicoloured bulbs hanging from balconies and trees, and even—in Oriental fashion—in the cemeteries, its long preparation beginning already in November, and its aftermath extending far into January. There is the climax of winter gloom, just before Christmas, with its sense of relief and expectancy, when the days start growing longer, week by week, presaging the 'nightless epoch' to which every Icelander looks forward all winter, however much he may be enjoying winter's thrills. In some narrow fiords on the north-west and east coasts there are farms and towns where the sun is not seen at all for two months or longer. In one of them, Ísafjördur, the reappearance of the sun on 25 January is celebrated with a special 'Sun Coffee' ceremony.

The strong feeling of expectancy lends a special flavour to winters in Iceland. It must have been even greater in the old days, before the advent of electricity, when the whole country lay more or less in darkness for months every winter. These very long winter nights no doubt had a profound influence on the imagination and literary activity of the inhabitants.

The oppression of winter darkness has now been largely relieved by modern technology, lighting up all densely populated areas and most of the rural farmsteads. But that does not preclude the old thrills out in the wild country—and there are plenty of those. The sense of being alone with the naked elements, whether you are skiing in the mountains, skating on a lake, riding the shaggy horses over a ridge or through a mountain pass, or just walking over snow-clad hills or along star-spangled beaches, it is there to challenge you, fill you with awe and elevation.

Winter in Iceland is a source of many dark mysteries, which will never be fully uncovered, but it is above all a time of continuous indoor entertainment, feverish intellectual activity and mental preparation for the promised respite of wakeful summer nights.

Note

1. This applies to the period 1921-64, while the climate after 1965 has been considerably cooler. Climatic variations—the fluctuations in the average annual temperature—are more pronounced in Iceland than in most other places, mainly owing to the fact that the country is located just south of the main channel through which the ice exits from the Arctic. The polar ice is constantly being carried southwards by ocean currents, and Iceland is in its path, the first to be hit. Fluctuations in the average annual temperature become smaller as the distance from this ice mass increases. In Britain, for instance, the deviation is only one-third of what it is in Iceland. The crucial difference between a warm period and a cold one is a matter of merely 1·5° C.: that is all it takes to tip the scales, and during the past centuries there have been many frightening examples of the consequences of this small drop in average annual temperature, especially while the country was mainly agricultural.

Select Bibliography of Works in English relating to Iceland

General Information

Berry, Erick, *The Land and People of Iceland*. Philadelphia-New York 1959.

Eldjárn, Kristján, *Iceland: Land in Creation*. Reykjavík 1967.

Gíslason, Gylfi Th., *Iceland 1918-1968*. London 1969.

— *The Problem of being an Icelander: Past, Present, Future*. Reykjavík 1973.

Griffiths, John C., *Modern Iceland*. New York 1969.

Björnsson, Björn Th., *Iceland*. New York 1967.

Briem, Helgi P., *Iceland and the Icelanders*. Maplewood, N.J. 1945.

Hansson, Ólafur, *Facts about Iceland*. Reykjavík 1954 and later.

Iceland, a Nation of Ancient Culture, a Country of Contrasts. Text by Bjarni Gudmundsson, photos by Thorsteinn Jósepsson. Reykjavík 1962.

Iceland Review (a quarterly News Summary on Icelandic Industries and Trade, Social and Cultural Affairs). Reykjavík 1963 ff.

Iceland To-day, the Land and the Nation, the Economy and Culture. Reykjavík 1961.

Iceland 874-1974 (handbook published by the Central Bank of Iceland on the occasion of the Eleventh Centenary of the Settlement of Iceland). Reykjavík 1975.

Kidson, Peter, *Iceland in a Nutshell: Complete Reference Guide*. Reykjavík 1971.

Lindroth, Hjalmar, *Iceland: a Land of Contrasts* (translated from the Swedish by Adolph B. Benson). New York 1937.

Magnússon, Sigurdur A., *Handy Facts on Iceland*. 2nd ed. Reykjavík 1972.

Samivel, *Golden Iceland*. Reykjavík 1967.

Stefansson, Vilhjalmur, *Iceland: the First American Republic*. New York 1939 and later editions.

Stewart, R.N., *Rivers in Iceland*. Reykjavík 1950.

Thórdarson, Björn, *Iceland Past and Present*. 3rd ed. Reykjavík 1953.

Thorsteinsson, Björn, and Thorsteinn Jósepsson, *Thingvellir: Birthplace of a Nation*. Berlin 1961.

Thorsteinsson, Björn, *By the Roadside: Descriptive Notes on the Route Reykjavík-Akureyri*. Reykjavík 1962.

Travels

Auden, W.H. and Louis MacNeice, *Letters from Iceland.* London 1937 (new ed. 1967).

Baring-Gould, S., *Iceland: its Scenes and Sagas.* London 1863.

Beckett, J. Angus, *Iceland Adventure: the Double Traverse of Vatnajökull by the Cambridge Expedition.* London 1934.

Bryans, Robert, *Summer Saga: a Journey in Iceland.* London 1960.

Bryce, James, 'Impressions of Iceland' (1872) in his *Memories of Travel.* London 1923.

Burton, Richard F., *Ultima Thule, or a Summer in Iceland.* 2 vols. London and Edinburgh 1875.

Chapman, O. M., *Across Iceland: the Land of Frost and Fire.* London 1930.

Coles, John, *Summer Travel in Iceland.* London 1882.

Collingwood, W.G. and Jón Stefánsson, *A Pilgrimage to the Saga-Steads of Iceland.* Ulverston 1899.

Dufferin, Lord, *Letters from High Latitudes.* London 1857 and later editions.

Forbes, Charles S., *Iceland: its Volcanoes, Geysers and Glaciers.* London 1860.

Golden, Grace Blaisdell, *Made in Iceland.* New York 1958.

Goodell, Jane, *They sent me to Iceland.* New York 1953.

Henderson, Ebenezer, *Iceland, or the Journal of a Residence in that Country during the Years 1814-1815.* 2 vols. Edinburgh 1818.

Hooker, William Jackson, *Journal of a Tour in Iceland in the Summer of 1809.* 2 vols. 2nd ed. London 1813.

Howell, Frederick W.W., *Icelandic Pictures Drawn with Pen and Pencil.* London 1893.

Leaf, Horace, *Iceland Yesterday and To-day.* London 1949.

Lewis, David, *Dreamer of the Day: to Iceland and back by Catamaran.* London 1964.

Mackenzie, George Stewart, *Travels on the Island of Iceland during the Summer 1810.* 2nd ed. Edinburgh 1812.

Morris, William, *Journals of Travels in Iceland 1870, 1873.* In *Collected Works of William Morris,* Vol. VIII. London 1911. New ed. 1969.

Oswald, E.J., *By Fell and Fjord, or Scenes and Studies in Iceland.* Edinburgh and London 1882.

Paijkull, C.W., *A Summer in Iceland* (translated from the Swedish by M. R. Barnard). London 1868.

Pfeiffer, Ida, *Visit to Iceland and the Scandinavian North.* 2nd ed. London 1853.

Radcliffe, Dorothy Una, *Iceland Spring.* London 1950.

Rothery, Agnes, *Iceland: Bastion of the North.* London 1955.

Russell, W.S.C., *Iceland: Horseback Tours in Saga-land.* Boston 1914.

Shepherd, C.N., *The North-west Peninsula of Iceland.* London 1867.

Sutton, George Miksch, *Iceland Summer: Adventures of a Bird Painter.* Oklahoma 1961.

Symington, Andrew James, *Pen and Pencil Sketches of Faroe and Iceland.* London 1862.

Taylor, Bayard, *Egypt and Iceland in the Year 1874.* 2nd ed. New York 1902.
Watts, W.L., *Across the Vatna Jökull.* London 1876.
— *Snioland or Iceland: its Jökulls and Fjalls.* London 1875.

Geography and Natural History

Ahlmann, Hans W:son and Sigurdur Thórarinsson, 'Vatnajökull. Scientific Results of the Swedish-Icelandic Investigations 1936-7-8.' Reprinted from *Geografiska Annaler* 1937-40. Stockholm 1943.
Anderson, Tempest, *Volcanic Studies in Many Lands.* London 1903.
Barth, Tom F. W., *Volcanic Geology: Hot Springs and Geysers of Iceland.* Washington 1950.
Björnsson, Sveinbjörn (ed.), *Iceland and Mid-Ocean Ridges.* Report of a Symposium. Reykjavík 1967.
The Botany of Iceland. Copenhagen 1912 ff.
Einarsson, Trausti, *A Survey of Gravity in Iceland.* Reykjavík 1954.
Einarsson, Thorleifur, *The Surtsey Eruption in Words and Pictures.* Reykjavík 1967.
— *The Eruption on Heimaey.* Reykjavík 1974.
The Eruption of Hekla 1947-1948. Reykjavík 1949 ff.
Gunnarsson, Árni, *Volcano: Ordeal by Fire in Iceland's Westmann Islands.* Reykjavík 1973.
Ostenfeld, C.A. and J. Gröntved, *The Flora of Iceland and the Faroes.* Copenhagen 1934.
Pálmson, Gudmundur, *Crustal Structure of Iceland from Explosion Seismology.* Reykjavík 1971.
Slater, Henry H., *Manual of Birds of Iceland.* Edinburgh 1901.
Steindórsson, Steindór, *Contribution to the Plant Geography and Flora of Iceland.* Reykjavík 1935-7.
Surtsey Research Progress Report. Reykjavík 1963 ff.
Thórarinsson, Sigurdur, *Askja on Fire.* Reykjavík 1963.
— *The Eruption of Hekla in Historical Time.* Reykjavík 1967.
— *Hekla: a Notorious Volcano.* Reykjavík 1970.
— *Hekla on Fire.* Munich 1956.
— *Surtsey: the New Island in the North Atlantic.* Reykjavík 1964 and later editions.
— *The Öraefajökull Eruption of 1362.* Reykjavík 1958.
— *Glacier: Adventure on Vatnajökull, Europe's Largest Ice Cap.* Colour Photography by Gunnar Hannesson. Reykjavík 1975.
Thorkelsson, Thorkell, *The Hot Springs of Iceland.* Copenhagen 1910.
— *On Thermal Activity in Iceland and Geysir Action.* Reykjavík 1940.
Tuxen, S.L., *The Hot Springs of Iceland.* Copenhagen 1944.
Zoology of Iceland. Copenhagen 1937 ff.

History and Economy

Brönsted, Johannes, *The Vikings* (translated by Kalle Skov). Paperback ed. London 1965.

Bryce, James, 'Primitive Iceland', in *Studies in History and Jurisprudence* I. London 1901.

Chamberlin, William Charles, *Economic Development of Iceland through World War II*. New York 1947.

Eldjárn, Kristján, *Ancient Art in Iceland* (introduction and texts by Eldjárn, photos by Hans Reich). Munich 1957.

Foote, Peter and D.M. Wilson, *The Viking Achievement*. London 1970.

Gathorne-Hardy, G.M., *The Norse Discoveries of America (The Wineland Sagas*, translated and discussed by G. M. Gathorne-Hardy, with a new Preface by the Author and a new Introduction by Gwyn Jones). Oxford 1970.

Gjerset, Knut; *History of Iceland*. New York 1925.

Grímsson, Thorkell, *National Museum of Iceland: Summary Guide to the Exhibition Rooms*. Reykjavík 1964.

Grönbech, V., *The Culture of the Teutons*. London-Copenhagen 1931.

Gröndal, Benedikt, *Iceland: from Neutrality to NATO Membership*. Oslo 1971.

Guthmundsson, Barthi, *The Origin of the Icelanders*. Lincoln 1967.

Hood, John C.F., *Icelandic Church Saga*. London 1946.

Ingstad, Helge, *Westward to Vinland*. London 1969.

Jack, Robert, *Arctic Living: the Story of Grímsey* (foreword by Vilhjalmur Stefansson). Toronto 1955.

Jensen, Elisabeth, *Iceland: Old-New Republic*. New York 1954.

Jóhannesson, Jón, *Íslendinga Saga: a History of the Old Icelandic Commonwealth* (translated by Haraldur Bessason). Manitoba 1974.

Johnson, Sveinbjörn, *Pioneers of Freedom*. Boston 1930.

Jones, Gwyn, *The Norse Atlantic Saga: Being the Norse Voyages of Discovery to Iceland, Greenland, America*. London 1964.

— *A History of the Vikings*. London, Oxford and New York 1973.

Jónsson, Vilmundur, *Health in Iceland*. Reykjavík 1940.

Magnusson, Magnus, *Viking Expansion Westwards*. London-Sydney-Toronto 1973.

Mawer, Allen, *The Vikings*. Cambridge 1913.

Olrik, Axel, *Viking Civilization*. London 1930.

Rehman, Edward, *The Norse Discoveries and Explorations in America*. California 1949.

Sawyer, P.H., *The Age of the Vikings*. 2nd ed. London 1971.

Sveinsson, Einar Ól., *The Age of the Sturlungs: Icelandic Civilization in the Thirteenth Century* (translated by Jóhann S. Hannesson). Ithaca, New York 1953.

Thórarinsson, Sigurdur, *A Thousand Years Struggle against Ice and Fire*. Reykjavík 1956.

Thorsteinsson, Thorsteinn, *Iceland and the War: in Sweden, Norway, Denmark and Iceland in the World War*. New Haven 1930.

Trial, T.G., *History of Education in Iceland*. Cambridge 1945.

Turville-Petre, G., *The Heroic Age of Scandinavia*. London 1951.

— *Myth and Religion in the North: the Religion of Ancient Scandinavia*. New York 1970.

On Old Icelandic Literature

Anderson, Theodore M., *The Icelandic Family Saga*. Cambridge, Mass. 1967.
— *The Problem of Icelandic Saga Origin. A Historical Survey*. New Haven and London 1964.
Bach, Giovanni, *The History of Scandinavian Literature*. Washington 1966.
Balchin, Nigel, 'The Irredeemable Crime. The Story of the Burnt Njal', in *Fatal Fascination: a Choice of Crime*. London 1964.
Bekker-Nielsen, Hans and Ole Widding, *Arne Magnusson: the Manuscript Collector* (translated by Robert W. Mattila). Odense, Denmark 1972.
Brady, Caroline, *The Legends of Ermanaric*. Berkeley and Los Angeles 1943.
Craigie, William A., *The Art of Poetry in Iceland*. Oxford 1937.
— *The Icelandic Sagas*. Cambridge 1913 (new ed., New York 1968).
Einarsson, Stefán, *A History of Icelandic Literature*. New York 1957.
Frazer, James G., *The Golden Bough*. Vols. I-XII. London 1911-15. (In the abridged one-volume edition, New York 1922 and later editions, see Chapters LXI, 'The Myth of Balder', and LXV, 'Balder and the Mistletoe'.)
Hallberg, Peter, *The Icelandic Saga*. Lincoln 1962.
— *Old Icelandic Poetry: Eddic Lay and Scaldic Verse*. Translated with a foreword by Paul Schach and Sonja Lindgrenson. Lincoln and London 1975.
Ker, William Paton, *Epic and Romance*. London 1922 (new ed., New York 1957).
— *The Dark Ages*. New York 1904.
Koht, Halvdan, *The Old Norse Sagas*. New York 1931.
King, Cynthia, *In the Morning of Time: The Story of the Norse God Balder*. New York 1970.
Kristjánsson, Jónas, *Icelandic Sagas and Manuscripts*. Reykjavík 1970.
Liestöl, Knut, *The Origin of the Icelandic Family Sagas*. Oslo 1930.
Martin, John Stanley, *Ragnarok: an Investigation into Old Norse Concepts of the Fate of the Gods*. Assen-Melbourne 1972.
Munch, Peter Andreas, *Norse Mythology: Legends of Gods and Heroes* (translated by Sigurd Bernhard Hustvedt). 3rd ed. New York 1954.
Nerman, Birger, *The Poetic Edda in the Light of Archaeology*. Coventry 1931 (Viking Society for Northern Research).
Phillpotts, Bertha S., *Edda and Saga*. London 1931.
— *The Elder Edda and Ancient Scandinavian Drama*. Cambridge 1920.
Raglan, Lord, *The Hero: a Study in Tradition, Myth, and Drama*. London 1936.
Schlauch, Margaret, *Romance in Iceland*. London 1934.
Sveinsson, Einar Ól., *Dating the Icelandic Sagas: an Essay in Method*. London 1958.
— *Njáls Saga: a Literary Masterpiece* (edited and translated by Paul Schach). Lincoln 1971.
Turville-Petre, G., *Origins of Icelandic Literature*. Oxford 1953.
Vries, Jan de, *Heroic Song and Heroic Legend*. London 1963.

Translations of Old Icelandic Literature

A Pageant of Old Scandinavia. Edited by Henry Goddard Leach. New York 1946.

Old Norse Poems. The most important Non-Skaldic Verse. Translated by Lee M. Hollander. New York 1936.

The Skalds. A Selection of their Poems with Introductions and Notes by Lee M. Hollander. Princeton 1945.

The Northmen Talk. A Choice of Tales for Iceland. Edited by Jacqueline Simpson. Foreword by Eric Linklater. London and New York 1965.

Icelandic Folktales and Legends. Translated with an Introduction by Jacqueline Simpson. London 1972.

Mead Moondaughter and other Icelandic Folk Tales. Translated by Alan Boucher. London 1967.

The Oxford Book of Scandinavian Verse. Oxford 1925.

An Anthology of Scandinavian Literature. From the Viking Period to the Twentieth Century. Selected and edited by Hallberg Hallmundsson. London and New York 1965.

Íslendingabók (Book of the Icelanders). Translated and edited by Halldór Hermannsson. Ithaca 1930 (*Islandica*).

The Book of Settlements—Landnámabók. Translated with an Introduction by Magnus Magnusson and Hermann Pálsson. London 1966 (Penguin Classics).

The Saga Library I-VI. Translated by William Morris and Eiríkr Magnússon. London 1891-1905.

Origines Islandicae I-II (26 Sagas). Edited and translated by Gudbrand Vigfusson and F. York Powell. Oxford 1905.

The Poetic Edda. Translated with an Introduction and Notes by Henry Adams Bellows. Fourth printing, New York 1957.

The Poetic Edda. Translated by Lee M. Hollander. 2nd ed. Austin, Texas 1964.

The Elder Edda. A Selection translated by Paul B. Taylor and W. H. Auden. London 1969.

The Poetic Edda. Vol. 1. *Heroic Poems.* Edited with Translation, Introduction and Commentary by Ursula Dronke. Oxford 1969.

Poems of the Vikings: The Elder Edda. Translated by Patricia Terry with an Introduction by Charles W. Dunn. Indiannapolis and New York 1969.

The Prose Edda. By Snorri Sturluson. Translated with an Introduction by Arthur G. Brodeur. Fifth printing, New York 1960.

The Prose Edda of Snorri Sturluson. Tales from Norse Mythology. Translated by Jean I. Young. Introduction by Sigurdur Nordal. Seventh printing, Cambridge 1973.

Heimskringla. History of the Kings of Norway. By Snorri Sturluson. Translated with Introduction and Notes by Lee M. Hollander. Austin, Texas 1964.

Heimskringla. The Olaf Sagas. Vols. I-II. By Snorri Sturluson. Translated by Samuel Laing. Revised with an Introduction and Notes by Jacqueline Simpson. London and New York 1964 (Everyman's Library).

King Harald's Saga. By Snorri Sturluson. Translated with an Introduction by Magnus Magnusson and Hermann Pálsson. London 1969 (Penguin Classics).

The Saga of the Volsungs and the Saga of Ragnar Lodbrok. Translated by Margaret Schlauch. New York 1930.

Four Icelandic Sagas. Translated with an Introduction by Gwyn Jones. New York 1935.

Voyages to Vinland (3 Sagas). Translated by Einar Haugen. New York 1942.

The Sagas of Kormák and the Sworn Brothers. Translated with Introduction and Notes by Lee M. Hollander. New York 1949.

Three Icelandic Sagas. Translated by M. H. Scargill and Margaret Schlauch. New York 1950.

Eirik the Red and Other Icelandic Sagas. Selected and translated with an Introduction by Gwyn Jones. London 1961.

The Vinland Sagas. The Norse Discovery of America (Grænlendinga Saga and Eirik's Saga). Translated with an Introduction by Magnus Magnusson and Hermann Pálsson. Third edition, London 1968 (Penguin Classics).

The Confederates and Hen-Thorir. Two Icelandic Sagas. Translated with an Introduction by Hermann Pálsson. Edinburgh 1975.

The Story of Burnt Njal. Translated by George W. Dasent. London 1949 (Everyman's Library).

Njál's Saga. Translated with Introduction and Notes by Carl F. Bayerschmidt and Lee M. Hollander. New York 1955.

Njál's Saga. Translated with an Introduction by Magnus Magnusson and Hermann Pálsson. Fourth edition, London 1967 (Penguin Classics).

Egil's Saga. Translated by E. R. Eddison. Cambridge 1930.

Egil's Saga. Translated with Introduction and Notes by Gwyn Jones. New York 1960.

The Laxdæla Saga. Translated by Thorstein Veblen. New York 1925.

The Laxdale Saga. Translated by Muriel Press. Edited with an Introduction and Index by Peter Foote. London and New York 1964 (Everyman's Library).

The Laxdoela Saga. Translated with Introduction and Notes by A. Margaret Arent. Seattle and New York 1964.

Laxdaela Saga. Translated with an Introduction by Magnus Magnusson and Hermann Pálsson. London 1969 (Penguin Classics).

The Saga of Grettir the Strong. Translated by G. A. Hight. Edited with Introduction, Notes and Indexes by Peter Foote. London and New York 1965. (Everyman's Library).

The Saga of Gisli Son of Sour. Translated by Ralph B. Allen. New York 1936.

The Saga of Gisli. Translated by George Johnston. With Notes and an Essay on the Saga of Gisli by Peter Foote. London 1965 (New edition 1973).

The Saga of Gunnlaug Serpent-Tongue. (Bi-lingual edition.) English text translated by R. !uirk. Edited with Introduction and Notes by Peter Foote. London 1957.

Eyrbyggja Saga. Translated by Paul Schach. Introduction and verse translations by Lee M. Hollander. Nebraska and New York 1959.

Eyrbyggja Saga. Translated by Hermann Pálsson and Paul Edwards. Edinburgh 1973.

The Vatnsdalers' Saga. Translated by Gwyn Jones. New York 1944.

The Saga of the Jómsvíkings. Translated by Lee M. Hollander. Austin, Texas 1955.

The Saga of Hrafn Sveinbjarnarson. Translated by Anne Tjomsland. Ithaca 1951 (*Islandica*).

Völsunga Saga: The Saga of the Volsungs. Edited and Translated with an Introduction, Notes and Appendices by R. G. Finch. London 1965.

The Saga of King Heidrek the Wise. Translated from the Icelandic with Introduction, Notes and Appendices by Christopher Tolkien. London 1960.

Gautreks Saga and other Medieval Tales. Translated with an Introduction by Hermann Pálsson and Paul Edwards. London and New York 1968.

Hrolf Gautreksson. A Viking Romance. Translated by Hermann Pálsson and Paul Edwards. Edinburgh 1972.

Sturlunga Saga. Vols. I-II. Translated by Gudbrand Vigfusson. Oxford 1878.

Lilja (The Lily). By Eysteinn Ásgrímsson. Edited and translated by Eiríkr Magnússon. London 1870.

Icelandic Christian Classics: The Lay of the Sun, the Lily. Translated by Charles Venn Pilchner. Oxford 1950.

The Life of Gudmund the Good Bishop of Holar. Translated by G. Turville-Petre and E. S. Olszewska. Coventry 1942 (The Viking Society for Northern Research).

Icelandic Meditations on the Passion. Selections from the Passion-Hymns by Hallgrím Pétursson. Translated by Charles V. Pilcher. New York 1923.

Hymns of the Passion. Meditations on the Passion of Christ. By Hallgrím Pétursson. Translated by Arthur Charles Cook. Reykjavík 1966.

.

On Modern Icelandic Literature

Beck, Richard, *History of Icelandic Poets 1800-1940*. Ithaca 1950.

Einarsson, Stefán, *History of Icelandic Prose Writers 1800-1940*. Ithaca 1950.

— *A History of Icelandic Literature*. New York 1957.

Magnússon, Sigurdur A., 'Icelandic Literature: Preserver of National Culture'. *Mosaic* Vol. I, No. 3, 1968. University of Manitoba Press.

— 'The Modern Icelandic Novel: From Isolation to Political Awareness'. *Mosaic* Vol. IV, No. 2, 1970.

— 'Halldór Laxness—Iceland's First Nobel Prize Winner'. *The American-Scandinavian Review* No.1, 1956 (New York).

— 'Modern Icelandic Poetry'. *Iceland Review* No. 2, 1966 (Reykjavík).

— 'Eyvind of the Hills'. *Iceland Review* No. 1, 1968.

— 'Gunnar Gunnarsson-Iceland's First International Novelist'. *Iceland Review* No. 1, 1973.

Translations of Modern Icelandic Literature

An Anthology of Scandinavian Literature. From the Viking Period to the Twentieth Century. Selected and edited by Hallberg Hallmundsson. London and New York 1965.

20th Century Scandinavian Poetry. 1900–1950. Edited by Martin S. Allwood. Mullsjö, Sweden 1950.

Icelandic Lyrics. Originals and Translations. Edited by Richard Beck. Reykjavík 1930.

The North American Book of Icelandic Verse. Translated by Watson Kirkconnell. New York 1930.

Icelandic Poems and Stories. Edited by Richard Beck. New York 1943 (New edition 1968).

Odes and Echoes. Translated by Paul Bjarnason. Vancouver, Canada 1954.

An Anthology of Icelandic Poetry. Edited by Eiríkur Benedikz. Reykjavík 1950.

Anthology of Icelandic Literature 1800–1950. Vols. I–II. Edited by Loftur Bjarnason. Berkeley, California 1961.

Seven Icelandic Short Stories. Edited by Á. Pétursson and S. J. Thorsteinsson. Reykjavík 1960.

Poems of Today. From Twenty-five Icelandic Poets. Selected and translated by Alan Boucher. Reykjavík 1970.

Short Stories of Today. By Twelve Modern Icelandic Authors. Selected and translated by Alan Boucher. Reykjavík 1972.

Icelandic Short Stories (25 authors). Selected, edited and partially translated by Evelyn Scherabon Firchow. Introduction by Sigurdur A. Magnússon. New York 1975.

Modern Scandinavian Plays ('Bishop Jón Arason' by Tryggvi Sveinbjörnsson, translated by Lee M. Hollander). New York 1954.

Fire and Ice. Three Icelandic Plays by Jóhann Sigurjónsson, Davíd Stefánsson and Agnar Thórdarson. With Introductions by Einar Haugen. Madison, Milwaukee and London 1967.

Modern Nordic Plays—Iceland (Plays by Halldór Laxness, Jökull Jakobsson, Erlingur E. Halldórsson, and Oddur Björnsson). Introduction by Sigurdur A. Magnússon. Oslo and Boston 1973.

Benediktsson, Einar, *Harp of the North* (Poems). Translated by Frederick T. Wood. Charlottesville, Virginia 1955.

Gudmundsson, Kristmann, *The Bridal Gown.* Translated by O. F. Theis. New York 1931.

— *Morning of Life.* Translated by Elizabeth Sprigge and Claude Napier. New York 1936.

— *Winged Citadel.* Translated by Barrows Mussey. New York 1940.

Gunnarsson, Gunnar, *Guest the One-Eyed.* London 1920.

— *The Sworn Brothers.* London 1920.

— *Seven Days' Darkness.* Translated by Roberts Tapley. New York 1930.

— *The Dark Mountains.* In *Hidden Treasures in Literature.* New York 1934.

— *The Night and the Dream.* Translated by Evelyn Ramsden. Indianapolis 1938.

— *Ships in the Sky*. Translated by Evelyn Ramsden. Indianapolis 1938.
— *The Good Shepherd*. Translated by Kenneth C. Kaufman. Indianapolis 1940.
— *The Black Cliffs*. Translated by Cecil Wood. Madison, Milwaukee and London 1967.
Kamban, Gudmundur, *Hadda Padda: A Drama*. Translated by Sadie Luise Peller. Foreword by Georg Brandes. New York 1917.
— *We Murderers* (A Play). Translated with an Introduction by Einar Haugen. Madison, Milwaukee and London 1970.
— *The Virgin of Skalholt* (A Novel). Translated by Evelyn Ramsden. Boston 1935.
— *I see a Wondrous Land* (A Novel). New York 1938.
Laxness, Halldór, *Salka Valka*. Translated by F. H. Lyons. London, New York and Boston 1936.
— *Independent People*. Translated by J. A. Thompson. London 1945. New York 1946. New Delhi 1957.
— *World Light*. Translated by Magnus Magnusson. Madison, Milwaukee and London 1969.
— *The Happy Warriors*. Translated by Katherine John. London 1958. Calcutta and Bombay 1960.
— *The Atom Station.* Translated by Magnus Magnusson. London 1961.
— *The Honour of the House*. Reykjavík 1959.
— *Paradise Reclaimed*. Translated by Magnus Magnusson. London and New York 1962.
— *The Fish Can Sing*. Translated by Magnus Magnusson. London 1966.
— *Christianity at Glacier*. Translated by Magnus Magnusson. Reykjavík 1972.
— *A Quire of Seven* (Short Stories). Translated by Alan Boucher. Reykjavík 1974.
Sigurjónsson, Jóhann, *Eyvindur of the Mountains*. Translated by Francis P. Magoun Jr. Reykjavík 1961.
— *Modern Icelandic Plays: Eyvind of the Hills. The Hraun Farm*. Translated by Henninge Krohn Schanche. New York 1916.
— *Loftur: A Play*. Translated by Jean Young and Eleanor Arkwright. Reading 1939.
Svensson, Jón, *Nonni and Manni*. Dublin 1938.
Thórdarson, Agnar, *The Sword* (A Novel). Translated with Introduction and Notes by Paul Schach. New York 1971.
Thórdarson, Thórbergur, *In Search of My Beloved*. Translated by Kenneth G. Chapman. New York 1967.
Vilhjálmsson, Thor, *Faces Reflected in a Drop* (Short Stories). Translated by Kenneth G. Chapman. Reykjavík 1966.

INDEX

ADILS, JÓN, 120–1
agriculture, 209–11, 240
Agústsson, Hördur, 200
air traffic, 208–9
Algerian pirates, 115–16
Alginate Industries (Scottish), 219–20
Algonquin Indians, 28
Althing: constitution, 13–15, 134, 145; dissolved, 123; re-established 131–3; legislative power, 133; millennium, 139; radio reports, 150
America, discovery of, 26–8
American occupation and military bases, 143, 184, 189, 194
Andvari, 181
Arason, Jon, bishop of Hólar, 108–13, 114, 177
Arason, Sigurd, 112
Arason, *see also* Jónsson, Björn, 110
Ari, 38
Arinbjarnar, Snorri, 199
Armann á Althingi, 129
Armstrong, Neil, 226
Arnadóttir, Nína Björk, 193
Arnamagnaean Institute, 155
Árnarson, Ingólf, 17, 29
Árnason, Jón, 130, 167
Árnason, Jón Gunnar, 202
Árnason, Jónas, 191–2
Asatrú (pagan cult), 148
Asgeirsson, Bragi, 200–1
Ásgrimsson, Eystein, 99
Ashkenazy, Vladimir, 206
Asmundsson, Grettir, *see* Grettir the Strong
astronauts, 226
Atlamál, 47

Attila the Hun, 50, 51
Auden, W. H., 75, 159
Aurora Borealis (Northern Lights), 137, 236, 241

BACON, FRANCIS, 200
Baffin Island, 27
Balchin, Nigel, 92
Balder's Dreams, 63
Bandamanna Saga, 95
banking, 221
Banks, Sir Joseph, 125
Bárdarson, Skúli, 34, 35
Benedict, Ruth, 171–2
Benediktsson, Einar, 137, 161
Beowulf, 46, 47, 54, 93
Bergsson, Gudbergur, 189
Bergsson or Bergthórson, Nikulás, 41
Bessastadir, 112
Bible, translations of, 109, 114
birds, 234–5
Bjarni the Mathematician, 42
Björn's Saga, 84, 85, 93, 96
Björnsson, Sveinn, 141
Björnsson, Oddur, 193–4
Black Death, 105, 106
Bödvarsson, Gudmundur, 182
Bödvarsson, Thórd, 33
Book of Settlements, 8, 9, 31, 93
book publishing, 177–80
Boy Scout Movement, 157
Brahe, Tycho, 114
Brandes, Georg, 136
Briem, Jóhann, 199–200
British occupation, 142–3
broadcasting, 148–50
Brunehild, wife of Sigebert, 52
Brynhild's Ride to Hel, 53
Budli, King, 52

Iceland, a nation-state of 250,000 people, has an importance in the world out of all proportion to its size. Because of its geographical situation it is a key member of NATO, and because of its heavy dependence on the fishing industry for its livelihood, it has been in serious conflict with more than one of its NATO allies.

Iceland is a country with unique geological features – great glaciers alongside active volcanoes; and with a cultural heritage which it is also no exaggeration to call unique – a country settled by Norsemen in the ninth century and where the language of the first settlers is still spoken – the home of the greatest literary outpouring of the Middle Ages and of one of the noblest polities, comparable ancient Athens – occupied and exploited by foreigners from the thirteenth to the twentieth century – and finally reborn with a fresh outburst of creative activity.

A well-balanced, comprehensive account in English of this extraordinary country has been lacking, and Sigurdur A. Magnússon, an Icelandic man of letters, has produced such a book – sympathetic as befits an Icelander but detached and sometimes critical. He examines first the original settlers and the great Commonwealth they produced, then "Myth and Legend" – medieval Icelandic poetry and its origins – and the Sagas. How decline followed the four centuries of Icelandic greatness is described, together with the long period of foreign rule, poverty and distress that continued until well into the nineteenth century. The next chapters describe the national renaissance in the nineteenth century; the society which has grown up in the twentieth century and how it functions; the contradictory, "Sphinx-like" character of the Icelanders themselves; the whole spectrum of the creative arts in the present century, and finally the infrastructure and physical features of the country.